PRIMACY OF THE EYE

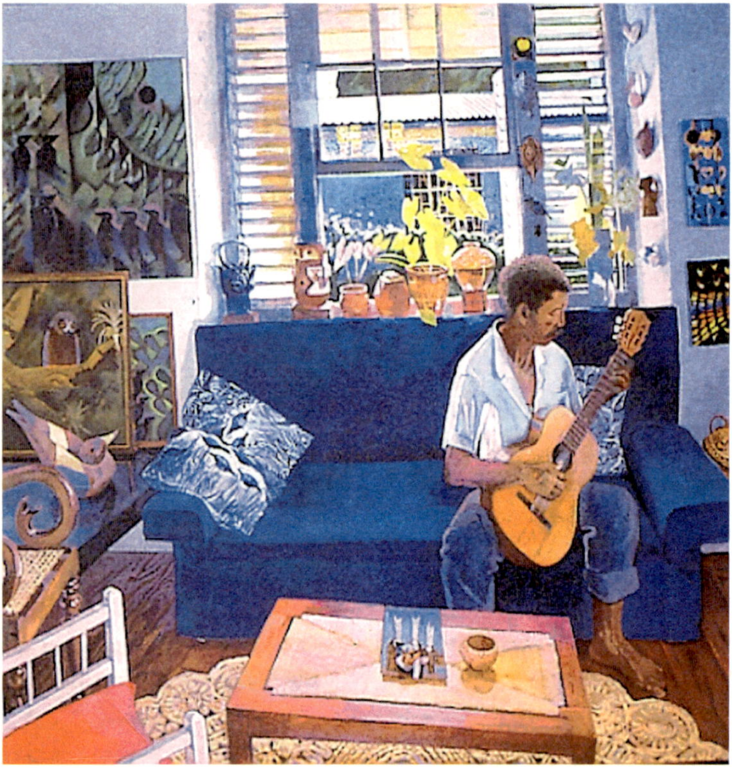

Alison Chapman-Andrews, **Imitation of Birds**
(portrait of Stanley) 1986, acrylics, 122x 122cm

PRIMACY OF THE EYE

THE ART OF STANLEY GREAVES

RUPERT ROOPNARAINE

PEEPAL TREE

First published in Great Britain in 2005
by Peepal Tree Press Ltd
17 King's Avenue
Leeds LS6 1QS
England

ISBN 1 900715 86 4

Peepal Tree gratefully acknowledges Arts Council support

CONTENTS

In memoriam
Martin Carter, 1927-1997

ACKNOWLEDGEMENTS

Some of the chapters that follow began life as catalogue notes and essays to accompany the exhibitions of the work of Stanley Greaves held over the course of twelve years, in Guyana, Barbados and London. The earliest dates from 1993 and forms the core of Chapter Seven, "Frontiers of Consciousness: explorations in Scale". The latest was written for the exhibition of the *There is a Meeting Here Tonight* and forms the main body of Chapter Ten. Sections of Chapter Nine, "Caribbean Folklore, Caribbean Ikons," draw on material from the catalogue essay for the Elders Exhibition in London in 1999. All have been substantially revised, expanded and in places corrected for the present publication. I thank the persons responsible for inviting me to contribute to the various catalogues: Castellani House and the Hadfield Gallery in Georgetown, the Barbados Museum, the South London Gallery and curator Godfried Donkor, and, most recently, Mervyn Awon and Therese Hadchity. The Management Committee of Castellani House has kindly permitted reproductions of several works in the National Collection.

I am indebted to Joan García and Janice De Nobrega for their labours in transcribing the first interviews with Stanley so many years ago when the project was in its infancy; to Bonita Bone Harris for companionship in the meditation on *White Hearts, Yellow Diamonds*; to Therese Hadchity, Anne Walmsley, and my son, Terry, for their attentiveness and solidarity, and for their refinements; to Ray Kril for his electronic recreation of the reproductions, and for providing the refuge of Javastraat; to Malaika Scott for patiently suffering the production of the several drafts, and for solace; to Christine, Jeremy and Mervyn Awon for the warmth and generosity with which they shared their home and access to its treasures; to Deodat Persaud for brotherhood and the lessons of the heart; and to Jocelyn Dow for caring in and out of season. The gentle insistences of Jeremy Poynting made this book worthier of its subject; without his work and that of Hannah Bannister at Peepal Tree Press, it would not have been made at all.

FOREWORD

Visual arts in the English-speaking Caribbean, the former British West Indies, have a short history. It was only in the 1920s and 1930s that pioneers within the region, trained in European art techniques or stimulated by reproductions of its masterpieces, began to teach art locally, to arrange exhibitions, and to set up art societies and classes. Such a recent start in art contrasts sharply with much earlier initiatives and far longer established visual practice in the Spanish and French-speaking Caribbean. The harvest of this 'intrusive and historically recent art' – so dubbed by Denis Williams of Guyana – has become increasingly visible over the past decade. Major international exhibitions with their catalogues (*Caribbean Visions,* 1995, *Caribe Insular*, 1999), and the regional art history, *Caribbean Art* by Veerle Poupeye (Thames and Hudsons' World of Art series, 1998) show work by artists from Jamaica to Guyana alongside work from Cuba to Martinique. Such a book, such exhibitions, give a sample or two at most of the region's leading artists. The lifetime's work of the first generation of artists in the English-speaking Caribbean is now ripe for close study and assessment. But such opportunities are few indeed. Retrospective exhibitions are rarely accompanied by a fully illustrated catalogue. Monographs can be counted on the fingers of one hand. *Primacy of the Eye*, this monograph on Stanley Greaves, is the first to illuminate an artist of the second generation, still making art. Rupert Roopnaraine's presentation of Greaves's art and writing about it sets a welcome model for such monographs. It reveals Greaves as an artist whose quality and range of visual production, underpinned by ceaseless research, experimentation – and looking, gives him a place of special significance in the art of the Caribbean.

Guyana, Greaves's home country, which belongs as much to South America as to the Caribbean, gave birth as British Guiana in the 1920s and 1930s to several artists of international renown: Denis Williams, master draftsman; Philip Moore, as accomplished in sculpture as in painting, untrained and wholly dependent on his 'visions'; Aubrey Williams and Frank Bowling, painters and supreme colourists, most at home in abstraction; Donald Locke, ceramist and sculptor. Greaves is known primarily as a painter. The series of 14 paintings, *There is a Meeting Here Tonight*, shown at three venues in the Caribbean in 2001/2 and then travelled to Europe, marks, in Roopnaraine's words, 'the high tide of his maturity.'

But one of the surprises of this monograph is the extent to which the art of Stanley Greaves reaches out beyond painting. His wooden sculpture, "Blue Soap" is known in Barbados. But there has been so much other work in sculpture, in a variety of materials, for so long. Sculpture was his focus during two spells of art studies overseas at Newcastle-on-Tyne in the UK and at Howard University in the US.

"When making drawings yourself, you should try to put into practice some of the principles you have learnt from this study of the great masterpieces of Art, and then some day you may perhaps be a celebrated West Indian artist." So concludes the final Picture Lesson – on Giovanni Bellini's "Angel with a Lute" – in Nelson's *West Indian Readers*. Greaves acknowledges his debt to these Picture Lessons for fuelling his interest in art, and has proved himself an exemplary student. In travels he has taken every opportunity to look, firsthand, at work in art which suggested solutions to what he wanted to express. He sees the art of the Caribbean as essentially eclectic and is confident in the right to borrow from other artists and from other cultural traditions – provided it is the approach which is appropriated, not stylistic features blindly copied. Artists to whom Greaves claims especial indebtedness are the European surrealists Magritte and de Chirico, and the Latin Americans Lam and Matta, themselves from formerly colonised countries, using modernism to forge a distinctive language. In his in-depth study of other artists, in the technical and philosophical explorations which have underpinned each new phase in his paintings and his three-dimensional work, Greaves is the antithesis of the self-taught, "intuitive" artists of the Caribbean. But the iconography and concerns of his work are unmistakably local. As he has said: "The task before Caribbean artists is to define the fundamentals of a Caribbean experience that cuts through and transcends the history of colonialism."

Rupert Roopnaraine is uniquely well equipped to write on the art of Stanley Greaves. He has looked closely at the work, and followed its progression, since 1960. His knowledge of art and art theory, his interest in philosophy, reflects some of Greaves's own concerns. Roopnaraine has already contributed the catalogue text for four of Greaves's recent exhibitions. Here he provides detailed, illuminating commentary on significant works within each stage of Greaves's production, with diversions into related art theory where appropriate. Roopnaraine's own active participation in politics and concern for appropriate political systems in Guyana, enables him to supply concise, informed accounts of recent political history, the context of Greaves's latest work. Roopnaraine's focus is on the work itself, with minimal biographical detail. Such detail as is needed for the understanding of the work is set out separately in a Brief Chronology, supplied by Greaves. The quotations from Greaves's notebooks, and the range of his writing set out in the Bibliography, substantiate Roopnaraine's claims for the unceasing intellectual work which has accompanied the making of art.

Roopnaraine recalls his first encounter with art by Stanley Greaves. Mine was very different, but is equally vivid: a drawing, heavily outlined, of a barefoot man, head in hand, seated on a wooden box, and a boy, standing in shoes, left hand free and forward – on the cover of *A Century of West Indian Education*, from my time as Longman's Caribbean publisher in the 1960s. I have known Greaves only since 1993. Research into the Caribbean Artists Movement prompted a wish to find out more about the region's visual artists. Everyone said that the key person in such a quest was Stanley Greaves. We have met and talked, in Barbados and in London, alongside an almost continuous exchange of letters, information and ideas ever since. Such exchanges, and chances to see Greaves's work, have transformed all my seeing. Everyday objects and familiar people constantly startle with their "acuities", their unexpected connections and metaphysical dimensions. After a lifetime of work in literature, I find the "primacy of the eye" has become insistent and disturbing.

Anne Walmsley
London, 2005

INTRODUCTION

He is schooled in the exploration of modern themes, expressionist, impressionist, constructivist, architectonic....But he wears these media or modes upon an inner grasp of form-within-yet-beyond-identical form. One senses in his work a true absorption of influences and a parting of the ways into other unsuspected vistas.

Wilson Harris on Stanley Greaves[1]

Days after the recent launching of Denis Williams's *Prehistoric Guyana*, his master work in archaeology, his friend Ian McDonald, the Caribbean novelist and poet, wrote with feeling of "one of the greatest scholarly and intellectual achievements by a Guyanese... an archaeologist and anthropologist of worldwide stature." In full awareness of the lowering horizon and the encroaching desert, McDonald laments the falling of two of Guyana's most towering trees: "Nobody except Martin Carter matched him as a creative presence in this nation. When these two men died within a year of each other in 1997/98 we could almost feel the world of art and sensibility in Guyana grow narrower in imagination, meaner in spirit, shallower in intellect, smaller in stature, weaker in all that inspires humanity to do its best."

There are moments in a people's history when more than usual care and energy must be devoted to asserting permanence in the midst of disintegration, and affirming continuity in the face of rupture. No-one saw this with greater clarity than the late A.J. Seymour, the legendary founder of the Caribbean's oldest literary magazine, *Kyk-over-al,* and the respected elder of the tribe of Guyanese poets. His "Editorial Notes" immediately following the invasion of British Guiana in October 1953 and the overthrow of the country's first elected government are elegiac in tone and conjure up a solemn parade of the fallen pioneers who blazed the trail of the country's cultural movement – the brothers Potter, Philip Pilgrim and, before them, Mac A Lawrence, A.R.F. Webber, Egbert Martin. Seymour's editorial is a praise-song of "the supremacy of the spirit over material things." "In this country," Seymour writes, "we have seen brilliant lights go out in the darkness and clocks have stopped on the wall." [2] In the face of rupture and defeat, the measured celebration of continuity. Herein lies the great value of Denis Williams's monument to origins and continuity.

It was in something of this spirit, in another dark time, that I turned to the work of Stanley Greaves and Martin Carter in 1985. In that season of waste and ashes that followed the assassination of Walter Rodney in Guyana and, not long after, the self-immolation of the Grenada revolution, it seemed important not only to advance on other fronts, but to assert on all fronts the primacy of the human and to celebrate the garden over the ashes. Greaves and Carter take their rightful place in the company of a remarkable post-colonial generation of Guyanese thinkers, writers and artists that includes, among its brightest lights, E.R Burrowes, Eusi Kwayana, Wilson Harris, Edgar Mittelholzer, Phillip Moore, A.J. Seymour, Aubrey Williams, Denis Williams, and like a meteor in the night sky, Walter Rodney.

One striking failure in Grenada was the failure to nourish our debates and our thinking from the well-springs of our own people's experience, to draw inspiration from our own thinkers and through them connect with the stubborn desire for material and spiritual decolonization that has continuously stirred in the Caribbean heart since the European conquest and the long night of slavery and indenture.

My 1985 essay, "Re-Reading Martin Carter", was written at the same time and under the same compulsions as the meditation on "Yellow Hearts, White Diamonds" that forms the core of Chapter Six, "Grids of Order" (see pp. 87-98). My *explication de texte* of the poem and of the painting was resolutely, and even perversely, formalist. No poem of Carter's had been more often declaimed or quoted. It was no longer read and no longer read anyone. The degradation of ordinary language was everywhere. Walter Rodney had spoken of the ways in which words that expressed the noblest of ideas and ideals had turned into their opposite in the mouths of the rulers. It seemed a necessary duty to defy this degradation on all fronts and at every level, even, in the essay on "You are Involved", by reclaiming and renewing the purity of the purest of words, the words of poetry, through an estranging process of analysis. My aim was to make strange the most familiar of poems by laying bare the workings of its words. At the heart of the examination of poem and painting was the grammar of word and of shape and colour. In the chapters that follow I have retained the formal and descriptive method in the discussions of the paintings and sculptures, extending into biographical explanations only when they added a necessary dimension to my understanding of the particular objects. In my treatment of the paintings I have drawn on the distinction made by Lucien Goldmann between *understanding* and *explanation*, where the former concerns itself with the internal relations of the object, and the latter with its external relations. In the language of philosophy, it is the distinction between *identity* and *relationship*. In these terms, my emphasis throughout has been on the identity of the paintings.

Wilson Harris's "true absorption of influences and a parting of the ways into other unsuspected vistas" speaks to the dialogue in Greaves' work between a world art historical tradition and an explicitly Caribbean frame of reference and iconography. Harris points us in the direction of Greaves' cosmological concerns. It is precisely such a dialogue that informs the mini-paintings of the 1986 exhibition, *Caribbean Metaphysic: another reality* and resonates at various points in explicit allusions to particular artistic traditions. A recurring motif throughout is the appropriation of particular elements of the *Vanitas* tradition of still-life painting that developed after the Reformation. The *Vanitas* still-life painting consists of a collection of objects chosen and arranged to remind the spectator of the transience of mortal life: *vanitas vanitatum* from Ecclesiastes. The objects of the tradition are readily recognized: skulls, mirrors, hourglass or clock, butterflies, flowers, leaves, guttering candles. When Greaves paints his leaf pinned to the table of *Caribbean Committee* (see p. 130), his brown drying leaf in the shape of the bird looking out from one of *Alison's Cups* (see p. 126), his butterfly inscribed with the pattern of the bent nail on the sensuous, erotic *Knot* (see p. 127), his biscuit burning instead of the candle in *The Doll*, he is setting up a dialogue with the *Vanitas* tradition in Western European painting. The dialogue is also established in Greaves's wood-carvings in the African manner and in his homage pots in tribute to the ancient potters of Jenne Jeno, discussed in Chapter Five.

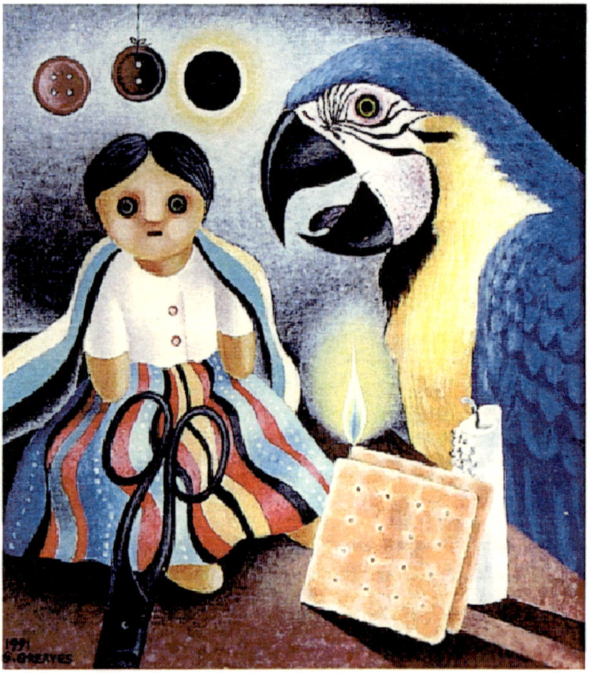

The Doll, 1991, acrylics, 25 x 23.5 cm

The "parting of the ways" occurs as Greaves is drawn deeper into the exploration of the magical and begins to sense that, in the words of Edouard Glissant, "a magical notion of reality is based on beliefs hidden deep in the collective past. It forms part of the present. But it proliferates also because the present is elusive and slips away from you. We do not know which of its motifs will be important to us."[3] As Greaves works through the implications of the absence as he sees it of a Caribbean metaphysic, a holistic system of beliefs and practices flowing from a cosmology that is uniquely Caribbean, the religious themes begin to assert themselves and point to a totalizing ideology "hidden deep in the collective past." Among the "unsuspected vistas" is a connectedness with the Caribbean religious underworld with its proliferation of secret cults – Vodun, Santeria, Pocomania, Shango and the Orishas, Obeah, Macumba, Cumina, and the rest. Of the mini-paintings, discussed in Chapter Eight, *The Doll* and *Jaguar Table* are explicitly obeah paintings; the *Magus with Reversed Bananas* (discussed in Chapter Nine), *The Manifesto* and *Political Protest* (discussed in Chapter Ten) are critical of the manipulation of the people's beliefs to serve narrow political ends. The paintings where Greaves sets out to invent the figures and episodes of a Caribbean folklore, such as *Caribbean Chimera, The Visitation* and *The Tree of Life*, are expressions of that magical notion of reality. The "beliefs hidden deep in the collective past" are the retentions of a whole world view, "a cosmic vision", deeply rooted in traditional African religion and culture. "In that vision," Gordon Lewis has written, "the human and the divine are encompassed together in holistic fashion. Man, nature, and society are seen as necessarily intermixed with each other. All of them compose the grand order of the universe... Man not only enters into a rich relationship with the invisible and supernatural world; he also is enabled to conclude, both in vodun and Santeria, an alliance of spirit with that world."[4] Greaves's obeah paintings derive from and connect with this belief system. Greaves is not unique among Caribbean artists for sensing this disconnectedness and discontinuity, the absence of and the yearning for a fixed Caribbean order. Wilson Harris and Kamau Braithwaite, each in his own terms, have elaborated their architectures of wholeness out of the fragments of the various narratives that converge in the Caribbean.

Wilson Harris is on firmest ground when he identifies the "architectonic" as a feature of Greaves's work. There is no "influence" that Greaves has absorbed more thoroughly and truly. From the early paintings of the 1950s to the most recent of 2004, the architectonic has been the dominant mode, revealing itself in the control over the rhythm of structure and composition, the organization of space and the placement of the figures. Throughout, there is a stillness in Greaves's figures, even when in the course of performing an action, that signals the architectonic.

It began as a boy's fascination with the idea of composition. Greaves recalls the "terrible reproductions" of the Picture Lessons in the *Nelson's West Indian Readers* of his childhood: "The paintings reproduced were taken from the national galleries of England and Scotland. Pictures by the pre-Raphaelites and others, Chardin, Velazquez, Rembrandt. Also of course, by the Dutch landscape painters and their English counterparts. The later Picture Lessons not only described these paintings but had diagrams showing how they were composed. And that was right up my alley: what are the fundamentals behind producing a painting."[5]

This study is an attempt to understand how this most accomplished of artists came to master those fundamentals and, in the course of a productive life, created a body of work that re-affirms the enduring value of acts of the imagination, Seymour's "supremacy of the spirit over material things."

END NOTES TO INTRODUCTION

1. Wilson Harris, *Selected Essays: The Unfinished Genesis of the Imagination*, ed. Andrew Bundy (Routledge, London, 1999), p. 224
2. A.J. Seymour, "Editorial Notes", *Kyk-over-al*, 1953
3. Edouard Glissant, *Caribbean Discourse, Selected Essays*, (Univ. Press of Virginia, 1989), p. 243
4. Gordon Lewis, *Main Currents in Caribbean Thought*, p. 194
5. Interview with Anne Walmsley, *Bomb* (Winter 2003/2004 No. 86)

CHAPTER ONE

THE GREAVES WORLD AND THE EARLY PAINTINGS

> *Art has never been an attempt to grasp reality as a whole – that is beyond our human capacity; it was never even an attempt to represent the totality of appearances; but rather it has been the piecemeal recognition and patient fixation of what is significant in human experience.*
>
> **Herbert Read**[1]

I. The Greaves World

I remember almost to the day when a Stanley Greaves painting first burned itself into my mind. It was a late afternoon in August 1960 when I encountered *Evolution*, a painting in the collection of Dr. Frank Williams, a discerning and early supporter of a generation of young Guyanese artists. Unframed, it was affixed to the northern wall of an airy, elegant drawing room in an old plantation house at Cove and John on the East Coast of Demerara, since demolished to give way to a pompous concrete citadel. Commissioned by Dr. Williams, it was the young painter's response to a passage in H.G. Wells's 1920 classic, *The Outline of History*.

It could have been the big green eye, innocent of expression with its perfectly curved lashes, looking back at me from the head of the foetus in the exact centre of the picture. Or the single giant leaf, going dry and brown at the edges, surprisingly tattered considering the supple strength of its stem curling like the neck of a bird from out of the white lips of a smooth, rounded, green seed. But it was not the eye of the foetus nor the leaf of the seed that drew me, but the long curving column

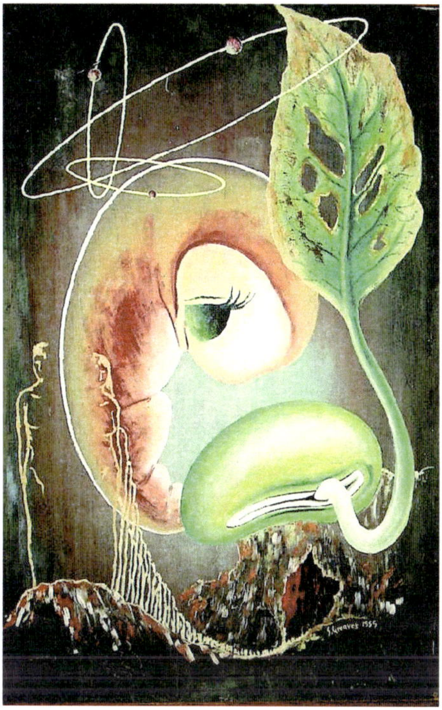

Evolution, 1955, Oils on hardboard

of human figures, in perfect perspective, diminishing in the distance, tall and looming on the crest of a rock in the left foreground. The column originated out of a hole in the side of a craggy mountain, a slash of bright red deep in the dark. The figures are in simple yellow outline, without detail, except for the first two where there is detail enough to distinguish man and woman. And in the top left of the picture, three orbital rings each with an astral body in motion. The largest of the rings loops around the sharp tip of the leaf. The rings are white, as is the outlined curve of the back of the foetus that is the segment of a fourth inter-locking ring.

Evolution, Greaves's meditation on the passage of Wells, is very much the young painter's respectful homage to Salvador Dalí. Among the painters who have impacted on his work, – José Clemente Orozco and Rudolfo Tamayo, Georgio de Chirico and Roberto Matta, – Dalí has remained for Greaves the grandmaster of technique and draughtsmanship under whose brush everyday objects and the ordinary things of the natural world were metamorphosed into luminous symbols and enigmatic dreamscapes. An entry in Greaves's journal, dated June 1984, records the following words of Dalí: "My whole ambition in the pictorial domain is to materialize the images of concrete irrationality with the most imperialistic fury of precision."[2]

In the many years of remembering Guyana away from Guyana, it was this painting, first seen on an August afternoon in the countryside long ago, that would bring the old house and much of the essence of colonial Guyana back into my mind. I was to see it again twenty years later – it was still there, gracing the Northern wall of the old house, a little the worse for wear, its old elegance faded – and I have come to realise that it had been, that afternoon, the first time that any painting at all had had such an effect and was to lodge such clear traces of itself in my mind. *Evolution* was painted in 1955, during the period of Greaves's apprenticeship and earliest investigations.

Looking at the painting now, in the company and context of his other works of that period, I am struck by the extent to which all these pieces, and indeed all the subsequent pieces over the years, in the full variety of their subjects, forms and materials, can be seen to constitute a world, with its own internal laws and rhythms, its own codes, its own distinctive aura, an imaginative universe renewing and enlarging itself in a restless dialogue with the real world of men and women and nature. Every exchange re-complicates the disposition of the elements of this imaginary world, and new lines of enquiry open up. The really important exchanges – and some are far more important than others – alter the very bases and parameters of the enquiry. On those occasions a kind of leap takes place, and a seminal work comes into the world.

Over the past fifty years, Greaves has released a steady stream of work: paintings, drawings, prints, carvings, ceramics, welded steel and mixed media fabrications. (I take no account here of his poetry, critical writings, or the journals and notebooks he has kept at his side through the years). Looked at in its entirety, and as it were all at once, his work is a strikingly self-contained whole within which variety and difference abound, but always inside the boundaries that circumscribe and enclose the whole.

With seemingly infinite scope for experimentation and refinement, his investigations unfold within a specific space of enquiry that may expand or contract, but that exists always in strict relation to a fixed centre. The Greaves world is distinguished by a clearly identifiable set of theoretical and technical preoccupations that sometimes prove to have existential implications. The iconographic environment is uniquely his own. The work seems powered by a narrow yet inexhaustible range of obsessions, marked by seriality and repetition as the enquiries deepen. From time to time, a work is produced that seems to turn inward and reflect on itself. Throughout there is a sense of a restless pushing outward of frontiers from a still centre.

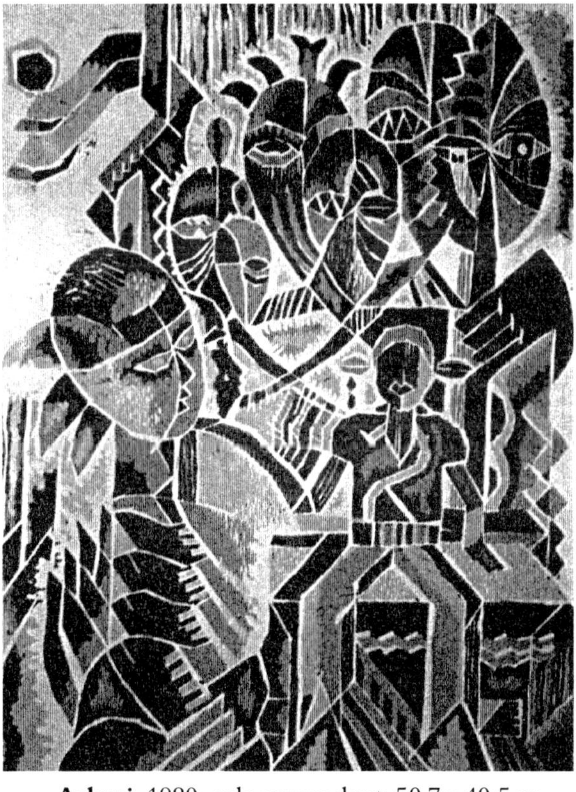

Askari, 1980, colour woodcut, 50.7 x 40.5cm.

As we begin our consideration of Greaves's work, it is useful to recognize what is to remain throughout an abiding preoccupation: the *method* and the *ethos* of production, the how and the why of the artistic act. *Askari*, (*Ancestral Images No. 4*), a 50.7 x 40.5 cm colour woodcut, is a reduction print, one of a series that Greaves executed in 1979-80 during a period of formal study at Howard University. A boy is sitting in the middle ground, slightly to the right of the print's centre. Around his head enigmatic shapes hover and swirl, shapes of masks/faces/shields/spears/leaves. The shield-faces are heart shaped and anticipate the explorations of the late 1980s. There are six of them, grouped in three pairs. Another pair of faces looms in the left foreground. These, like the small boy's, are depicted in considerable detail, amounting even to expressiveness in the face closest to the spectator, as it watches over the scene, protectively. It is the figure of the mother. The other face, her companion's, is in sharp profile. Mother, companion and child are the only figures depicted in a naturalistic way: the head-tie of the mother is one such detail. These three figures exist on the plane of reality. They are of this human world. The other three pairs that occupy the entire space above the boy's head are abstracted, sexless, and are not of this world. They are organised in ascending order, each pair larger than the one preceding.

While the first two pairs are the same way up with the points downward, the final pair are head to toe: the second of the two, or the last of the six, is inverted and more like a leaf/spear. In a picture full of eyes, the boy's face is eyeless. Instead, two eyes are off to the left and right of this face, one brown, the other green. They are closed, with teardrops falling from the right one.

The picture is muted in tone and colour and has a strange, otherworldly aura. For this ancestral study Greaves has chosen yellow ochre, green and brown, the colours of earth and vegetation. Brown, the darkest and last to be applied, tinges everything. The final brown asserts the relation of this colour with the yellow and green. It is entirely in keeping with the integration of Greaves's world that this is the identical palette used three years earlier in the *Canecutters* of 1977 (see p. 51). The mysterious power of *Askari* is partly accounted for by the tension between activity and passivity, busy-ness and repose, experience and innocence, which is the informing principle that structures the print. It is a picture about receptivity, about receiving and absorbing from the forces of knowledge the energy and guidance human beings need if they are not to flounder in the confusion of the world. The picture dramatizes the externalization of the desires of the self and the journeying inward of the self's experience. The figures, some of them stern and menacing, that hover around the head of the small boy are the ancestors, the truth-bearing spirits through which human beings, as part of all being, connect with all that has been, all that is and all that will be. The mother figure draws her power and authority from them, graphically expressed in the sweeping lines that connect her to them. It is a small boy who is receiving the ancestors, not a grown man. The young boy, innocent, open, usually at the foot of an elder, is a recurring figure in the early paintings. He is the initiand.

A study on the theme of initiation, *Askari* expresses and celebrates the guardian aspect of the ancestral spirits. It is also a study on the theme of guardianship. These wraiths are one with the forest, arising out of it and ready to melt back into it in the twinkling of an eye. They are at home. Where the ancestors dwell, all is harmony and immanence. Theirs is that epic place that was before the fissure of self and world. This idea of a complete fusion with the environment of life, the dissolving of lines of separation, is central to many of Greaves' most important paintings.

It is not surprising to find the signs of so many of Greaves's established themes and permanent interests inscribed in *Askari*. His deep interest in African origins has never waned. In this case, his fascination is with what he saw as the significance of the Askari's curious social location in the activities of penetration and conquest. Who were the Askaris? Greaves had in mind the African tribesmen who accompanied the white hunter on his safari, first guiding him to the quarry and then providing the ultimate protection, even at the cost of their own lives. Should the white hunter come under attack, his Askari would if necessary place himself in the path of the charging animal. "The Askari was the white hunter's hunter, his eyes and ears and right hand. He was in fact his guardian."[3]

Askari is a reduction print, end result of a process of production uniquely well suited to Greaves's interest in the dynamics of production. The printing of each successive colour means a reduction of the actual printing surface of the block. The first colour put down will therefore establish the number of prints that can be made. Once completed, the edition cannot be repeated. Because the printing block is progressively consumed in the process, *the final prints are the only prints.* It is a reflection, from within the very process of production and reproduction, on the question of the authority and finality of the original. The print of *Askari* which is before me as I write is number 8 of the 10.

It is easy to understand Greaves' attraction to the reduction print as a process of labour, with its delicate woodcarving and the sensual contact with tools and materials it requires. The streaks in some areas of the picture and the sharp, hard angularity of the edges are accounted for by the particular type of block that was used. Unlike the *Ancestral Images No. 3*, another reduction print of the time, made from a linoleum block, *Askari* was printed from a plywood block. The streaky effect and the hard, sharp edges, even of the circles and curves, were imposed by the grain of the plywood. In a moving and evocative essay on Shiko Munakata, the Japanese master of the woodcut, Arthur Danto refers to this as the transferring of "the life of the wood" on to the print.[4]

Greaves would have been drawn to the restricted colour possibilities that brought the exacting monochromatic ideal closer. It would have been no less a question of rigour and limits and the discipline of application. To produce a colour print requires repeated rubbings, as many times as there are colours. This calls for a high degree of co-ordination and precision of registration. This would be required – as is the case in the traditional colour print – even when different blocks are used, each for the application of a single colour. In the case of the reduction print, the printing process was interspersed and integrated with bouts of carving and gouging, thereby imposing greater demands on accuracy of registration. Greaves's temperament, it has to be said, was well suited to this "mechanization of the process of creation", as Danto calls it.

With its inbuilt immunity to commodification (mass-production), the reduction print *Askari* raises the question of artistic uniqueness, and the finality of the act of production. I have used the word "investigation" on more than one occasion to indicate the intellectual curiosity, that sense of theoretical restlessness that is at the heart of Greaves's project. Note the tenacity with which he sets out, in the paintings of the 1950s, of which *Preacher* and *Beggar and Urchin* (see p. 30) are typical, to resolve certain problems that begin, or at any rate which propose themselves initially, as problems of technique.

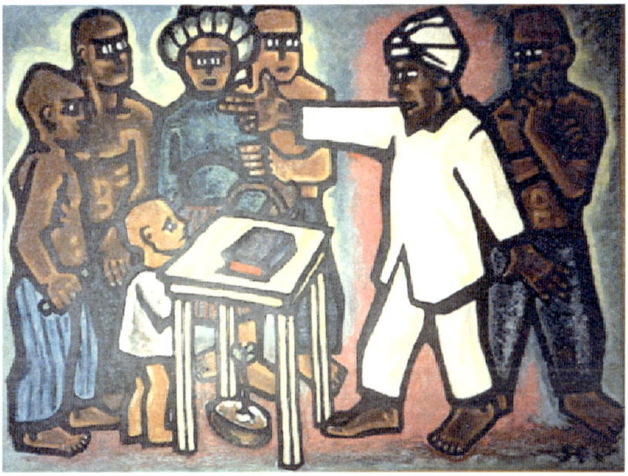

Preacher, 1958, oils, 91.5 x 122cm

I have in mind here the outlining of the figures. In a practical sense, this is the challenge Greaves sets himself in these early paintings. In one of the few contemporary commentaries on Greaves's work, Basil Hinds, that diligent servant of art, called these paintings the "People of the Pavement" series.[5] In painting after painting, notwithstanding the variation of scene, action and characters, nor the differences of strength and tone and emphasis, the essential problem of the outlining of the figures is pursued with what can be recognized as Greaves's studious persistence. This problem will eventually resolve itself in two approaches, or better, in two forms: into considerations of the edge, as in the "latticed" Mazaruni paintings of the late seventies, *Canecutters*, (see p. 51) *Black Beetle* (1977), *Channaman* (1978, see p. 52). And, secondly, into propositions about the inter-connectedness of people with the space they inhabit, about the dissolving of the lines of separation and difference that stand in the way of oneness and community. So what began as a matter of technique has revealed itself a matter of vision. In the best sense, Greaves is a painter of ideas, not a thesis painter. The intellectual investigations are rooted in the soil of form and technique and spring from it, and nothing is forced.

II. The early paintings

The *People of the Pavement* paintings are confidently executed, centred in the lives of the ordinary people. Greaves was born and grew up in the city. Like the late and revered Martin Carter, he was a man of the pavement, alert to the humour and despair and daily drama of the tenement yards and market places. In these first paintings, perhaps his best known to his Guyanese audience, Greaves is very much the public painter: bold social themes – labour, poverty, popular religion – dramatically, even theatrically expressed in a readily accessible idiom. The work of the great Mexican muralists, Orozco in particular, is a strong influence. This organic interest in the lives of ordinary working people – organic because he is of them and they are never for him mere spectacle (as in the romantic mode of some genre painting) – is to remain with Greaves throughout. Decades later, expressing himself in a more stylised and abstract idiom and moving away from groups to single figures, his subjects are the pavement vendor, channaman, grass-cutter, fried fish seller, sugar-worker, hat-man. With this group of paintings, beginning with the 1958 *Preacher*, including *Beggar and Urchin*, *The Weeding Gang* (see p. 28) and ending with the 1962 *People of the Garden City* (seep. 29), Greaves embarked on what were to become his life-long researches. Here at the very outset, the themes and motifs are introduced and the technical investigations launched.

For all their simplicity of design and narrative presentation, *Preacher* and *Beggar and Urchin* also set out to resolve the particular problem at hand: how to treat the spaces between figures. Common to both is the black outlining of the figures. It is not the last time that the sign-painter's son, remembering

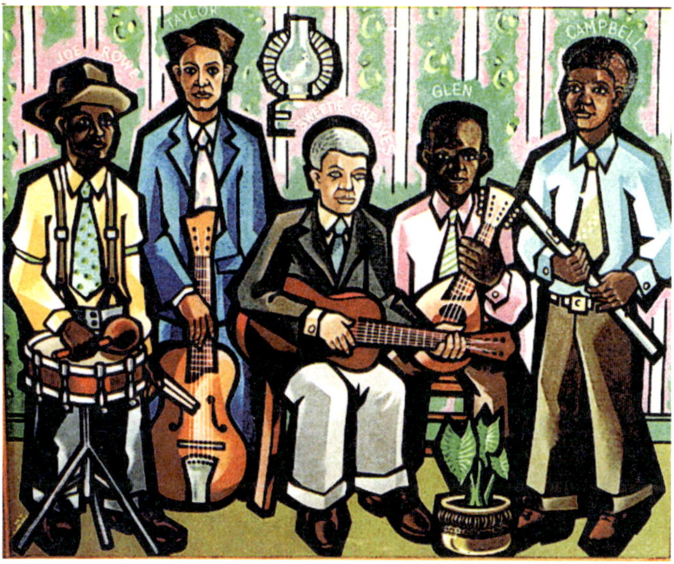

Old Time String Band, 1977, oils, 95.5 x 122cm

the lettering experiences of his boyhood, will be drawn to the black outline.

The tribute to the group of artisan musicians which included his father, 'Sweetie' Greaves, *Old Time String Band,* with its heavily outlined figures, was conceptualised in a technical sense as part of the *People of the Pavement* series. It was executed some twenty years later, after the last surviving member of the group had died. Greaves has commented on the anachronism: "Seeing that the painting was conceptualized and visualized such a long time ago, I could not bring myself to treat it using the new compositional technique I was developing. In a manner of speaking the work therefore is anachronistic in style." Greaves inscribed their names in the painting as a mark of commemoration and respect for these sons of the working people "who were determined not to allow a life of drudgery to destroy their sense of the beautiful and their ability to express this feeling through music."[6] This problem of the defining of the figures will undergo a further refinement and complication, in the series of mini-paintings of a decade later, notably *Biscuit Story No. 1* (1991, see p. 125). There, what began three decades earlier as a technical exploration has grown into

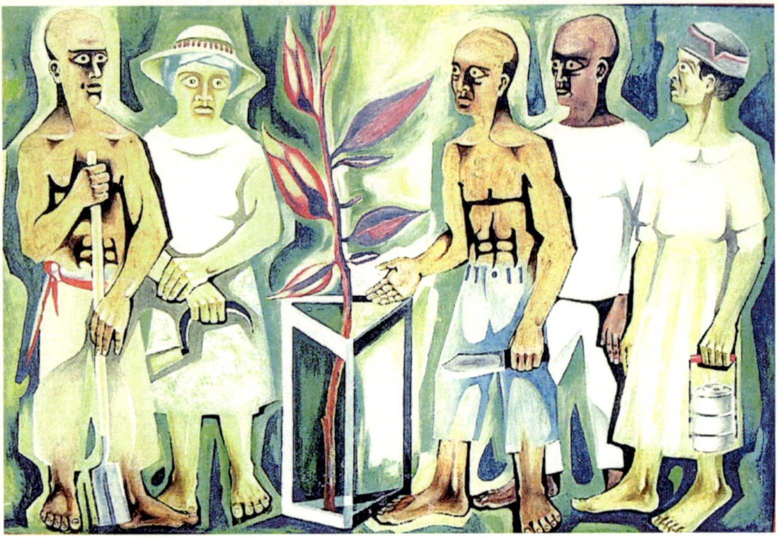

The Weeding Gang, 1961, oils, 81 x 122cm

bold propositions about the identity and relationship of real objects in an imaginary space. From there space itself moves to the centre of the enquiry.

In the two paintings that follow, the heavy black outline gives way to haloes of green in *The Weeding Gang* and to red and blue outlined areas in *People of the Garden City.* These are complementary pieces, expressing and uniting opposite poles: natural/mineral, creation/destruction, life/death. In the first, agricultural workers, tools in hand, are in the Botanic Gardens in Georgetown. They are gathered around a blooming plant, Greaves' botanical invention.

The central figure, pruning knife in hand, is taken with the splendid new shoots of life and is showing them off. Within the group of city paintings, *Weeding Gang* is a kind of pastoral interlude, a *locus amoenus* amid the surrounding bustle. The ironically titled *People of the Garden City*, with its images of despair and dislocation, is at once the most achieved and the most disturbing of the early paintings. (Ironical because Georgetown, with its wide tree-lined avenues and flowering yards, is frequently described as the Garden City of the Caribbean). No drama, no narrative, no sense of community; only starkness, stasis, isolation. The four figures, each immured in its own panel, tell of atomisation.

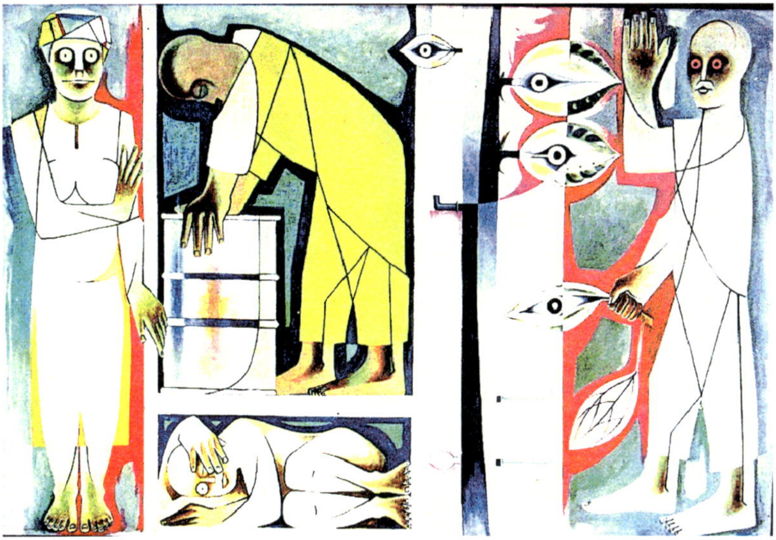

People of the Garden City, 1962, oils, 81 x 122 cm

In the upper central panel, a man forages in a garbage bin. It does not seem to have yielded much. In the lower panel, a naked figure is curled in a foetal position in a niche in a wall, one eye closed, the other looking out.

In the right panel, the iconoclast, eyes aglow with terrible purpose, tears off the leaves sprouting from a lamppost. The leaves, originating in the iron rungs of the post, are in the process of mutating from mineral to vegetal state; they have eyes and cross over to the animal world: iron→leaf→eye.

In the left panel, a woman with a Madrasi head-tie draws the curtain and invites our contemplation of those cast out from the garden, the dispossessed of the city, a prophecy come true in the Guyana of the eighties and nineties. We will encounter this garbage bin again, thirty-two years later, bearing new burdens of meaning.

It would be instructive to trace the evolution of motifs that recur throughout the paintings: the potted plant, the cage, the bird, the foot, the leaf – the simple things of this world which accumulate a radiant power from painting to painting. See how the leaf grows, now alone on a branch, now multiplying, now magically sprouting from a staff. In *Magic Pepper Tree* (1976), leaves spread open like fans, trinities of leaves and

Magic Pepper Tree, 1976, Oils, 81.2 x 61cm

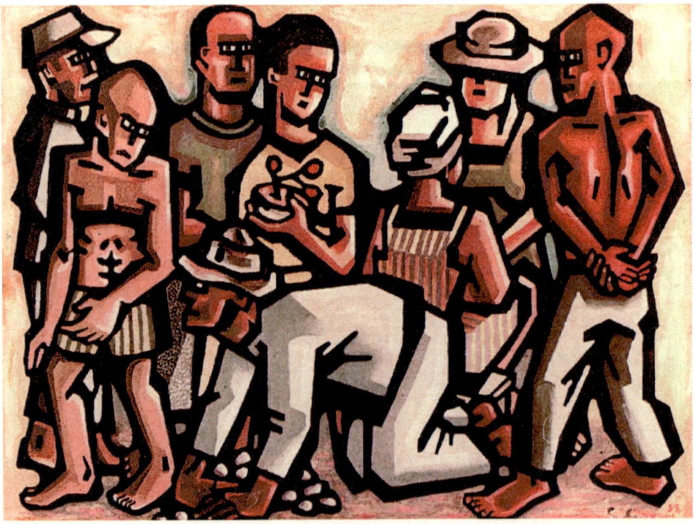

Beggar and Urchin, 1958, Oils, 81 x 122cm

branches, and are mysteriously unattached to their branches. Where leaf should meet branch, a hot space, a field of force. In *Big Bread* (see p.32) there are five plants whose stems and leaves are haloed with the same light that glows around the great plaited loaf from which they sprout.

It would also be useful to examine the pictorial representation of self-consciousness within the paintings, places where the picture takes account of its relationship to the viewer. Certain of Greaves's paintings are self-reflexive in this sense. This can be seen in the early observer figures.

In *Beggar and Urchin* (1958) he is standing off to the right, hands clasped behind his back, not of the scene, but its essential witness. In a later painting of the same period, *Beggars*, he

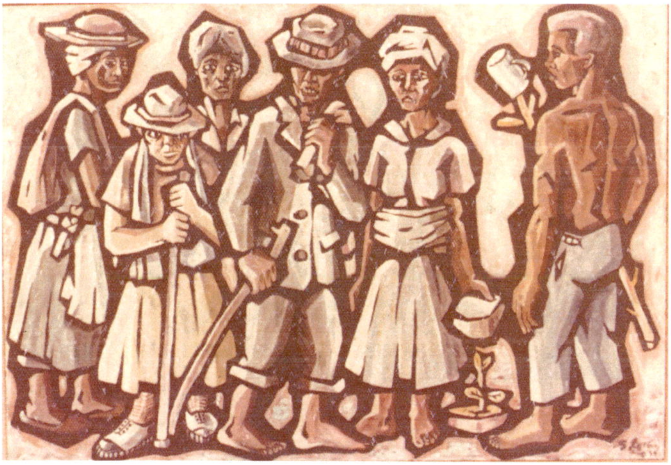

Beggars, 1959, oils, 81x122cm

becomes involved in the scene, an actor in the drama of the street. And see how at the very moment that he stops being a mere witness and joins in the activity of the world, another figure from within the group stares out of the picture, directly at the viewer who in turn is drawn closer to the action. In the process, the viewer has changed places with the former witnesses to become the street's latest spectator.

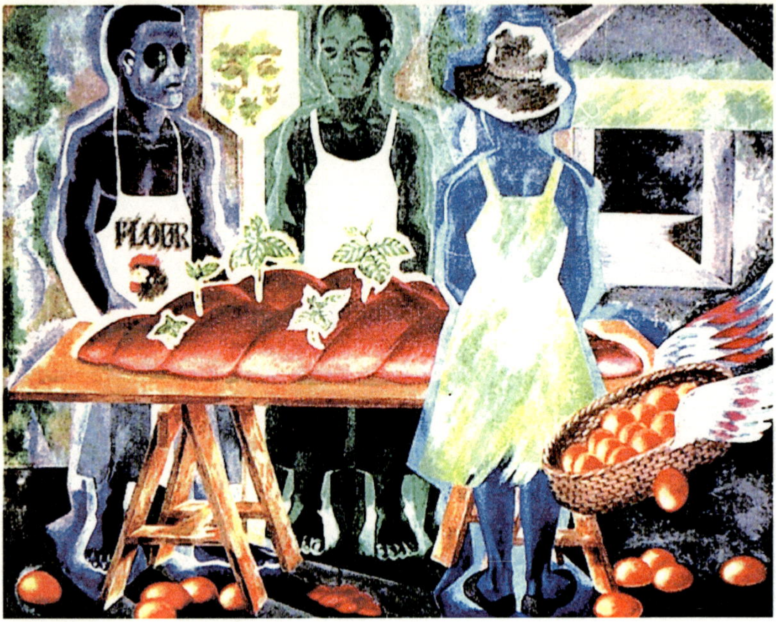

Big Bread, 1972, Oils, 85.7 x 113.2cm

The self-reflexivity is there in *Big Bread*, in the little loaf lying quietly and out of sight under the baker's table where the big loaf is laid out, a perfect little replica of the grand original. It is a surprisingly whimsical presentation for such a serious picture. *Big Bread*, with its religious allegory and private symbolism, was painted in 1971 out of Greaves's experience of his father's dead body laid out on the mortuary table.

Greaves's is an exceptional art, passionately committed to the truth of form that is at once the truth of vision. I venture this: if all other records of modern Guyanese life were to disappear, a study of Greaves's paintings of compassion of the fifties and sixties would be enough to tell us how we lived, what yards and houses we inhabited, what tools our hands held, what musical instruments consoled us, what forms of commerce we engaged in, what hats and pants and dresses and shoes we wore, what leaves and birds and flowers lit up our lives.

With the *People of the Pavement* paintings, Greaves was well launched on his long journey. It has not ended. In 2001, in the midst of the political turmoil in Guyana and Trinidad, exhibitions of the *There is a Meeting here Tonight* series opened in Georgetown and Port of Spain. These most explicitly political of paintings show Greaves, in the high tide of his maturity, returning to public themes in a direct and easily accessible idiom, insisting that art, whatever else it may do, also has an ancient duty: to boldly proclaim difficult truths and so change the way we experience the world.

ENDNOTES TO CHAPTER ONE

1. Herbert Read, *Icon and Idea – The Function of Art in the Development of Human Consciousness*, (Faber and Faber, London, 1955), p.18.

2. SG, journal entry, June 1984.

3. SG, in conversation.

4. Arthur C. Danto, *Philosophizing Art* (Berkeley: Univ. of California Press, 1999), p.173 ("Munakata in New York").

5. Basil Hinds (1919-81 b. Guyana) was a member of the British Guiana Arts and Crafts Society and Guyanese Art Group; he liked working in gouache (water-based powder colour). Hinds was a teacher, and later headmaster in primary education. A lover of classical music and jazz , he produced regular radio programs. He was also a commentator on art, music and drama, sometimes under several pseudonyms. He gained an Art Teacher's Diploma from Bristol University, UK, and taught at the Teachers' Training College and Queen's College in Georgetown. He curated art exhibitions and was Art Examiner for General Certificate Examinations at Ordinary and Advanced Levels. He later became cultural liaison officer with the United States Information service.

6. Stanley Greaves, "Iconographical Determinants in my work," MFA Thesis, Howard University, 1980.

CHAPTER TWO

EXTENDING INTO THREE DIMENSIONS I

> *It is perhaps not necessary to observe further that art is a highly contagious 'disease' – that the eye of the artist feeds unconsciously on whatever formal motes come its way. To strive to be uninfluenced by the work of one's predecessors or contemporaries is neither possible nor desirable, all questions of traditionalism apart. Artists confront their destiny – the general history of the civilization of which they are a part – with a certain unity.*
>
> **Herbert Read**[1]

In the luminous essay he contributed to the monograph that accompanied the 1998 Aubrey Williams exhibition at the Whitechapel Gallery in London, the late Denis Williams, nearing the end of a remarkable life, reflected with some feeling on the predicament confronting the Caribbean artist newly arrived in London in the fifties and sixties. "Unlike the West Indian 'migrants with manuscripts'," he wrote, "the West Indian painter in the metropolis creates problems for himself by adopting paradigms that result from an evolutionary agenda outside of his history and impossible for him to share." The writers went "for recognition" and the musicians "to impress." They did not go to learn their trade. "West Indian painters, by contrast, practising an intrusive and historically recent art, did not enjoy a similar assurance; they knew next to nothing about the Renaissance and its aftermath. They knew nothing at all about the academies. Thus, they most certainly went to Britain to learn."[2] Aubrey Williams had arrived in Britain in 1952. His first solo exhibition, at the New Vision Centre Gallery, took place six years later.[3]

Almost exactly ten years later, in the summer of 1962, the 26 year old Stanley Greaves set out for London; he spent a year there before going on to the University of Newcastle-upon-Tyne to read for a degree in Fine Art and a Diploma in Art Education. He was to remain there until 1968. For the year that he was in London, awaiting admission to the university, Greaves did no painting but busied himself visiting the city's museums and galleries, able now to stand in front of paintings and sculptures he had so far experienced only in reproduction in books and magazines. In the contemporary British art scene, Pop Art was in its heyday. Greaves was able to see work by the major artists in the Pop Art movement and was particularly interested in Derek Boshier and David Hockney. The young Frank Bowling, born in Guyana, was making a name for himself in London at the time. To Greaves his work seemed essentially part of the British art scene. When he arrived at the University of Newcastle he found that Richard Hamilton, the doyen of the Pop Art movement, was the principal tutor in painting. Hamilton's painting *Just What Is It that Makes Today's Home so Different, so Appealing?*, with its references to consumerism and popular culture, is held to be the first of the Pop Art works. The imagery of Pop Art drew on the everyday objects of the consumer society, from Campbell Soup cans to comic strips and advertisements. Although Greaves became interested in the manner the human figure was treated by some of the Young Contemporaries, it did not take him long to recognize that the ideological premises and technical concerns of Pop Art, its roots in the material consumer culture of Europe and North America, had no relevance or resonance for him as someone from an underdeveloped, colonial society. In his own words, Greaves found himself "the invisible man" in Richard Hamilton's class at Newcastle.

The year he spent in London before going up to Newcastle proved to be invaluable. More than anything else, it brought him face to face not only with the work of the masters old and new, but with what it meant to be an artist, and how he saw his relationship to the world of art. While he certainly went to Britain to learn, Greaves had left Guyana not as a novice but as a practising artist who, from the time he was fourteen years old, had sat at the feet of the pioneering E.R. Burrowes, founder of the Working People's Art Class and mentor to a generation of Guyanese artists[4]. He had been submitting pieces to the Working People's Art Class annual exhibitions since 1951. The Second Group Show of Paintings, with Michael Leila, Ron Savory, and Emerson Samuels had opened at Bookers Universal Building in Georgetown in 1960. He had also shown work at the Department of Culture annual exhibitions from 1959 to 1962, the year he left for London. By the time he set out for Britain in 1962, Greaves had already produced a number of impressive paintings in which he had begun to define himself and mark out the zones of his work to come.

Is it any wonder that the painter of the *People of the Pavement* felt a stranger in the strange land of Pop Art? Greaves did not feel that having Richard Hamilton as tutor would develop his work, but happily, turning away from painting studies opened up the opportunity to pursue woodcarving. With the encouragement of Murray McCheyne, he switched to formal studies in sculpture at Newcastle and eventually majored in it. Here too, he was not a complete newcomer. Woodcarving had been in fact among his first enthusiasms. As a boy he would dawdle on his way to school to observe tiny Chinese trade carvings of the Buddha, the fisherman, the farmer with his oxen, marvelling at their detail and naturalistic representation. His most prized possession was the carving tool he had fashioned out of a penknife, one blade sharpened and shaped into a chisel. After showing some of his carvings to Burrowes, the schoolboy Greaves was presented by the great man with a set of carving tools. It was to prove an act of great prescience on Burrowes's part. In Guyana in the early 1950s, Greaves began with relief carvings, in the tradition of the Croatian sculptor Ivan Mestrovic. From Burrowes's well-stocked library, he pored over the reproductions of the work of the German sculptor, Ernst Barlach, and took careful note of the medieval wood carving tradition. He was drawn to direct carving, admiring in particular the naturalistic pieces that bore the marks of the chisel. In Guyana, UK Art magazines such as *Studio* and *Studio International* were made available through the British Council. Through them he studied the work of Barbara Hepworth and admired its simplified outlines of basic organic forms. Newcastle, for the next two years, allowed for deeper exploration.

He elected to write his Honours Thesis on the work of Constantin Brancusi, the pathfinder and first of the moderns in sculpture. He chose well. Henry Moore has spoken of Brancusi's historic importance: "Since the Gothic, European sculpture had become overgrown with moss, weeds – all sorts of surface excrescences which completely concealed shape. It has been Brancusi's mission to get rid of this overgrowth, and to make us once more shape-conscious."[5] Greaves has never lost his deep admiration for Brancusi's achievement, his monk-like devotion to the purity of organic form and to the labour of sculpture. Most crucially, drawing on the ancient word-carving traditions of his native Romania, Brancusi had ushered in a revival of carving, displacing modeling as the fundamental determinant of sculpture.

Greaves's other focus at Newcastle was on the constructive method of producing sculpture where pieces are fitted together using carpentering techniques; and on the combining of materials

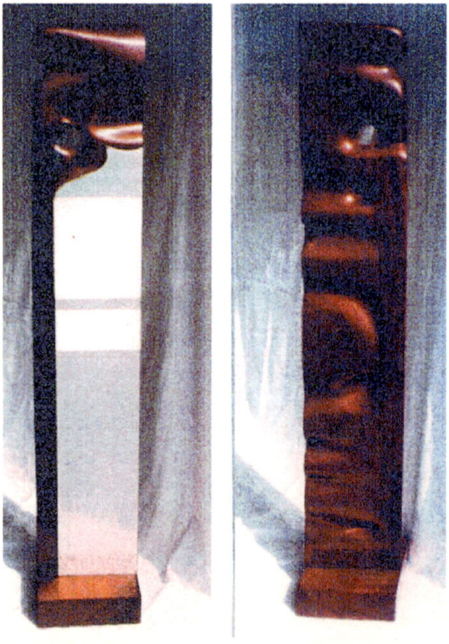

Amatuk, 1967, mahogany and mixed media, h. 152.5cm

of different kinds, mixed media fabrications. He made use mainly of aluminium, formica and wood, constructing the pieces separately and fitting them together. The elegant *Amatuk* (1967), inspired by a waterfall in the Guyanese rainforest, with its carved undulations in mahogany, its sections of aluminium and formica, fitted into the plinth, is typical of his work in this manner. The carpentry involved was such that after some thirty-five years, the carved slab slots into the solid plinth as securely as it ever did.

The austere, almost minimalist *Standing Figure* (1967) is his crucifixion, the carved abstracted body of Christ fitted into the louvred cross. The most powerful of the Newcastle constructions, *Slave Stock* (1965), out of mahogany, arborite and plywood, was inspired by the slave whip in the Georgetown Museum, with its handle wrapped in leather thongs and copper wire, resembling barbed wire, an abstraction of the barbed thongs of the slave whip. The sculpture is some 3 feet high, an inverted L shape out of mahogany. The axis of the horizontal part of the L is bent to about 15 degrees out of true, avoiding the flattening of the L shape. Through this upturned L are

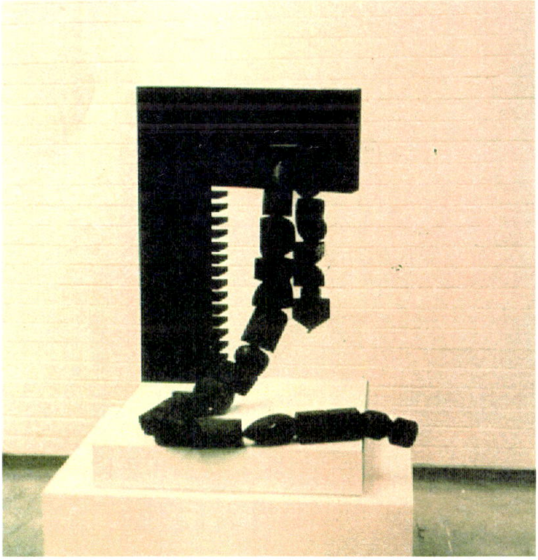

Slave Stock, 1964, mahogany, 101.6 cm

strung small, carved abstract shapes, irregular in form, like some fantastic necklace hanging down.

The inverted L shape form and the strung forms rest on a three feet square platform covered with formica, the white of the formica played off against the darkness of the wood. It is Greaves's most achieved mixed media construction and an image of frightful power. While at Newcastle he went on to extend the range of materials, producing the see-through form, *Ralegh's Dream*, an open-ended box with a false perspective that opened to reveal a carved shape like a hook or anchor with a few pieces hanging from it. The top and bottom of the two half-doors were covered with mirrors that created reflected images of the carved shapes inside the box. *Ralegh's Dream* makes reference to the mad chimeras Ralegh chased in his quest for Manoa: hook and anchor for the ships he used in his Orinoco *entradas*, mirrors and false perspectives signifying all the wrong leads and ultimate futility of the quest. Greaves was to resume work in the see-through form many years later in Guyana, when he executed *Diamond Box*.

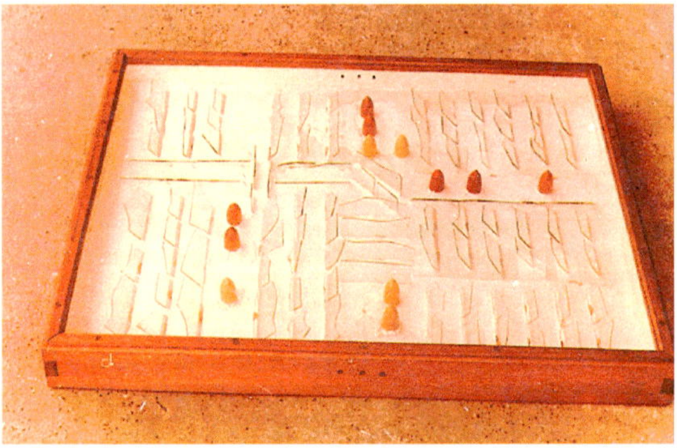

Diamond Box, 1970, mixed media construction, 72.6 x 61 x 7.6 cm

The flat wood and glass construction, reminiscent of Giacometti's "sculpture-as-board-game" pieces, projects some of the qualities of diamonds, transparent, hard and facetted. The shards of glass embedded in plaster-of-paris represent the peril of diving down to the bottom of a fast-flowing river in the search for the diamond-bearing gravel. The glass pieces were presented in a pattern drawn from the louvre and lattice effect he was to explore more fully in the *Mazaruni* paintings of the seventies (see pp. 49-59). The painted bullet-shaped wooden pieces, in addition to creating a sense of tension in the object, represent the different stones found alongside the diamonds on the riverbed.

By the time Greaves returned to Guyana in 1968, the winds of black power were gusting through the region, leading to convulsions in Trinidad in 1970 and the radicalisation of a new generation of Caribbean activists and intellectuals. Eyes were turned to Africa. Controversy swirled around issues of Pan-Africanism. In this atmosphere, Greaves, like others, began to examine anew the way African art had impacted on the art of Europe in the first years of the century, particularly among

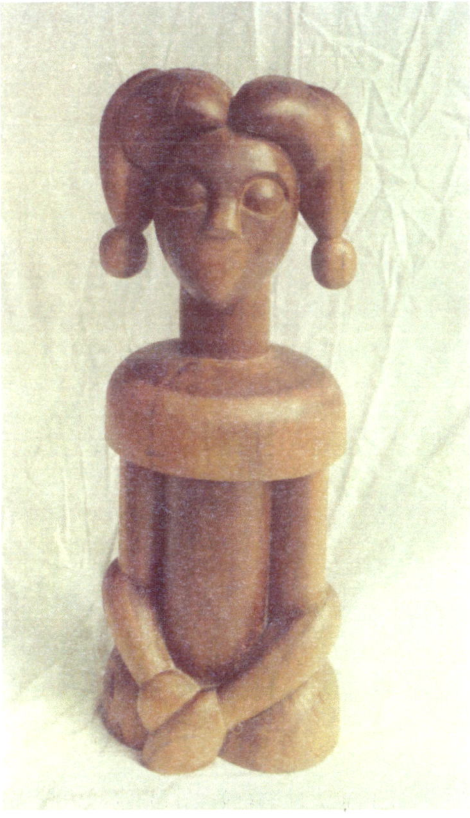

Sonya, 1976, cedar wood, h.

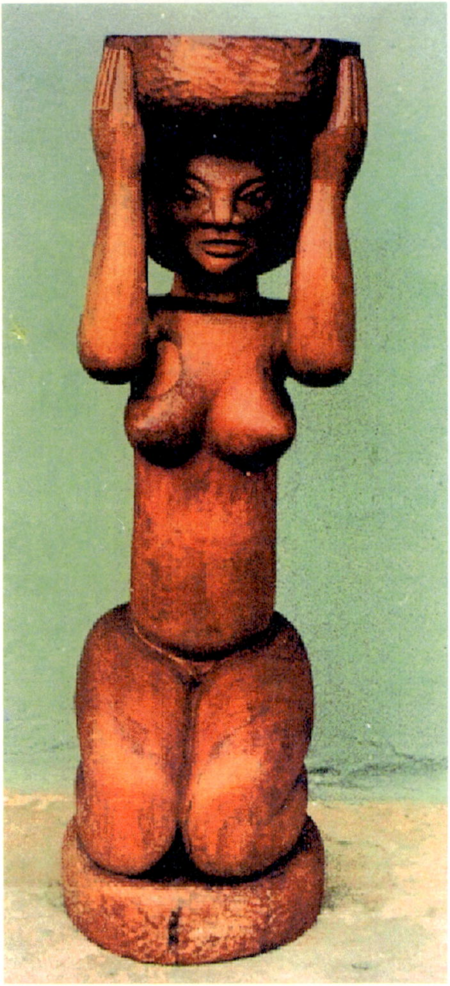

Orisha, 1976, cedar wood, h. 66.6cm

the Modernists. He paid particular attention to the manner in which form in African sculpture was conceptualised and presented. Greaves writes: "The style held the interest because the spiritual ideology informing the production was not accessible... What I 'borrowed' was the approach to the perception and analysis of form and applied it to my own area of interest, be it traditional sculptural techniques or modernist practice as in constructions (which had been informed by 'primitive' work from Africa as well as the Pacific islands."[7] The realisation of form and the actual presentation of sculptural values were to remain central concerns. Between 1976 and 1978, he executed three pieces derivative of aspects of traditional West African carving: *Little Man, Orissa* and *Sonya.*

The figures are non-naturalistic, tending towards abstracting parts of the human body into geometric forms, seen specifically in *Sonya.* Round forms, befitting a female, exaggerated plaits, semi-abstract features and a frontal presentation draw on the African sculptural traditions in both *Orissa* and *Sonya.* In the latter, Greaves's last effort in single figure carving in the African manner, the form is more abstract and geometrical, more in keeping with modernist appropriations than African art.

Ancestral Figures combines shapes carved in a West African manner with construction by carpentering techniques. It is an attempt at creating a form that is not determined by the basic cylindrical form of the block of tree trunk. In this piece, two of the carved shapes and the foot of the stool are painted in colours characteristic of Yoruba sculpture in Dahomey. The

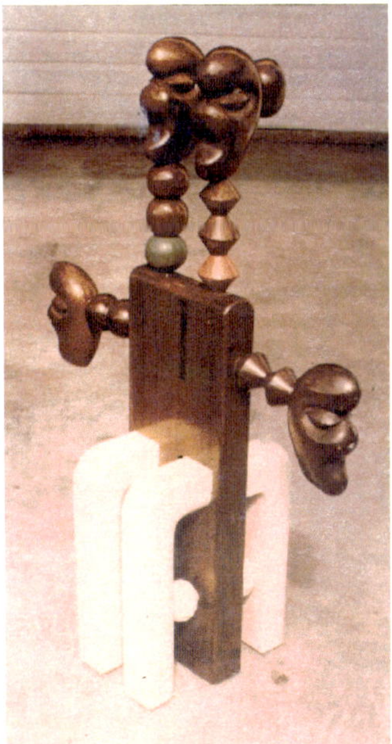

Ancestral Figures, 1976, mahogany and paint, h. 110cm

colours have symbolic value: white for the ancestral spirits represented by the four little carved, stylised heads within the legs of the stool, the maternal and paternal grandparents. Mother and father are at the top, the mother with her neck shaped by the rounded beads, the father's by conical beads. Her bead is green, his red. At their sides, two children, one male and one female, stick out like arms. The piece is at once stool and standing two-headed figure. "The basic conformity of *Ancestral Figures* to a chair", Greaves has written, "is meant to symbolically represent the stability that comes to us through communicating with the ancestral spirits."[6] The round beads of the female and the angular beads of the male establish between them that tension that characterises African sculpture.

His journey into African artistic traditions led to deeper researches into African cosmology. Soon he was making connections and drawing comparisons with the cosmology of the Americas. He was especially intrigued by the concept of sacrifice, what he called "the idea of people who voluntarily sacrificed their lives for a spiritual principle."[7] He cites the case of West Africa where a king, if his people were suffering, is deemed to have come to the end of his tenure and to have fulfilled his earthly duties. After the Elders so pronounce, the king would be presented with a bowl of poison by the women elders who remained outside his door until he drank. After his removal, a new king was elected. Dynasties were not permitted, so all the dead king's direct blood relations were removed from the royal line. They would be treated with respect, but no longer wield any power. Power was invested in the new king who then chose his court. Greaves was struck by the similarity to the investiture of the Mayan Corn God, Xipu-Toltec.

Each year young men vied for the honour to be designated Corn God whose word for the following year would be law. At the end of that year, the young Corn God was sacrificed and his skin flayed. The officiating priest would be wrapped in the flayed skin and become the authority in the interregnum, the acting Corn God until the skin rotted off his back. The new Corn God would then be chosen, a new young man to represent the fresh corn growing. Just as the corn sheds that husk, so the new god too will have to shed the husk in order to let a new corn come through.

The canvas skin is stretched by cords on a board. Shapes made of different materials – wood, aluminium and cotton stitched in like a knap of a rug – against the blood-red board complete the construction. Greaves was in the end dissatisfied with the Xipu-Toltec pieces. He found them too elegant of construction, the artistry standing in the way of the sense of horror he set out to convey. "They were not horrible enough", he says.[8] He was to write later: "The aesthetic determinants have dominated the piece and the result lacks the kind of felt tension one should experience in the face of a sacrifice that has been made. The canvas as skin, the red background as blood are obvious analogies. The internal pieces of wood, metal and wool, however, do not provide the tension that is needed. They are resting too easily on eyes and mind."[9] To achieve the effect he wanted would require execution in an expressionist mode which he admitted to finding the most difficult of methods in the realm of sculpture. "To work in that expressionist mode means you really have to begin throwing different kinds of materials together to bring out the horrors as I perceive it, of this self-sacrifice, of the entrails, the blood."[10] He felt in the end that it might be a topic better executed in painting.

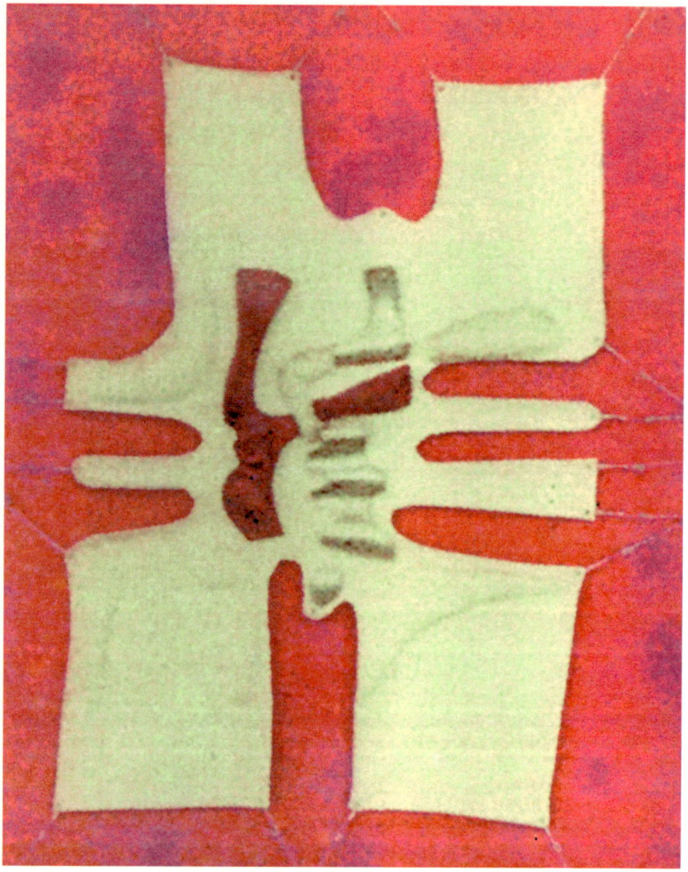

Flayed Culture God, Xipu-Toltec,
1970, mixed media construction, 101.5 x 85cm

ENDNOTES TO CHAPTER TWO

1. Herbert Read, *Modern Sculpture* (London: Thames and Hudson, 1964), p. 168

2. Denis Williams, C.C.H., D.Litt. (Guyana, 1923 – 1998) was a member of the Guiana Arts and Crafts Society and the Guyanese Art Group in the 1940s. Attended Camberwell School of Art 1946-48 on the first British Council Scholarship for art offered in British Guiana. Major appointments were: 1950-57 lecturer at Central School of Fine Art London; in Africa from 57-62 at the School of Fine Art in Karthoum; lecturer 62-66, University of Ife; 66-67, University of Lagos. Returned to Guyana 1967. He researched Amerindian petroglyphs to 1974 when he was made Director of Art. Founded the Burrowes School of Art in 1975, very enthusiastic about the way young artists in Guyana went about developing and expressing their visions. Founded the Walter Roth Museum of Anthropology 1977. Visiting research scholar, Smithsonian Institute 1980. Between 1955-96 was the recipient of several research grants in Africa and Guyana. Apart from his art work and published research in African and Amerindian art/craft, Williams also wrote some short stories and two novels, *Other Leopards*, and while in Nigeria, *The Third Temptation*. Other publications include *Giglioli in Guyana 1922-1972* (biography); *Image and Idea in the Arts of the Caribbean* (1970); *Habitat and Culture in Ancient Guyana* (1985); *Amazonia Petroglyphs* (1985); *Prehistoric Culture of the Iwokrama Rain Forest Reserve* (1996); and frequent articles in *Archaelogy and Anthropology: Journal of the Walter Roth Museum of Archaeology and Anthropology*. His *Icon and Image* on the classical forms of African art in metal is a pioneering work. He wrote several essays and catalogue notes on the Visual Arts in Guyana. In the late 1940s, early 1950s his work was highly praised by artist and critic Wyndham Lewis and in 1950 his painting "The Human World" made the *Time* magazine cover. It was bought by public subscription in Guyana and became the start of the National Collection.

3. Aubrey Williams (1926-1990, b. Guyana), as a young man, participated in Burrowes's *Working People's Art Class* (see note below). Trained as an agronomist, he was employed as an agricultural officer. Posted to Hosororo, a villlage in Guyana's remote North West District, he lived among the Warau Amerindians and began his lifelong interest in Amerindian culture. He moved to England in 1952 to pursue his career as an artist. He was a member of the *Caribbean Artists Movement*. His major works were the paintings in his *Shostakovich* and *Olmec-Maya* series.

4. Edward Rupert Burrowes (1900-66 b. Barbados) arrived in Guyana as a young child and remained living with his godparents. Possessing a sharp intellect, he became knowledgeable and well-informed; he was well read in English Literature and History, and was a bible scholar. He joined the British Guiana Arts and Crafts Society that later became the Guyanese Art Group. In 1945 he formed his own group to bring art to the masses – the Working Peoples' Art Class. Burrowes had several careers – artist, master tailor, lay preacher, journalist, radio broadcaster, art teacher, and education officer. He had a remarkable bass singing voice but turned down an offer to go to sing in Italy. He was awarded a British Council Scholarship in art 1949-50; he studied at St. Martins and at the Brighton College of Art. He was always willing to impart what he had learnt. He was awarded the OBE by the Queen in 1954 for his work as artist and teacher. Burrowes taught at the Teachers' Training College and at Queen's College, the premier boys' school in the country. He came to be revered as the "Father of Art" in Guyana. Burrowes worked in several media, mainly painting and some sculpture and block printing. The School of Art in Guyana is named after him.

5. Henry Moore, "The Sculptor Speaks", 1937. Quoted in Herschel Chipp, *Theories in Modern Art* (Berkeley: University of California Press, 1984), p. 595.

6. SG, "Iconographical Determinants in my work," MFA Thesis, Howard University, 1980.

7. SG, in conversation.

8. SG, written note, 2004.

9. SG. "Iconographical Determinants in my work".

10. SG, in conversation.

CHAPTER THREE

CRISIS AND RENEWAL: THE MAZARUNI PAINTINGS

Greaves's return to Guyana in 1968 after the Newcastle experience did not lead to a resumption of painting. On the contrary, the years from 1968 to 1976 proved to be years of drought for the painter of the *People of the Pavement.* A cartoon for a larger work, *Sale of the Village*, submitted in 1968/9 for a mural competition for the Crichlow Labour College, confirmed the loss of verve and direction. He was attempting to resume the modality of the figure paintings of a decade earlier, but the cartoon lacked wholeness and strength. He was to conclude later that he was looking at Guyana, the well-spring of his inspiration, "not as a person who was sensitive to his environment, but as a painter who was interested in the effects of painting." He reflected on this season of drought: "When I was in Britain, my body was in Britain, but my soul was still in Guyana. When I returned to Guyana, I left my soul in Britain and I had to get it back."[1]

The turning point came not in a studio but in the Guyana bush. Accompanying his friend and former pupil, the photographer Bobby Fernandes and Isaac Jerry, a legendary Amerindian path-finder, Greaves travelled into the deep interior: up the Mazaruni River by boat and on foot to Imbaimadai, Maipuri, Chinakruk, Jawalla. He immersed himself in the forest. "Water, rock, trees, giant trees. For about three days I was lost in space and time. Chronological time just disappeared. I had strange dreams." He emerged from the bush and, soon after, executed *Mazaruni*, a seminal painting that triggered new explorations, new directions. "I looked at this painting and said, yes, body and soul are now back together." It was a transforming and liberating experience. "I had regained my sight," he was to write years later.[2]

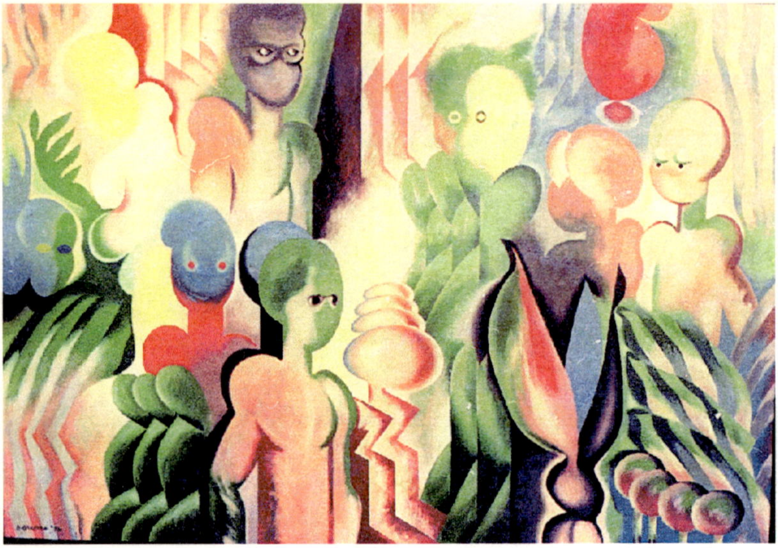

Mazaruni, Oils 80 x 60cm

There could be no return to the idiom of the figure paintings of the fifties. Instead, the trapezoidal forms of the broken jasper rocks, with their perfectly straight lines, pointed the way forward to *Black Ants and Diamonds, Canecutters, Channaman, Black Sunflowers*, *Traffic Lights and Banana Trees* and *Swamp Birds,* among the most important.

Canecutters is a dramatic expression of an idea central to Greaves's conception of being in the world: the labourers are smudged with the ash of the burnt cane, subhuman stalks emptied of individual identity, indistinguishable from the burnt-out cane they have produced and become. Cutlasses slash diagonally at the vertical stalks of cane, creating a sense of menace. What Greaves came to call his lattice technique, consisting of geometrically precise verticals and diagonals, elaborates a distinctive idiom. "I was discussing this 'lattice' effect with Martin Carter," he records in his journal, "and gave examples of it seen in nature – palm fronds, ripples, spider's web, network of cracks on the end grain of wood, turtle's shell, bark of some trees, e.g. samaan, mango. As I see it now, I have to find out more about the effect by producing more work, and then relating what I have discovered to problems of existence and being."[3] In the paintings of this period, issues of composition

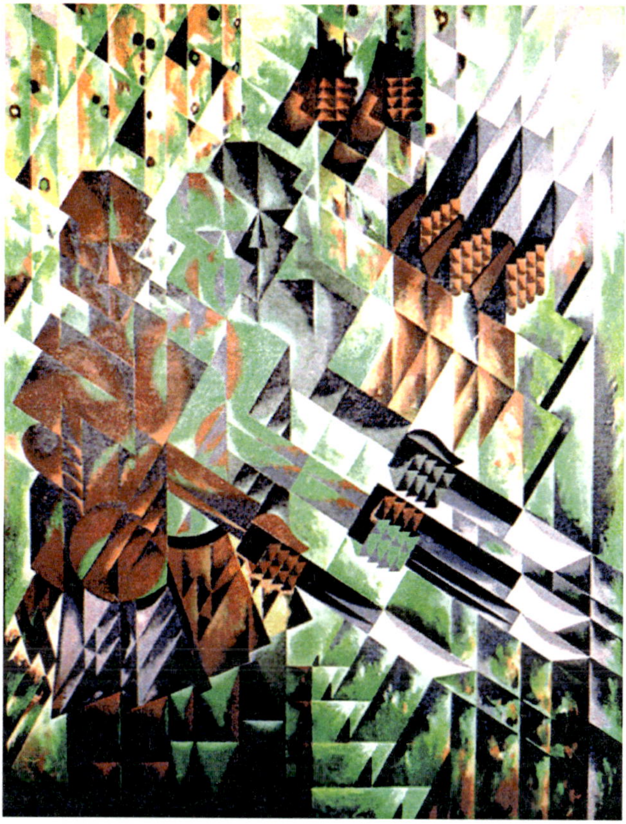

Canecutters, 1977, Oils, 114.2 x 84.4cm

move to the forefront of Greaves's concerns. *Channaman* and *Canecutters* are also exercises in geometry. Narration and psychological or symbolic content give way to the formal organisation of shape and colour.

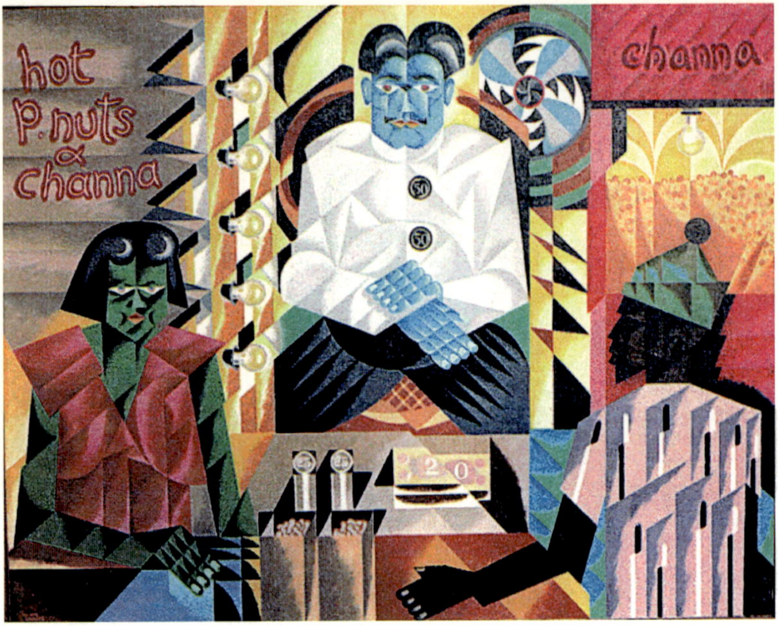

Channaman, 1978, Oils, 122 x 91.5 cm

In *Channaman*, the scene is familiar enough: the interior of a shop selling nuts and boiled chick peas (channa). In the iconography of the painting, the proprietor, with fifty-cent coins for buttons, surrounded by bright lights, is the high priest in his temple of Mammon. His acolyte serves a customer his two bags of channa. While it is thematically linked to the *Beggar and Urchin*, the stylistic concerns of *Channaman* are of a different order. The lattice effect, though resembling features of Analytical Cubism and Futurism, developed out of Greaves's own perceptions of the natural world. "I noticed for example, that whenever I viewed anything through the fronds of palm leaves I would get a kind of rhythmic fragmented effect. The same thing was true when viewing things through picket fences." The concentrated use of the lattice effect in the paintings of this period moved Greaves far beyond the formal and stylistic techniques of the *People of the Pavement* series, allowing him "to activate the picture plane in a way that [his] former technique of using a heavy black outline could not."[4]

Black Sunflowers was painted in tribute to Walter Rodney, the Guyanese historian and political activist who was blown up by an assassin's bomb on June 13, 1980, at the age of 38.[5] W-A-R spelled out at the center of the three sunflowers black with grief, are Rodney's initials: Walter Anthony Rodney. The warrior's belt buckle, almost coded in a Cyrillic typescript, spells b-o-m-b. Gripping a machete and hooked stick, his weeding tools, the figure of the gardener is at once heroic and strangely innocent. *Black Sunflowers* subdues the usual compositional and formal concerns of the lattice paintings and moves in the direction of story telling.

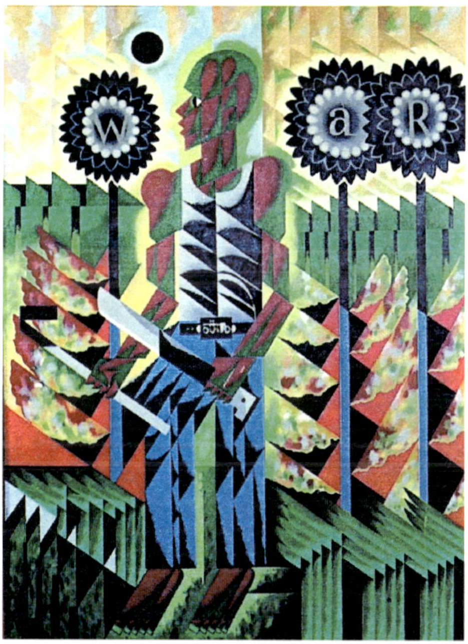

Black Sunflowers, 1981, Oils, 122 x 91.5 cm

A journal entry of 14 January 1978 opens up another dimension of this technical matter which is more than technique: "For some time now," he writes, "after reviewing my paintings of the "People of the Pavement" series, I have come to the conclusion that there are a number of things which went wrong with them. Most of these 'faults' are technical, but the most serious lies in the manner in which I perceived people – black people, coloured people of all shades from black to near white. I had devised a certain formula which I then used in such a manner that my perception of people had to be distorted in order to suit the formula – heavy black outlines. Such a technique did not allow me to paint black people, and one had to be content with brown people." He returns to the subject three days later on January 17 when he goes further: "...I had worked out a theoretical solution to the problem. Where the colour of the people was very dark I gave them a pale grey outline, combining this with the black outline for the figures of a lighter tonality. This was only a partial solution which was not satisfactory. As I thought about the problem of painting black people, I came to the view that in order to bring out the surface features, you had to concentrate on the areas that reflected light whereas in the person of lighter tonality you concentrated on areas of shadow."[6]

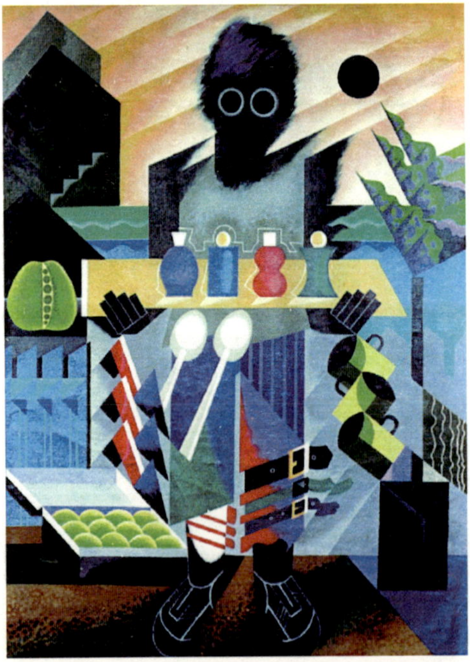

Caribbean Man No. 2, 1983, acrylics, 91.5 x 71cm

Caribbean Man No 2 is a black man painted black, as yet featureless but for the wire rim of his sunglasses. In the later paintings, *Hat Man* (1992, see p. 136), *Magus with Reversed Bananas* (1995, see p. 137), *Banana Manna* (1995, see p. 138) and *Election Results* (1997, see p. 181), modeled black faces, sternly expressive, signal Greaves's resolution of the "technical fault" he had come to perceive in the earliest figure paintings of the fifties: the need to include areas reflecting light. As the final painting in the Mazaruni sequence, *Caribbean Man* brings to a close the geometric explorations and compositional concerns of *Channaman* and *Canecutters.* The lattice effect persists in the treatment of the sky and the houses on the horizon, but it is now only one of the stylistic elements within the painting, and not the dominant one. Instead, there is now a complication of the picture plane, a new depth, a new concern with space and dimensionality. The abstractly rendered figure is set in a landscape complete with sun, sky, sea and horizon. This relation between the figure and the space it inhabits anticipates the central preoccupation of the figure paintings that Greaves is to execute in the late nineties, *Hat Man, Magus with Reversed Bananas, Banana Manna* and *Madonna with Pumpkin.*

Traffic Lights and Banana Trees (1978) and *Swamp Birds* (1981) are essays in design and rhythm pure and simple. They are free of storytelling and empty of immediate social content. *Traffic Lights and Banana Trees* was triggered by a scene at a main Georgetown intersection that Greaves passed every day on his way to Queen's College: a traffic light sprouting out of a clump of banana trees. He found it a strange conjunction between nature and man-made artifact where the latter was an intrusion. By the time he came to paint *Traffic Lights and Banana Trees* Greaves was moving away from the lattice effect, drawn to the rhythm of contrast and repetition.

In *Swamp Birds*, the curved neck and lower body of the birds, rhyming with the curved branches with leaves sprouting like wings, are played off against the straight lines of the beak, legs and upper body. The shape of the body is multiplied and repeated in the shape of the feathers of the wing, establishing rhythms that are explicitly related to serial movement like the frames of a movie film, except that in the painting Greaves, to avoid monotony, has made subtle variations on each bird, notably in the legs and the organization of the coloured shapes at the bottom. *Swamp Birds*, in the attention to colour, promises a new direction. Greaves remembers Denis Williams admiring the harmonies in the painting. *Traffic Lights and Banana Trees* and *Swamp Birds* are essays in rhythm, which were to lead eventually to the symmetries of the *Hearts and Diamonds* series.

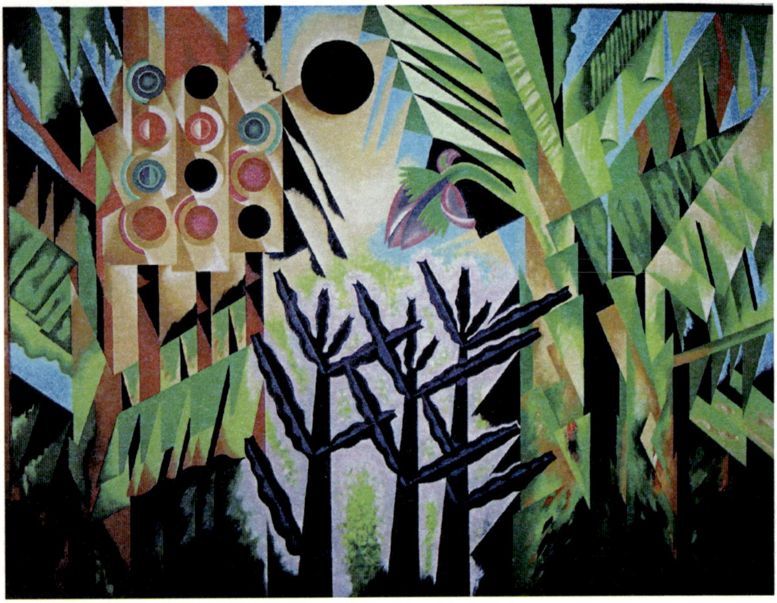

Traffic Lights and Banana Trees.
Oils on canvas on masonite, 93.5 x 122 cm. 1978

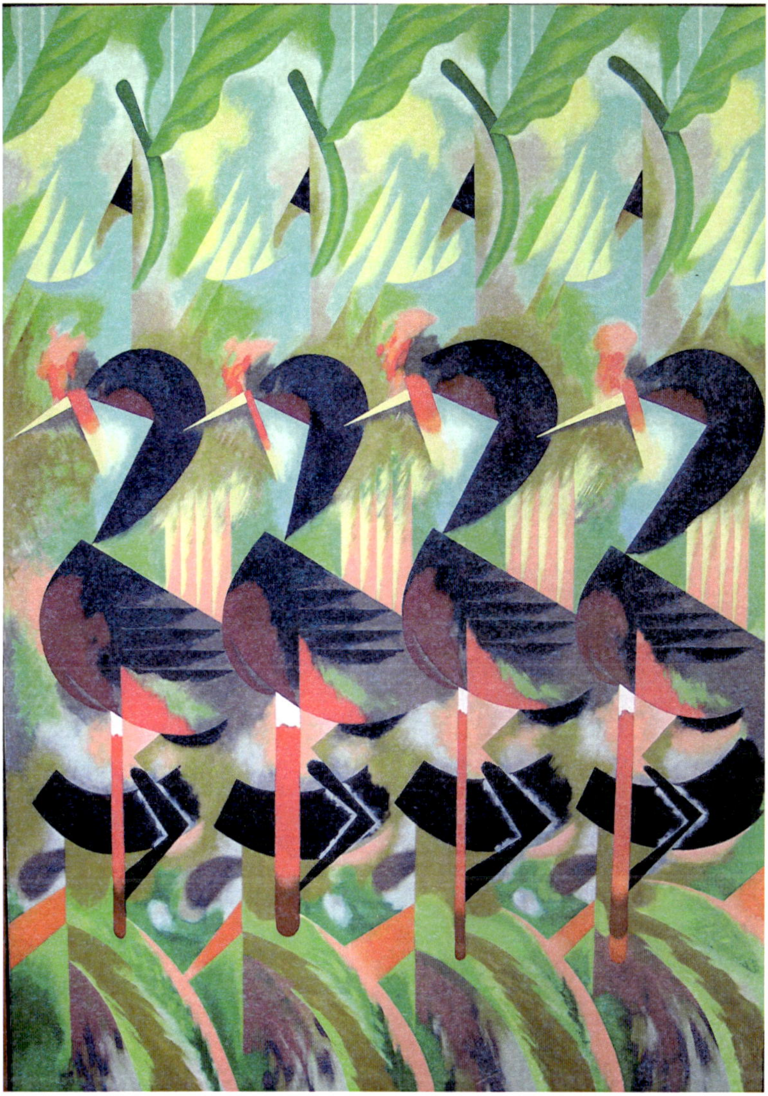

Swamp Birds. Oils on canvas on masonite, 122 x 89.5 cm. 1981

ENDNOTES TO CHAPTER THREE

1. SG, In conversation

2. SG, Journal

3. Ibid.

4. Ibid.

5. Walter Rodney (1942-1980) was assassinated in the heart of Georgetown on the night of June 13, 1980. Rodney had returned to the country of his birth after leaving Dar-es-Salaam where he had been teaching at the University of Tanzania and participating centrally in the ideological debates of the early Nyerere years. He had gone to Tanzania after being declared *persona non grata* by the government of Hugh Shearer in Jamaica, where Rodney had been lecturing in African history, in the lecture halls of the campus as well as in the ghettoes of Kingston. He was denied the position of Professor of History at the University of Guyana but remained to play a leading role in the democratic opposition to the Forbes Burnham dictatorship. A founding member and co-leader of the Working People's Alliance, Rodney led the civil rebellion against the dictatorship in 1979. Arrested and charged (along with the author and Dr. Omawale) with arson, he was killed in a bomb explosion before the end of the trial. In addition to scores of articles on African and Guyanese history, Rodney is the author of the classics *How Europe Underdeveloped Africa, Groundings with my Brothers, History of the Upper Guinea Coast* and *The History of the Guyanese Working People.*

6. SG, journal.

CHAPTER FOUR
EXTENDING INTO THREE DIMENSIONS II

Every material has its own individual qualities. It is only when the sculptor works direct, when there is an active relationship with his material, that the material can take its place in the shaping of an idea.

Henry Moore[1]

In 1979, Greaves was awarded a Fullbright Fellowship, enabling him to spend the year at Howard University, Washington DC, pursuing the Master of Fine Arts degree. At Howard his main interests were in welded sculpture, printmaking, carving in stone and wood, and ceramics.

Among the major works he executed that year were *Stone Flower* and *Jaguar*, stoneware pieces that were his first important work in ceramics. These two pieces, Greaves's attempt to transform a poetic image into something three dimensional, derive from "Longtime", one of his poems of 1980.

> Jaguar, stone-flower,
> you have been a long time coming.
> Each day is today
> for tomorrow never comes
> to steal my shadow
> of exultant bouquets.[2]

Stone Flower was the first of what was to become the Orchid Pot series. Orchids and the blossom of the cannonball tree inspired the mushroom-like forms growing out of the bark of the tree, with its markings and protuberances like buds and flowers.

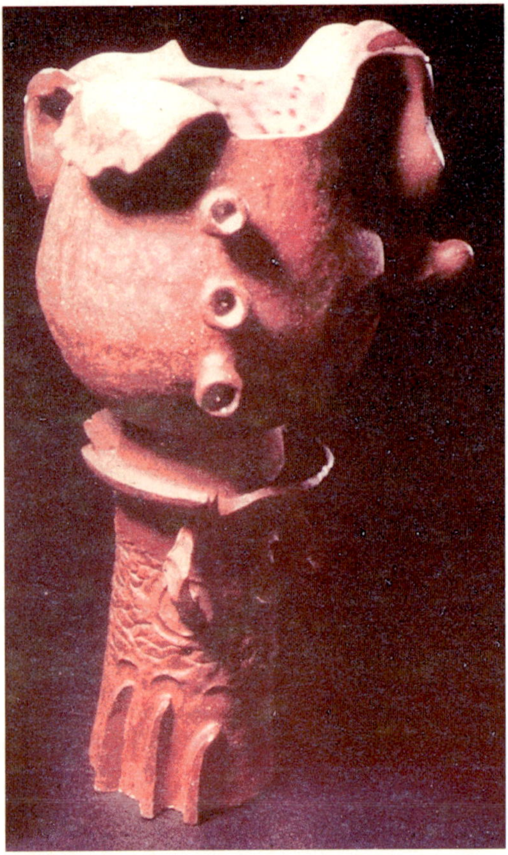

Stone Flower, 1980, terra cotta, h. 45.7cm

In executing the jaguar head, he drew on his knowledge of the jaguar cult of Mesoamerica and its highly stylised carvings. The triangle formed by the three protuberances on the forehead, the spots of the jaguar, holds together the ears, eyes and nose, imposing a unity, and exposing a tension between a movement towards the centre and one away from it: ears→eyes→nose↔nose→eyes→ears. This mythical jaguar with two pairs of ears was intended for ritual use: a bowl of incense was to be placed inside the hollow of the head to allow smoke flow out of the eyes, nostrils and ears.

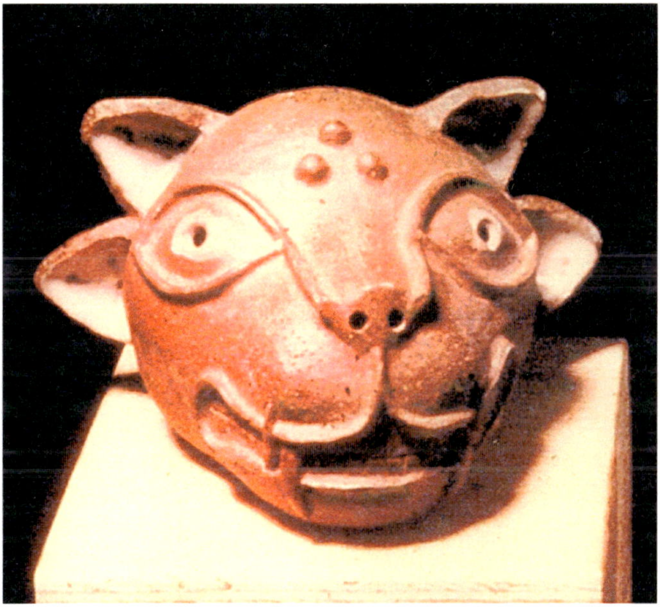

Two-eared Jaguar, 1980, terra cotta

In the two stoneware pieces, *Stone Flower* and *Two-eared Jaguar,* Greaves was exploring the stylised forms of Mesoamerica. To compare and contrast the stylistic technique of African sculpture, he produced a number of carvings in that manner.

Man and Bird was carved from a gift of greenheart wood from his tutor at Howard. In the carving, a man's face is metamorphosed into a bird. The little bird on top of his head has the face and feet of a man, a direct allusion to Egyptian mythology: Ka, the spirit bird of the soul. Greaves also intended a reference to a Zen poem of a man dreaming he was a butterfly or a butterfly dreaming he was a man. The passage of one being into another is a kind of transmutation that is an extension of Greaves's interest in the creation of tension through the interplay of different materials, as in the mixed media fabrications. In *Man and Bird,* it is the interplay of different concepts of being.

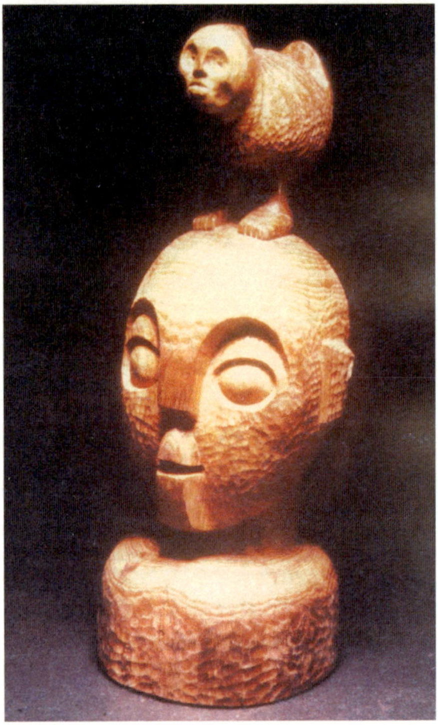

Man and Bird, 1980, greenheart wood, h. 47 cm

The year at Howard also saw him opening up a new field of enquiry, or rather pursuing his ongoing enquiries in a new medium: welded sculpture. For the lover of materials, the versatility of metal, its docility, was irresistible. He had been daunted only by the practical requirements, – unobtainable in Guyana – the equipment for cutting and bending the steel, and a forge for heating it so that pieces could be shaped with a hammer to produce rounded concave and convex forms. Bending wire and mild steel rods into shape and welding the assembled pieces together was a process not dissimilar in some ways from the carpentering techniques he had used for his earlier wooden constructions. Welded sculpture was an exciting new departure for Greaves. Sculpture up to this point had meant direct carving or modelling in terra cotta. It had also meant working within the traditional conception of sculpture as an art of solid form, of volume, "whether real or virtual", as Rosalind Krauss reminds us.[3] Writing in 1964, Herbert Read judged that "almost four-fifth of all contemporary sculpture [was] made of metal of some kind. It is possible to speak of a 'New Iron Age'."[4] And he went on to put his "devastating question": "to what extent does the art remain in any traditional (or semantic) sense *sculpture*? From its inception in pre-historic times down through the ages and until comparatively recently sculpture was conceived as an art of solid form, of *mass,* and its virtues were related to spatial occupancy." The new *"linear sculpture"* he saw as "essentially open in form, dynamic in intention", seeking to "disguise its mass and ponderability. It is not cohesive but cursive – a scribble in the air." In turning to metal, Greaves was joining the stream of the new generation of sculptors who were taking up the technique perfected in the late 1920s by the Spanish sculptor, Julio Gonzalez, of directly welding together metal sheets and rods. "In Gonzalez's hands," writes Rosalind Krauss, "the technical innovation of "direct-metal" sculpture contained within it a directive to make transparent or open sculpture, or as Gonzalez put it, 'to draw in space.'"[5] In his welded metal work, Greaves was exploring the possibilities of creating pieces that were basically linear but presented mass or volume as in solid work. In the most successful of the pieces, the values of both linearity and volume are maintained.

For his final presentation at Howard, Greaves had started with the intention of creating an installation, a room called the Amazon with welded free-form ants spread throughout the room, a marching army of ants. In the end he produced only two. In spite of reservations about trying to be expressive in sculpture, Greaves wanted the black ant to convey a sense of energy and militancy: the pieces constructing the figure, cut with a welding torch, were left rough-edged. The visual effect a roomful of these would, no doubt, have satisfied Greaves's intention. However, the limits of time and the need to explore other forms led him to abandon the idea, moving instead to a form inspired by the heliconia.

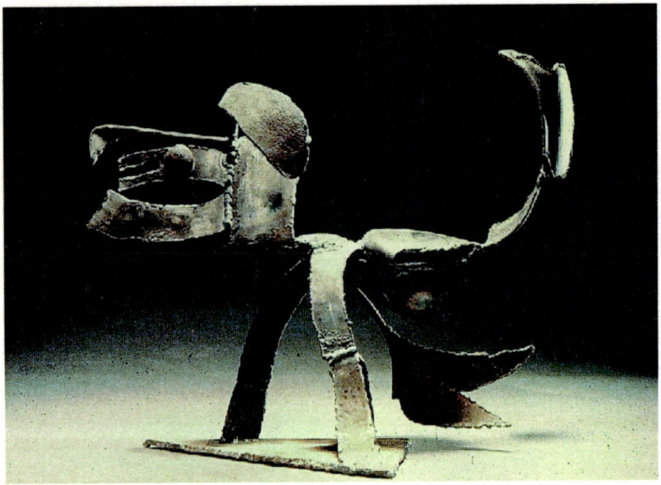

Black Ant, 1979, welded steel, h. 33.4cm

Heliconia was intended as a maquette for a fountain, designed to be in the middle of a mist spray. From this water would collect on the metal 'leaves' and drip down from leaf to leaf. The entire sculpture was intended to stand in the middle of a pool. Greaves would have liked to execute it on a monumental scale, with shaped steel over twenty feet high, but this would have called for industrial techniques. The piece is a virtual transcription of the bracts of the plant which Greaves felt was "a natural piece of sculpture." *Heliconia* occupies a conical space in which two different shapes play against each other like call and response, diminishing in scale to the crowning piece. The overall effect is an essay in close harmony.

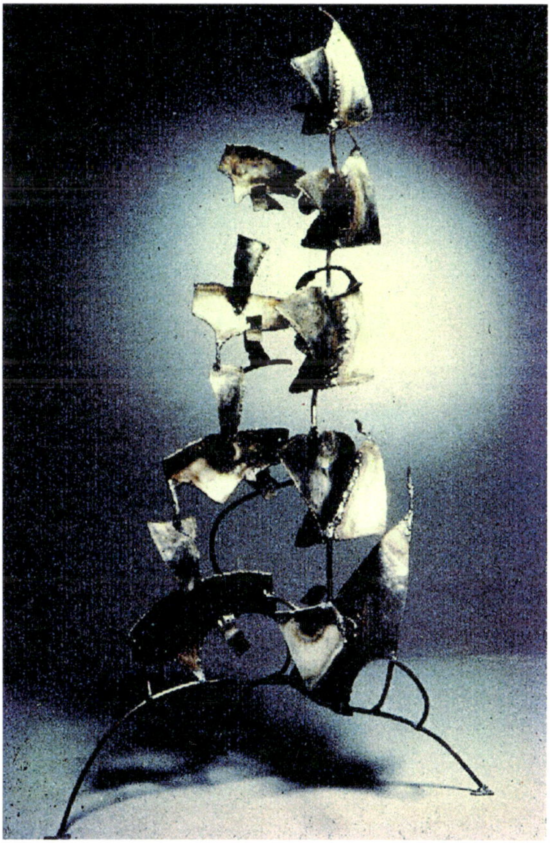

Heliconia. 1979, welded steel, h. 101cm

He then moved into some open form pieces using steel rods. *Ancestral Figures*, developed out of a silk-screen image, retains the two-dimensionality of a graphic sign. Constructed on two planes intersecting along the same vertical axis, *Ancestral Figures* is two images in one: a standing figure, and also a face, with eyes, nose and mouth. Face and form interlock to produce a complex whole. Each of the intersecting planes demonstrates that interest in symmetry which later on produced the *Hearts and Diamonds* series of paintings. Linear and fragile, *Ancestral Figures* is closer to Herbert Read's "scribble in the air" than to the sculpture of mass and volume.

Many years later, in Barbados, he left the figurative even further behind when he executed *Peas for El Dorado*, a mixture of carved wooden shapes and welded steel rods that is more abstract sign than figure.

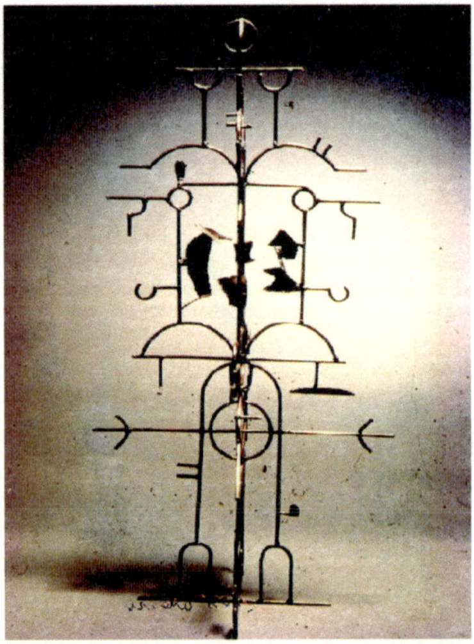

Ancestral Figures, 1980, welded steel, h. 110cm

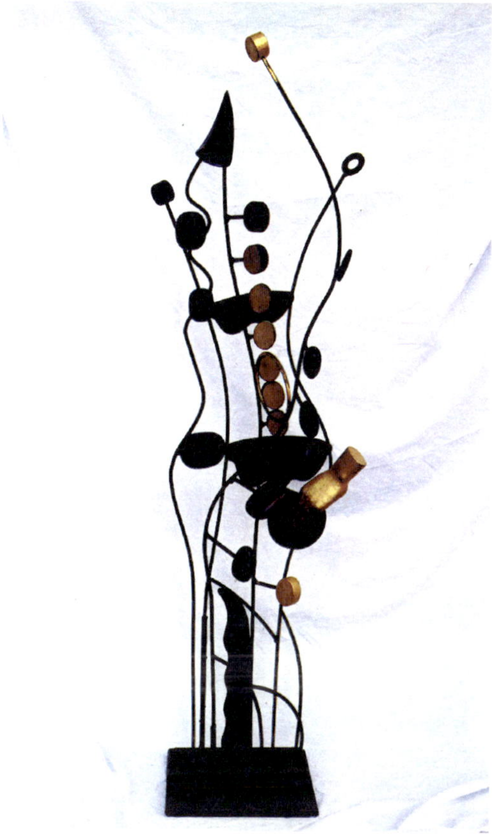

Peas for El Dorado, 1993, mixed media, h. 131cm

The gilded hand of El Dorado holds a giant pea, one of the pea shapes strung along the open wire form, with the wire itself describing the outline of a pea pod from different angles. Entered in the Barbados National Art Competition, it made little impression on the judges who seemed unready for sculpture that was so uncompromisingly non-representational and abstract.

In his later mixed media constructions, also part of his work at Howard, he has gone beyond the mahogany, aluminium and formica of his Newcastle days and utilised mahogany, canvas, wool and wire (*Flayed Culture God - Xipe Toltec,* 1970), mahogany, glass, plaster and paint (*Diamond Box,* 1970), wood, painted tin, wire (*Dancing Figures,* 1974).

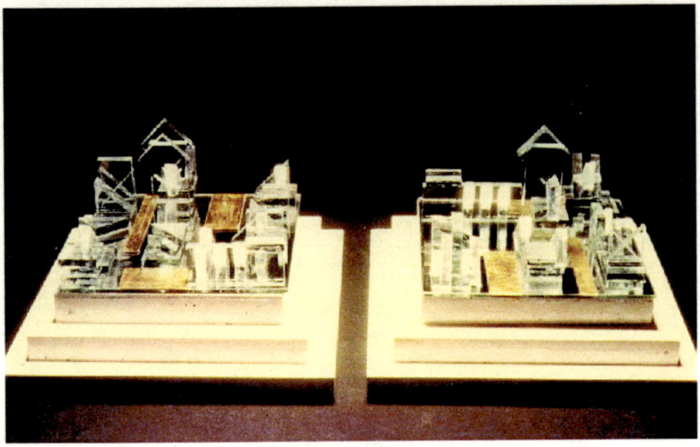

Twin Towers of the Martyrs,
1980, mixed media construction, h. 16.6cm

One of his Howard mixed-media pieces, using glass, wood and a mirror was *Twin Towers of the Martyrs*. This was drawn from an episode in the conquest of Mexico. The piece depicts the two towers defending the citadel through which the Spanish troops had to pass. At every step of the way they were met by the fierce resistance of the Aztec warriors who fought to the death to drive them out.

In the mixed media pieces, Greaves is drawn to the idea of tension produced by the interaction of the different materials: "I like the idea of using materials of a different resonance because they do create a certain kind of tension and you must have that tension in sculpted pieces for them not to become flabby. And for me it is the way in which forms accrete. You put forms together and the forms made of one material create a kind of dialogue with other forms made of a different material. The two of them have to live together in the same work."[6] It is, in the realm of the material as well as in philosophy, a proposition about the unity of opposites. It is as though at certain key moments of his investigations, the resolution of some sculptural problems demands that particular equilibrium of forces exerted among different materials when they are brought into relation one to the other. The presentation of the ensuing dynamic of tension is what holds the work together, as in *Amatuk* (see p. 38).

Whether carving in wood and stone, or modelling clay or welding metal, Greaves has always been seduced by the contact with materials: "The sensual pleasure," he has said, "comes from shaping things, iron, metal, wood, stone, and especially clay, shaping these things, putting them together, working out the techniques to fit these things together." He contrasts the restrictions of his painting technique with the freedom of three-dimensional work: "Painting for me is almost totally a mechanical act. I am totally focussed on what comes off at the end of the brush, how to push this thing or manipulate this thing around, so I don't have time to be indulging in sensuous fantasies and sensations. I do not think that the paintings I do can accommodate that. Working with materials for me is determined by ideas. Different ideas will need to be executed using different kinds of materials. I find this exciting because it helps to create a certain element of tension in the work, an element of dimension, of time into the work."[7]

ENDNOTES TO CHAPTER FOUR

1. Quoted in Herbert Read, *Modern Sculpture* (London: Thames and Hudson, 1964), p. 143.

2. Stanley Greaves, *Horizons, Selected Poems 1969-1998* (Leeds: Peepal Tree Press, 2002), p. 82.

3. Rosalind E. Kraus, *Passages in Modern Sculpture* (Cambridge, Mass: MIT Press, 1981), p. 147.

4. Herbert Read, *Modern Sculpture*, p. 238.

5. Rosalind E. Krauss, *Passages in Modern Sculpture*, p. 132.

6. SG, in conversation.

7. Ibid.

CHAPTER FIVE

TRADITION AND TECHNIQUE IN CERAMICS

> *...pottery, the most indestructible of all arts...*
>
> **Herbert Read**

> *My earliest adventures were as a boy trying to make pots like the marabuntas make. I was quite intrigued that this insect without any brains, as I thought, without any fingers, can actually make a pot with a lip. How do they understand geometry?*
>
> **Stanley Greaves**[1]

When he returned to Guyana in 1968 (where he resumed work as a teacher), Greaves found the opportunity to resume in earnest the work in clay he had begun at Howard. Long an admirer of the work of Stephanie Correia, the Amerindian potter and painter, Greaves attached himself to the Correia workshop where Stephanie worked with her two sons, both potters in their own right.[2] Informal meetings were held where techniques and concepts were discussed and shared. In the early days with Burrowes he had been put off by the plasticity of the material, preferring the resistance of stone and wood. The experience with clay at Howard had changed all that. Now, observing the work of the Correias, he saw the possibilities for his own work in the potter's medium.

With his keen interest in the inherent quality of the material combined with his drive to acquire a sound understanding and mastery of the techniques and processes demanded if creative ideas were to be given form, Greaves was well equipped for his excursion into studio pottery. In contrast to the great potters of the past whose creations were intended to meet specific social needs and requirements, whose production was for use, anonymous and social, Greaves's work as a studio potter was bound by no such necessity, enabling him to give free rein to his imagination, creating artistic objects derived from individual concerns and stamped with his unique personality. Free, too, of the stylistic constraints that imposed limits on the ancient potters, the studio potter can range far and wide, drawing inspiration and making use of techniques and processes taken from any historical period, from any civilisation. In fact, over the century since clay became a medium of artistic expression, potters have been engaged in a dialogue with the ancient traditions, appropriating techniques and processes to give form to their unique visions. For Greaves, work in clay has remained a central activity over the years and at the core of his continuing dialogue with the cultures of ancient civilisations.

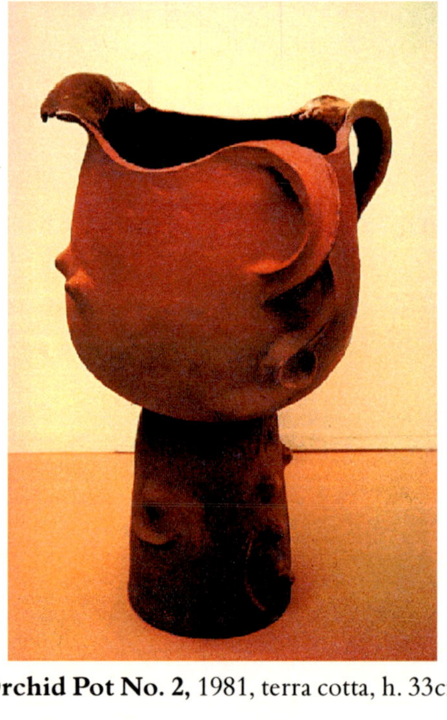

Orchid Pot No. 2, 1981, terra cotta, h. 33cm

Orchid Pot No. 2 was among the earliest of Greaves's work in this period. A number of *Orchid* pots were to follow some years later, after Greaves had re-located to Barbados. Working with Bill Grace, the Barbadian ceramist[3], in the early eighties, he began to explore the possibilities he had imagined in the Correia workshop and went on to produce a steady stream of pots and dishes. Based on his observation of the forms of orchids and his fascination with the uniqueness of their creativity, — ("One feels they can actually think after seeing the stratagems adopted for survival and propagation...most imaginative. It removes orchids from the ordinary realm of flowers."[4]) – the *Orchid Pot* series is a reaffirmation of Greaves's belief that nature is the ultimate creator of geometric and organic form. It is enough to note the development of forms on the rims of the pots based on observation of the petal arrangements on the orchids themselves. This is evident in *Orchid Pot* 2, a seminal pot that contained ideas subsequently developed in other pots in the series. Despite the amount of modelling on its surface, the pot has a strong sculptural presence. The same is true of No. 5 in the series. In both pots there is that element of two different forms coming together to form one object. This provides a kind of excitement for the eye.

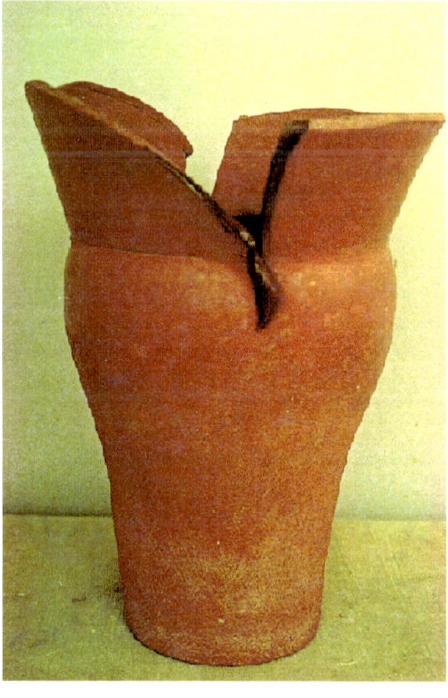

Orchid Pot No. 5, 1990, terra cotta, h. 32.7cm

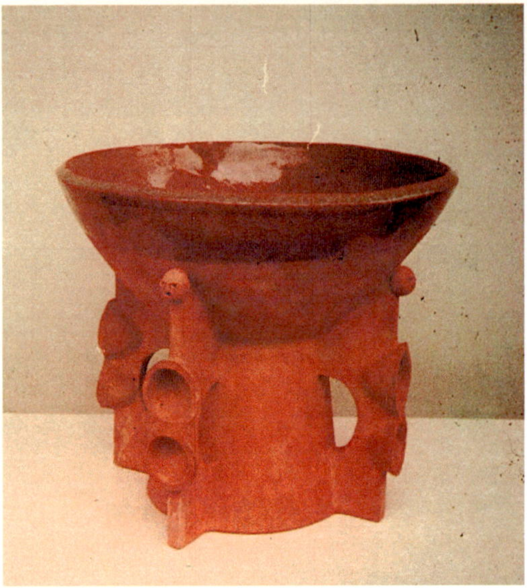

Great Pot No 2, 1983, terra cotta, h.23cm

In the 1980s, his experience of the Guatemalan work in the Natural History Museum in New York confirmed his use of terra cotta as the medium best suited to resolve certain sculptural concerns about the plasticity of form.

His *Great Pot No. 2*, with its flanges and little conical pots stuck on to them, drew on his experience of the virtuoso terra cotta objects from Guatemala, in particular the ornaments on the figures on the elaborate Mayan headdresses done in clay. *Great Pot No. 2* continues with some of the concerns of *Orchid Pot* 2, such as the bowl form surmounting a base, but the rhythmic elements of the former are more ordered and not as organically informal as the latter. The form of the pot is based on the cast iron pots common in the colonies. The title alludes to the Great Houses of the old slave plantations, their tables arrayed with European crockery. The Great House is the colonial edifice. In Greaves's words, "*Great Pot* was an attempt to bring together two levels of society: those who inhabited the Great House and those who served it. The form of the pot serves the latter, the title the former." After the departure of the colonial rulers, power passed to the local elite. These new residents of the Great House act out the old customs with gusto, remembering the graces and gestures of power. Mimicry of the slave master was a rehearsal for taking up and exercising his power.

Experimenting with free forms of different kinds, Greaves executed the most sculptural of pots, with analogies to carving in wood or stone, the *Dry Leaf Dish.*

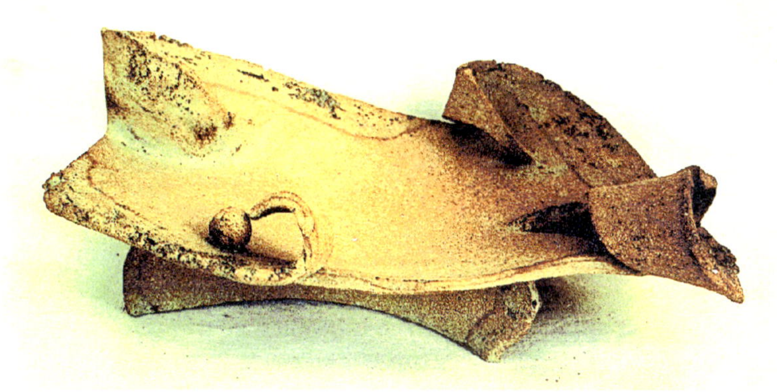

Dry Leaf Dish, 1986, stone-ware, l.30cm

Beginning with a flat piece of clay, he cut pieces on it, twisting and shaping them, adding nothing, manipulating one piece of material to create a complex shape. In using a flat piece of clay to produce a form without adding any other material was an exploration into the concept of transformation from a two to a three-dimensional format. The stoneware *Dry Leaf Dish* bears little relationship to classical pottery. It is a straight investigation into form and the possibilities stemming from his reading about topology. Enough of a dish to be called a dish, the piece plays on the difference between the utilitarian and the abstract in pottery. The idea of truth of form to material is hardly novel; yet it retains some significance for Greaves, now that he lives and works in Barbados where such a notion remains largely unexamined.

Greaves's work in clay led him to the study of the forms of ancient pots: the early historic pots from the Tigris and the Euphrates, from the old Syrian/Babylonian cultures, from Iran and Iraq, from Mesoamerica, China and the Indus valley, from the Nile. In the forms of ancient pottery, Greaves found an alternative to the extravagances and whimsy of current trends in ceramics in the USA. He found inspiration in the integrity of form and surface effects in the work of the ancient potters. In his Homage series of pots, Greaves was paying his respects to these unknown potters of the past, and reflecting some characteristics of the cultures to which they refer through forms and motifs. He pays tribute to the potters of Mesopotamia (*Susa,* see p. 80), of Mali (*Jenne Jenno,* see p. 81), of the Amazon (*Arawak,* see p. 82) and the in finest of the series, *Mycerinus No. 2,* to the potters of Egypt. However, in this pot, named after a Pharaoh from Nubia, Greaves bases its form not on Egyptian pots but rather on the elegant form of the Pharaoh's crown of Upper Egypt. As such, an exception among the Homage pots, it is also the pot that intentionally comes closest to being a pure "art" piece. With its plugs of ebony tipped with gold leaf, *Mycerinus No. 2* is an essay in pure form where the surface of the pot allows the eye to range in a sensuous manner over the entire surface interrupted only by the two flanges, one on each side, presenting a rhythmic sequence provided by the ebony plugs. The pot itself has a flattened lateral form like a fish. The side view is therefore the most telling aspect of its presence. The shaped foot not only helps to stabilize the pot but also makes an aesthetic statement of its own, flaring in the opposite direction to the rest of the pot. The burnished surface is impeccable: "paying my respects to Magdalene Odundo," says Greaves, refering to the work of a distinguished Kenyan potter. Greaves shares some of her major concerns: emphasis on sculptural values, burnished unglazed surfaces, sparse modelled decorative elements, and the joys of hand-building, sensing the nature of clay through the action of fingers alone, undistracted by the sensation produced by throwing on the wheel. His studies in the handling of the clay by the ancient potters led to the *Bird Pot*, the *Turtle Pot*, and the sculptural *Leaf Pot. Orchid Pot No. 4*, with its extravagant and sculptural upper part is based on a classical asymmetrical form.

In the *Yam Pot* series he develops the sculptural pot even further, remembering the relief work done by Isamu Noguchi

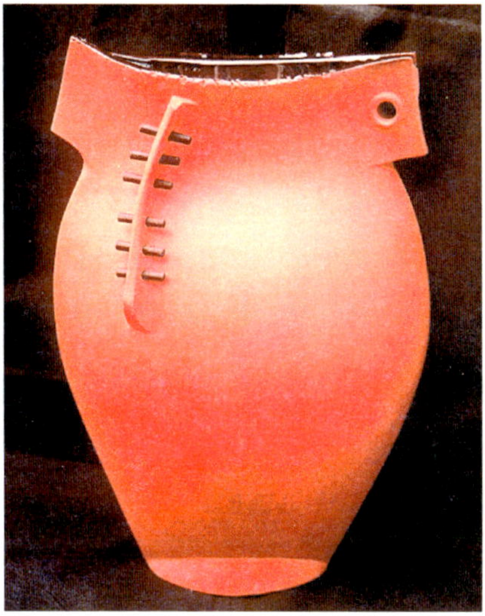

Mycerinus, No. 2, 1998, terra cotta, h. 46.5cm

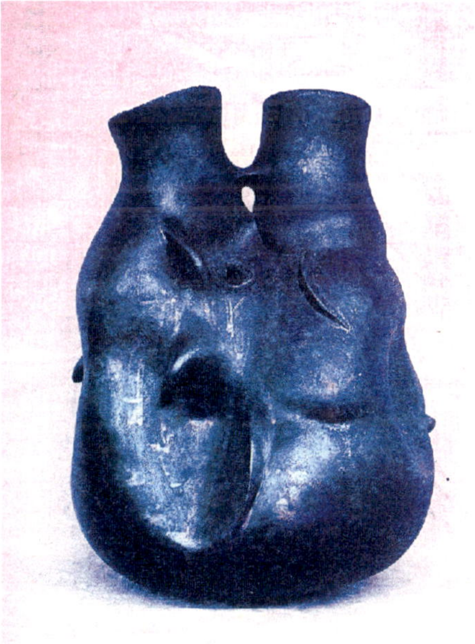

Yam Pot, 1992, terra cotta, glazed, h. 37cm

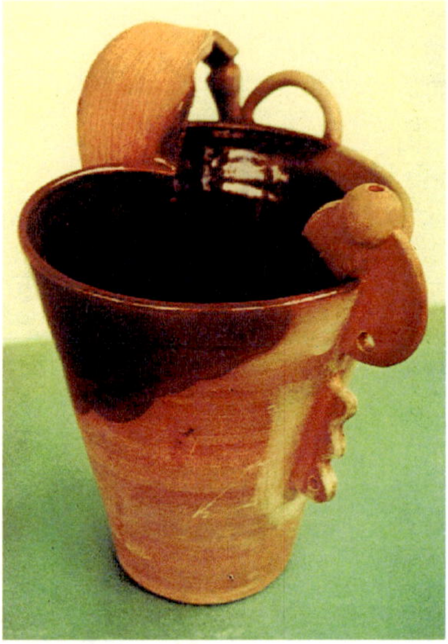

Cocktail Vase, 1988, terra cotta, h. 24.2cm

for some models he executed for playgrounds, where there were forms to be developed in concrete, little crescent and cone shapes like thorns coming off the bark of sandbox trees.

More playfully, he produced the whimsical *Cocktail Pots*, basic conical forms on to which shapes extrapolated from the slice of lemon and the olive are worked. The eye is kept seduced

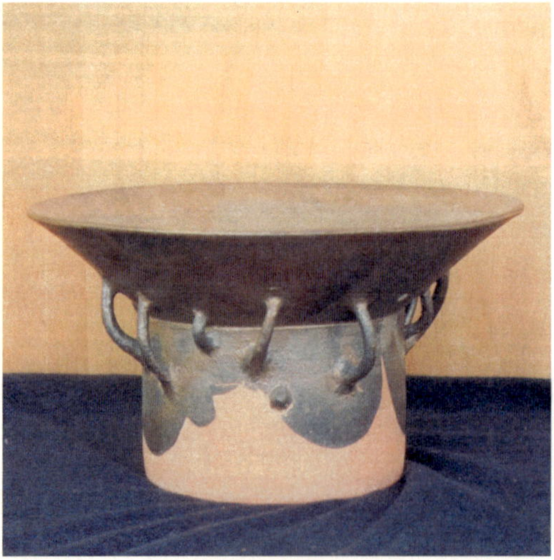

Banyan Pot

by changes in direction on the rim of the pot by forms that are a mixture of the organic and the geometric. *Banyan Pot* was intended as a prototype for a series based on the great Barbadian fig-trees he admired ("the most impressive sculptural thing on the face of the earth here in Barbados"), and for which the island was named – *Barbados*, the bearded ones.

The pot takes as its point of departure the aerial roots that drop from the branches of the trees and take root into the ground. The open dish-like form rests on a conical form, linked to it in a random sequence by the slender aerial roots and stems. The stems mediate the dialogue that is established between the dish and the cone.

Homage Pots

I do not seek to follow in the footsteps of the masters; I seek what they sought.
Matsuo Bashô

It is, though, in the Homage series that Greaves found the greatest satisfaction. The *Susa Pot*, a classical tumbler form with markings, salutes the potters of Mesopotamia.

Jenne Jenno was inspired and based on classical African forms, Jenne Jeno being an old city in Mali and an important centre of traditional pottery. In *Jenne Jenno* he repeats the traditional round, gourd-like shape and the conical neck of African pots. The nodules on the neck refer to the once traditional use of scarification as a means of stating one's status. Some excitement is provided by the use of two different kinds of modelled applied decorations, presenting two different rhythms. The nodules on the neck and the bars on the body of the pot are in a close design relationship with the surrounding areas.

In the *Arawak* pots, he sets out to do two things; first, to build a pot in the Amerindian tradition where images are sculpted into the surface, shaped perhaps to represent faces, a variant on the technique of sprigging where pre-formed decorative elements made of clay are added to the surface of the vessel before firing. In another tradition, that of *sgraffito* decoration,

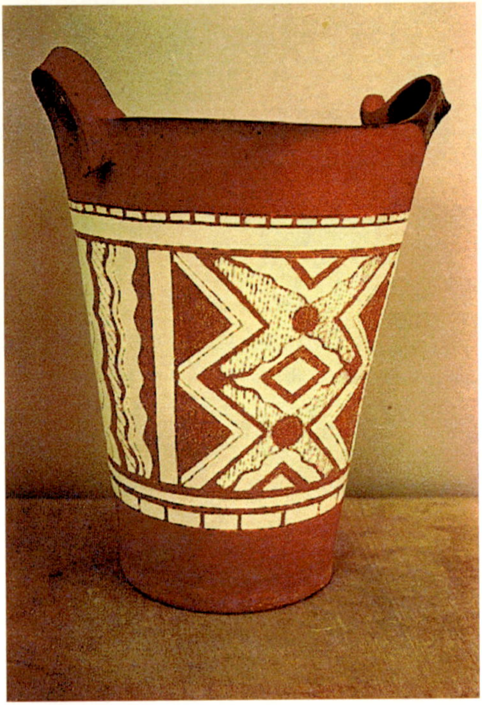

Susa Pot, 1990, terra cotta, white slip, h. 35cm

a white clay slip is applied to the pot and areas then cut out so that the terra cotta emerges to produce the contrasting red and white. Before firing, when the pot is half dry, the white slip is applied and burnished to avoid flaking, then cut into the required patterns. It is a strict procedure, an additional satisfaction for Greaves, the most meticulous of craftsmen. In the *Arawak* pot of 1990, Greaves's intention was to produce a body based on a combination of re-curves to create a sensuous effect enhanced by decorative elements that echoed those curves. It resulted in the liveliest of pots.

The pots in the Homage series are all symmetrical, though hand-built; a method that Greaves chose over the wheel which he found too confining. Of the two basic methods of hand-building – coil and slab construction – Greaves chose the latter as it allowed the pot to be built up faster, without the pressing and smoothing that coil construction would have required to

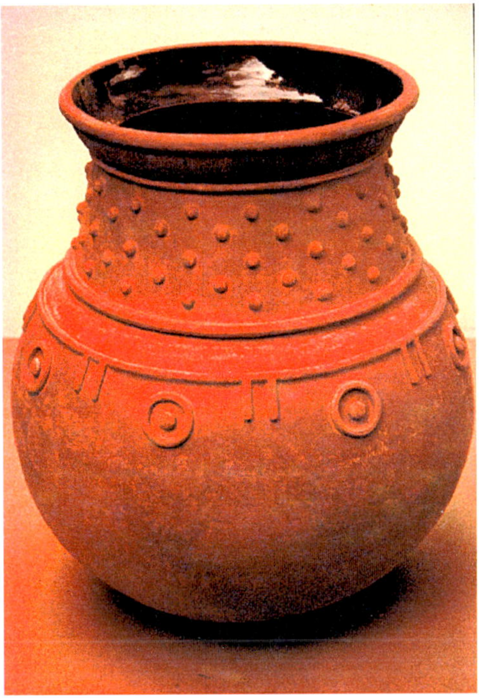

Jenne Jenno, 1990, terra cotta, h. 36.5cm

eliminate the ridges between the coils. From the time of the potters in the early agricultural villages of late neolithic and chalcolithic Mesopotamia and of Predynastic Egypt, the "first to develop a more professional level of production, with a degree of craft specialisation," slab construction has been the preferred technique for the creation of large open-mouthed vessels that allowed the hands easy access to the interior as well as the exterior of the object.[5] Hand-building, above all else, allowed for greater manipulative freedom in the creation of forms. Even for the symmetrical pots in this series, ideal for wheel production, Greaves chose to build by hand, sacrificing mechanical regularity for the more human look of profiles softened by slight occasional irregularities. His use of glaze is restricted to the inside of the pots, preferring to reserve the surface for graphic and modelled decoration and to preserve the inherent beauty of the terracotta itself. For his explorations

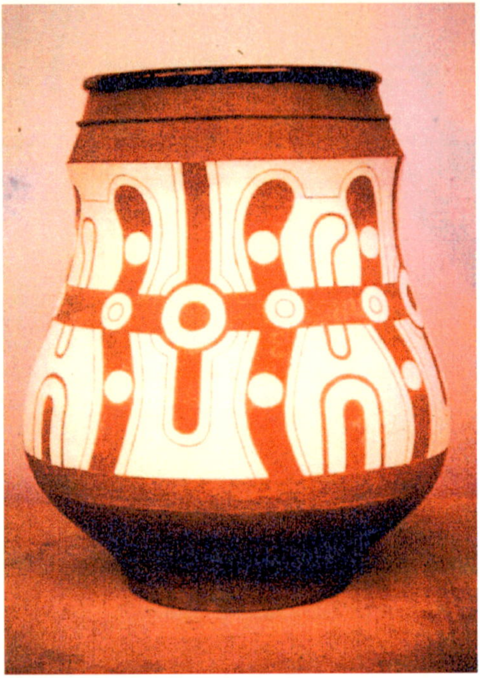

Arawak, 1990, terracotta, white slip, h. 35.5cm

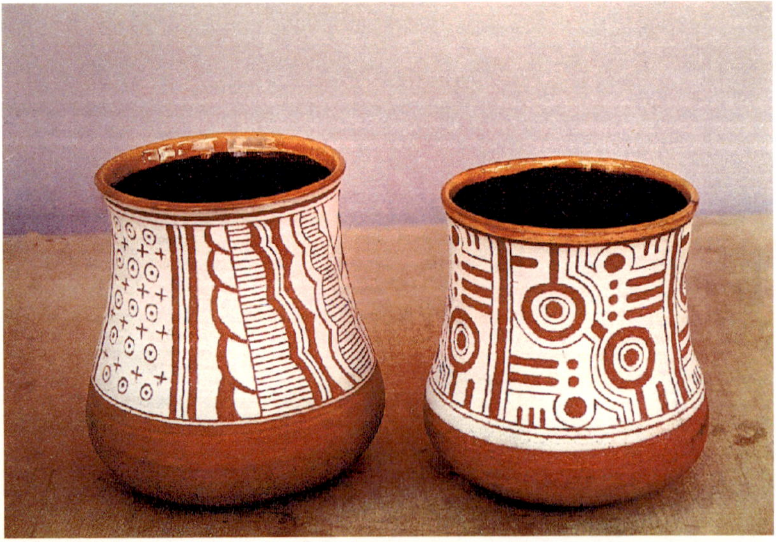

Vines & Frogs' Eggs, 1990,
terra cotta, white slip, 12.5cm

Raindrops, 1990,
terra cotta, white slip h. 9.5 cm

in pottery, he has roamed far and wide, across ages and traditions, feeling free to appropriate any technique he found for his own free expression. In the use of the white slip and terra cotta, he was following an Amerindian tradition, a method of creating design, but the forms and designs were his own.

This appropriation of traditional procedures to express his own ideas can be well illustrated by a number of pots he built using the white slip and terra cotta technique: *Raindrops* with its circular patterns and little round dots, and *Vines and Frogs' Eggs,* where images from the natural world, rain, vines, frogs' eggs, are invented and not appropriated from Amerindian ceramic motifs. It is the approach to the creation of imagery and design that Greaves appropriates, not the designs themselves. The forms of the pot are configured to the palm of the hand, making them more intimate than the larger Homage pots.

Similar is his *Benab* pot, where the form is based on the open conical head-dress of the Brazilian Indian chief. From the lugs, beads and feather forms are hung, an old decorative technique revived by Stephanie Correia. In this pot, he has appropriated the Amerindian dancing figure, but the figure

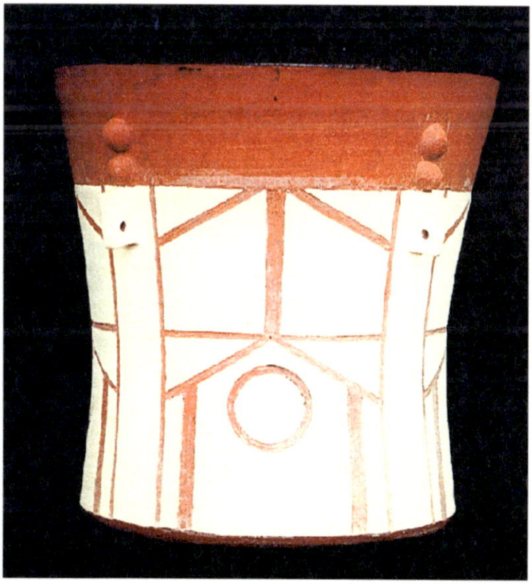

Benab. 1992, terra cotta, white slip, h. 15.2 cm

is cut in half and reversed, with the leg half-turned upside down. Here he has also used a geometrical linearity to present outlines of houses, a visual link with the title of the work. The severity of profile of this pot stems from exponential curves that seem to pick up speed as they move from the bottom to the top.

Matters of technique and process apart, Greaves's explorations into the ancient traditions permitted him a privileged entry into the social and cultural world of societies distant in time and place, from dynastic Egypt, Mali and Mesopotamia and the Islamic world to Mesoamerica and the Far East, providing a substratum of experience and memory that continues to feed his imagination. Through his study and creative engagement with world ceramic traditions, Greaves was able to deepen his knowledge of the technological, economic and cultural development of individual societies, both of the distant past and of the present. In this respect, Greaves's work connects to those historiographic and ethnographic approaches where the study of world ceramic traditions has long been recognized as an indispensable tool for accessing and deepening our knowledge of the technological, economic and cultural development of individual societies, past and present.

In his "Comments" to accompany the list of works on show at the exhibition in Georgetown, Guyana to commemorate his 60th birthday, Greaves writes of his "efforts to reveal the relationship between intellect and imagination" and of his "conceptual or ideational approach to the production of art." Marx says somewhere that the creation of the humblest architect differs from the architectural wonder of a spider's web, in that the architect creates twice, once in the mind and then in the outside world. The notebooks and journals he has kept over the years show Greaves to be the least spontaneous of artists. Every painting, every sculpture, every pot is premeditated and meditated upon, as ideas and concepts and visions are considered. Colours and their values are tested and resolved upon, mechanics and technicalities of construction are worked out in fine detail. Very little is left to chance. The final production is just that: the end of a process which, if we study the notebooks, we can follow in its raw development. And it is here, in the final execution, that technique comes into its own. "There is no excuse," Greaves writes, "for not pursuing mastery of technique."[6] In this regard I have been struck by an entry of October 1992 in his journal. He enters the words of Count Bernard de Clavière d'Huist, an *animalier*: "Painting is mental. Compared to that, execution is nothing. But between the moment you have it all in your mind and the moment you start to paint is a world. Yet sometimes I cannot start, I am so afraid – not to be able to reach technically the level of my vision." Greaves' commentary on the Count's words follow, and they are humbling: "I agree with what he says except for the 'yet sometimes I cannot start.' Starting is not a problem. The problem is the limitations of my technical skill which now about thirty-six years later informs me that I have *only just started* (his emphasis). There is no point in even trying to accelerate this process."[7]

ENDNOTES TO CHAPTER FIVE

1. SG, in conversation.

2. Stephanie Correia (1930-1999) was a ceramist, painter, sculptor and poet. She was born in Guyana of a Spanish Arawak father and a mother of Portuguese descent. Her father, Stephen Campbell, was the first Amerindian legislator in the British Guiana House of Assembly. She attended primary school on the Pomeroon River and was appointed a pupil teacher at the Martindale Roman Catholic School. She attended the Teachers' Training College in 1950 where she was taught by E.R. Burrowes. In 1975 she taught as a part-time teacher at the Burrowes School of Art, founded by Denis Williams. Her work has been shown at exhibitions of the Guyanese Women Artist Association, Carifta 1972, and at the Carifesta celebrations in 1976 in Jamaica and 1981 in Barbados.

3. Bill Grace (b.1953 Barbados) studied at Acadia University, Canada, Universidad de Valencia, Spain, and Nova Scotia College of Art and Design; he served a 4 year apprenticeship with John Reeve who had studied with Bernard Leach: this provided him with a connection to the pottery traditions of Japan. He believes in the role chance played in creating art work. Back in Barbados he set up studio and also did part time-teaching at the Barbados Community College. A first-rate ceramist, master of form and glazing techniques. Exhibited in Barbados, Israel, USA.

4. SG, In conversation.

5. Ian Freestone and David Gaimster, Editors, *Pottery in the Making: world ceramic traditions*, London: British Museum Press, 1997, p. 45.

6. SG, "Comments," *Exhibition Catalogue,* Hadfield Gallery and Castellani House, Georgetown, 1994.

7. SG, journal, entry of October 1992.

CHAPTER SIX

GRIDS OF ORDER: EXPLORATIONS IN SYMMETRY

Theory is never in advance of practice in art, never drags practice in its train, but vice versa. Everything depends on feeling, especially at first. What is right artistically can only be attained through feeling, particularly at the outset.

Wassily Kandinsky[1]

Strange happenstance: a little doodle of a heart shape with a diamond form inside of it suddenly caught my fancy, as simple as that, a heart shape with a diamond in it and that doodle led me into a whole new world, the exploration of symmetry in painting...symmetry and, of course, its opposite, things which are asymmetrical, and so all of those elements were examined in that series of paintings.

Stanley Greaves [2]

From the evidence of the finished work, as well as of the notebooks and journal in which for years he has confided his thoughts, recorded fragments of the thoughts of others and done his studies and sketches, the 80s were difficult if not crisis years for Greaves. The Mazaruni paintings (see pp. 50-57) had ended the long drought and he was seeing and painting again. But the times also demanded the resolution of other deep internal conflicts. The vehicle for these new explorations delivered itself serendipitously, the "strange happenstance." Intensely over two years and sporadically over several more, Greaves pursued the Hearts and Diamonds explorations in symmetry and order.

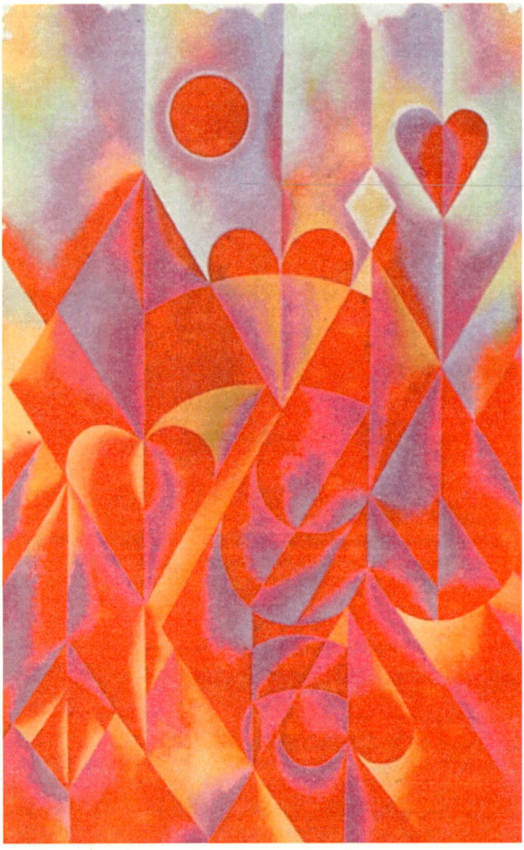

Tantric Landscape, 1985, acrylics, 84 x 57.6cm

The paintings of the 1950s, with their bold reds and greens and blacks, showed little evidence of interest in the expressive use of colour. The main problem then was the place where colours met, not the colours themselves. However, concern with colour as a signifier has played an increasingly important role in his work. His most recent work where paint is being applied in thin glazes with greyed colours shows great constraint. It is as though, out of a kind of artistic rectitude, he is in rebellion against the lack of necessity, that anarchy of possibilities which confront the painter who is free to paint a human face green, yellow, aquamarine. There is even a witticism along these lines in his *Channaman* of 1978 (see pp. 52), where the IndoGuyanese channaman's face and hands are bright blue, the colour of Lord Shiva's throat. Greaves has spoken of his ambition to make use strictly and only of the colours of nature – the browns of mud, the greens of ferns, the perfectly modulated greys of a moth's wing. He believes that purely monochromatic paintings are his eventual destination. But in the *Hearts and Diamonds* series, Greaves explores the expressive possibilities of colour, freeing the colours, allowing them to blend and flow, nudging them here and there, guiding them to mingle and separate. This use of colour in the *Hearts and Diamonds* paintings raises questions that go far beyond technique, questions that go to the heart of the artist's relation to his art – what is his art for?

In work after work Greaves expresses his "fascination" with what he identifies as an aesthetic as well as a mathematical principle: "the principle of symmetry (which is) an aspect of harmony." Greaves sees these researches extending to related principles: "reflection, refraction, inversion, progression, chance and inferences of infinity." The paintings search out the forms that express "man's need for order and for transcendence." They are to be "looked *into*", not only "looked *at.*"[3] But for all the concern with order, these are strange and troubling pictures. The symmetries of *Hearts and Diamonds* may be grids of order brought down on chaos, yet the chaos over-spills the templates of order. Nor can all their joy of design conceal the spirit's desolation at their heart. In *Mountain of Hearts and Diamonds*, high over the radiant mountainside, the black sun that held dominion over the landscapes of yesteryear is today's black heart.

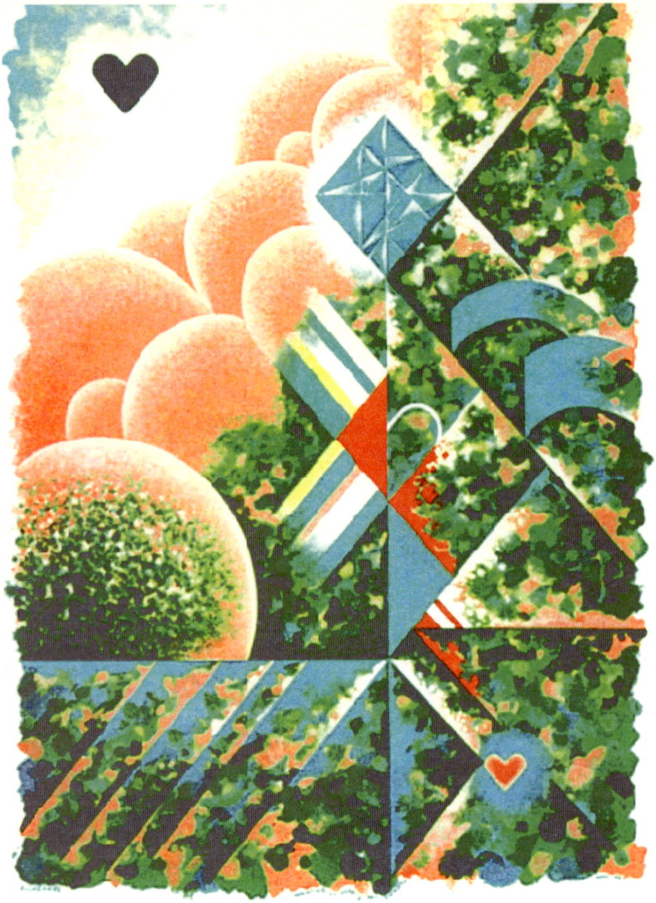

Mountain of Hearts and Diamonds, 1987, acrylics, 80.5 x 57.5cm

What is the source of this dread that haunts canvas after canvas in this extraordinary series of paintings? Take *Yellow Hearts/White Diamonds*, painted in March 1985. It is a seminal painting. Intricate patterns of blue lines of an even thickness stand out boldly from a background of colours used in different tonalities and hues, moving from deep orange to yellow and orange red, and from white to neutral shades of orange. It does not take us long to realise that this is no innocent background.

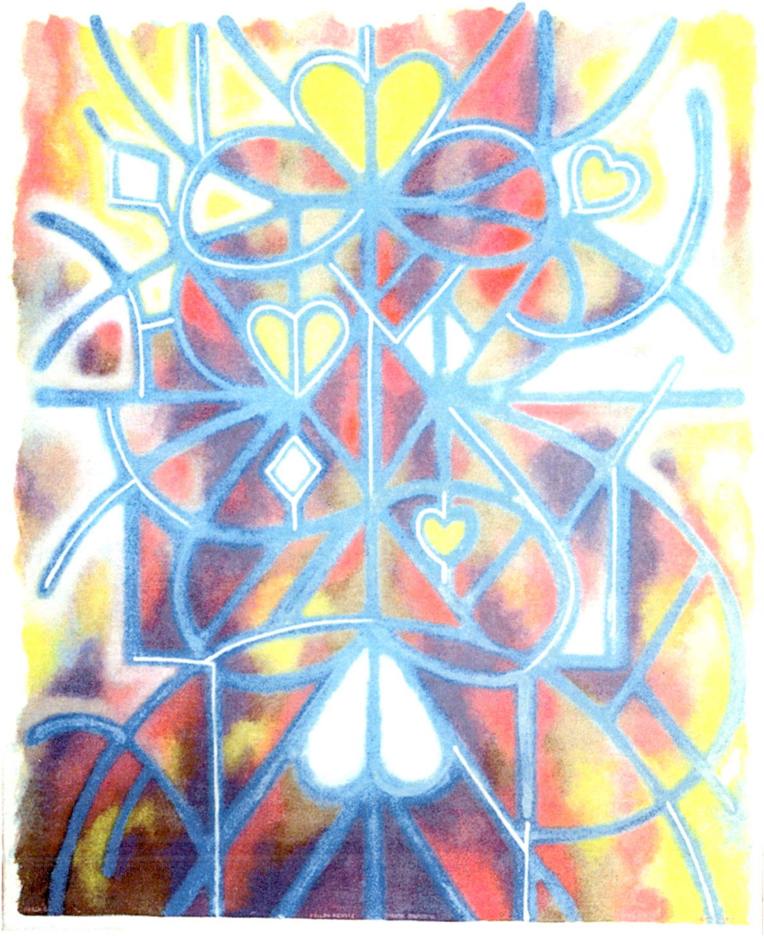

Yellow Hearts, White Diamonds, 1985, acrylics, 113 x 96.5 cm

It is nothing less than the depiction, entirely through the use of colour, of the vertiginous space of chaos and contingency. Whereas the blue of the grid is stable, as befits the primary instrument of order, the orange ranges vertically along the black and white tonal axis, and horizontally along the hues axis from yellow through red to red purple. This is readily seen as soon as we refer to the Newtonian colour wheel.

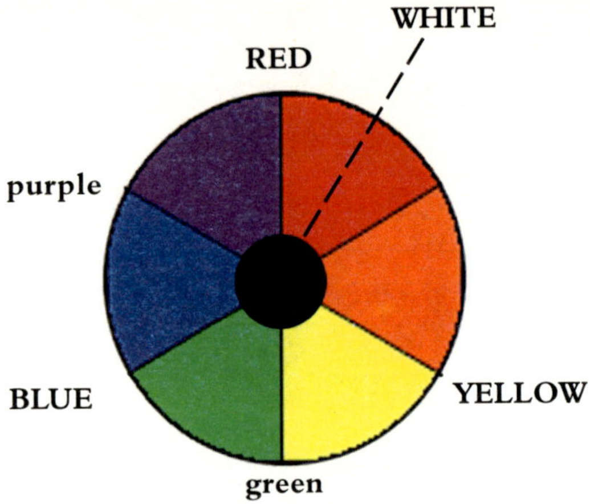

This mobility of the secondary orange along the vertical (from patches of white to neutral shades) and the horizontal (from yellow to orange red) is in marked contrast to the fixed and primary blue. Orange is taken through a range of hues and tonalities: in its movement along the hues axis to red-purple, it stops at a point where red is a kind of burden of the past and purple a promise of the future. Most significantly of all, orange in its true spectrum aspect is absent from the painting. Orange is implied in the tension between yellow and red, the occluded middle. It is an orange of the mind. It is a methodical exploration. Even as this background of mobile orange signifies the zone of contingency it does so by means of systematic method, raging against disorder within its very articulation.

The grid of blue is brought down on to the pulsing orange. It is not a true spectrum blue. It is a blue whose intensity is held in check by the patches of neutral shades surrounding some if its sections. It has also been lightened by the admixture of yellow. At the level of pure form, the blue lines are both straight and curved, now meeting at acute angles, now describing segments of incomplete circles and ovals. The entire structure rests on the point of a triangle enclosing two smaller triangles with which it shares a base. A parabola, a perfect semi-circle, meets the apex of the large triangle exactly at its midpoint. This point is also the midpoint of the slightly curved segment of the parabola that is the base of another triangle. From the apex of this smaller triangle, two triangles fold outwards to form a diamond. Four hearts, right side up, are blocked in with various tones of yellow. Each is outlined or partly outlined in a fine white line that runs along the centre of sections of the blue lines and curves, forcing these sections out further from the canvas. This has the effect of introducing an additional dimension to the blue plane. One heart, blocked in white and upturned, fills the apex of the first large triangle at the bottom, balancing the large yellow heart at the top. Three small diamonds are blocked in white and again are variously outlined in white lines running through the blue. At the centre of the pattern, structuring it, is a cross, its vertical running from top to bottom and dividing the painting exactly in half; its horizontal, interrupted at the intersecting right angle to accommodate the central diamond, runs straight across the canvas from left to right. The bottom of the picture is a straight line of colours meeting the white of the canvas. The other three sides are unfinished, smudges of colour untidy on the white. The painting, which is four feet high and three feet wide, is a maze through which the eye hunts for pattern and the mind for meaning. The eye comes to rest in relief on the perfect semi-circle crowning the perfect triangle at the base.

"Form alone", Kandinsky has written, "even though totally abstract and geometrical, has a power of inner suggestion. A triangle (without the accessory consideration of its being acute or obtuse-angled or equilateral) has a spiritual value of its own."[4]

The painting is framed on its four sides by a border of the unpainted white of the canvas. It has been noted how arbitrarily the paint meets the canvas at three of the four sides, marking that "erosion of the contours" that has haunted the modern philosophic mind from Nietzsche to the existentialists. But this framing is important for another reason: it establishes the plane (the empty canvas) *above* and *below* which the two other planes of the picture exist. The significance of this assertion of the three planes of the picture becomes clear as soon as it is recognized that the painting itself consists essentially of two planes separated by a *volume of space*. Of what do these planes consist?

First, there is the blue plane, the plane of the grid of order. At the top left and right of the picture, arcs of the blue grid are haloed in white and white tinged with blue and purple. These haloes exist on the same plane as the blue arcs which they surround. So too do the white and yellow hearts and the white diamonds. Two of the yellow hearts and a single white diamond are "*complete*" as forms of yellow and white. The other hearts and diamonds are intimations, rendered incomplete by the blue lines of the grid that mark them off and divide them.

Then there is the orange plane, the plane of organised chaos. Both the yellow of the hearts and the white of the diamonds are among the colours mingling and spreading on this plane. It is as though the white and yellow have been drawn up through the volume of space that hangs between the planes, to be caught and held in the blue grid of the first plane. A similar movement between the two planes occurs in sections of this second plane, where the dark shades of orange-purple are not allowed to "bleed over" into the adjacent sections. Instead, a discontinuity: patches of light yellow orange, where the light yellow orange is on the first plane. This movement across the space that separates the two planes is the essential dynamism of the picture. It is also the source of anxiety, the space of vertigo. Hence, the reassurance of the borders of white of the original canvas. It is after all only paint on a canvas surface. It is a place to anchor. Another important relation between the two planes is that of conflict, expressed by the juxtaposition of discordant colours. Areas where the blue of the grid is adjacent to the red of the background establish one of the two major discords in the painting. The other is the blue/yellow discord, this time occurring at the level of the first plane. The yellows, like the blue, are reduced in intensity. Hence, they are less "disquieting". (Kandinsky: "Yellow, when directly observed [in some kind of geometrical form], is disquieting to the spectator, pricking him, stimulating him, revealing the nature of the power expressed in this colour...This property of yellow, a colour that inclines considerably toward the brighter tones, can be raised to such a pitch of intensity unbearable to the eye and to the spirit."[5]) Kandinsky acknowledges that his assertions regarding colour are "the results of empirical-spiritual experience and not based upon any positive science." He takes as a starting point what he calls "the first great division": between colours that are "warm" and those that are "cold": "In the most general terms, the warmth or coldness of a colour is due to its inclination toward yellow or toward blue." He identifies a "horizontal movement", the warm colours "moving in this horizontal plane in the direction of the spectator, striving toward him; the cold, away from him." He goes on to identify a second movement that concerns yellow and blue, "their eccentric or concentric motion": "If one makes two circles of the same size and fills one with yellow and the other with blue, one notices after only a short period of concentration upon these circles that the yellow streams outward, moves away from the center, and approaches almost visibly toward the spectator. The blue, however, develops a centripetal movement (like a snail disappearing into its shell), and withdraws from the spectator."[6]

In the case of the painting under discussion, the blue is not permitted to withdraw. It is held in check by its linearity. Large swatches of blue would have had a tendency to retreat, but *lines* of blue reduce the movement away and into itself. The blue is held even as it strains to leave. This is a point of tension in the picture and resembles in its function the zones of strife where discordant colours meet. This tension is most dramatically expressed in the yellow hearts and white diamonds glowing on the plane of the grid. As we have seen, two of the hearts and one diamond are complete forms of hearts and diamonds. They bear no marks of the grid. The other three hearts and the other diamond are caught and held in the grid, as yet unfree to emerge as final forms. The movement of the yellow began in the depths of the lower plane and moved up through the illusionary space to the upper plane where it is partially held and partially free.

Finally, of the pairs of complementary colours, blue and orange have for Greaves a particular and transcendental resonance. Characteristically, nature is the point of departure: the colour harmony of this painting was supplied to Greaves by the colours of the macaw, seen in the hinterland of Guyana, with its brilliant blue back, its breast of brilliant golden orange and the neutrals (black and white) of its head.

The yellow hearts and white diamonds are jewels come up from the deep. The painting suggests that victory over the fear of the abyss may lie in a kind of surrender to it. Within itself, the painting indicates the paths of future exploration: they begin precisely at the points of strife and discord. It is for this reason that I have called this painting seminal*: it contains its own future*. Kandinsky, finally:

> *The more freely abstract the form becomes, the purer, and also the more primitive it sounds. Therefore, in a composition in which corporeal elements are more or less superfluous, they can be more or less omitted and replaced by purely abstract forms, or by corporeal forms that have been completely abstracted. In every instance of this kind of transposition, or composition using purely abstract forms, the only judge, guide, and arbitrator should be one's feelings. Moreover, the more the artist utilizes these abstracted or abstract forms, the more at home he becomes in this sphere, and the deeper he is able to penetrate it. The spectator too, guided by the artist, likewise increases his knowledge of this abstract language and finally masters it.*[7]

Greaves's researches were pursued with extraordinary single-mindedness in the *Hearts and Diamonds* series, showing that the informing intelligence was more restless than ever, the rhythm of enquiry quickened by the urgency of the quest for repose. By March 1988, there were nineteen paintings in the series. In 1986 he began to explore the themes of hearts and diamonds in sculptural forms.

That year he executed three Hearts and Diamonds stoneware pieces – two bowls and a pedestal dish. Also in 1986, he completed the first of the two mixed-media pieces on the theme – a vase with wooden plugs. He continued the following year with several pieces of earthenware – four dishes and two pairs of

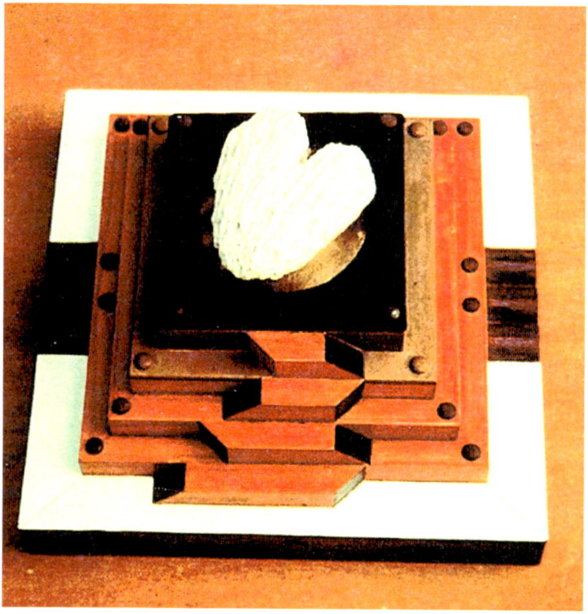

Pyramid of the Heart, 1988,
mixed media construction, 31 x 31 x h. 18cm

loving cups. And then, the second mixed-media piece – *Pyramid of the Heart* (wood, velvet, mirror, glass and coral), proposing a summary and a resolution of problems that had arisen in the course of the sculptural investigations. He had called on the pyramid before, in 1980, at Howard University, the season of *Askari: Pyramid of Power* (glass and wood) draws together wood and crystal to celebrate that glory of symmetry that the pyramid enshrines.

In many of these hypnotic paintings, Greaves looks to art and the history of art for the alleviation of anxieties of the self and the resolution of intellectual conflicts. In a score of paintings, stoneware pieces and mixed media sculpture, he searched out the consolations of form and colour and shape and texture. And he chose to do this in the mode and language of abstract art and modern existentialist philosophy. The *Hearts and Diamonds* series were the last of his Guyana paintings to be painted in Guyana.

ENDNOTES TO CHAPTER SIX

1. Wassily Kandinsky, *On the Spiritual in Art,* in *Complete Writings on Art,* p. 176.

2. SG, journal.

3. Ibid.

4. Kandinsky, p.163.

5. Ibid, p. 177-179.

6. Ibid, p. 180.

7. Ibid. p. 169.

CHAPTER SEVEN

BETWEEN THE BLOT AND THE LINE: PEN AND INK DRAWINGS

The nib has an elasticity meant for writing, and that is why I have always used pen and ink: it is a form of writing. But unlike writing, drawing makes up its own syntax as it goes along. The line can't be reasoned in the mind. It can only be reasoned on paper.

Saul Steinberg[1]

In the pen and ink drawings I became more and more interested in the relation of the blot to the line, the tension and the dialogue between them.

Stanley Greaves[2]

Greaves relocated to Barbados in 1987. "The perfect studio," he called it. Having navigated his way out of the maze of the *Hearts and Diamonds* complexities, the last major series of work he produced before leaving Guyana, he returned to the simplicity and directness of pen and ink to produce the first key work in his new surroundings, the 36 drawings that comprise the *Birds of Black* series, exhibited at the Barbados Museum in 1989.

It was not his first extended work in pen and ink. Soon after returning to Guyana from Howard University in the mid-seventies, he discovered that his colleague at the University of Guyana, Rayman Mandal, was on the verge of publishing a new group of poems by Martin Carter, *Poems of Affinity,*[3] with an introduction by the late W.I. Carr, then professor of English Literature at the Turkeyen campus. Greaves offered to provide pen and ink drawings to accompany the text. The *Affinity* drawings can properly be considered the start of Greaves's explorations of the expressive possibilities of pen and ink, though his first encounter with pen and ink drawing had been as a boy at St. Stanislaus College in Georgetown. He remembers the "exquisite" illustrations in his Siepmann's French Reader, pen and ink renderings in a highly realistic manner. Tenniel's stylised illustrations of *Alice in Wonderland* were another source of fascination, as were the highly stylised renderings of the popular *Tarzan* comic strips of the day. Some years later, he was to fall under the spell of Aubrey Beardsley's drawings with their single unvaried tone of pure and strong black lines.

It is immediately obvious that Greaves's free drawing style is as different as can be from his strict painting style. For the meticulous painter whose every minute brush-stroke was pre-meditated and tightly controlled, where the story, not the presentation of paint, has been the dominant preoccupation, the *Affinity* drawings permitted him a freedom and spontaneity of mark that both satisfied expressionist urges – what Philip Rawson calls "an unformulated yearning for the liberated hand"[4] – and opened up new areas of technical exploration.

In what sense can these drawings be said to *illustrate* the poems? There is no attempt to tell the story of the poem in visual images, to translate. Instead, what Greaves presents is a visual image to rhyme with the verbal image at the emotional centre of the poem, set in relation to images that record certain details of the environment of the poem. Describing the illustrations added to poems, stories and romances in medieval European manuscripts, Philip Rawson writes:

> "...[the] manuscript illuminations...must be regarded as drawings in their own right. This is because, although they are connected to the text or arise from it, what they do is to add something purely visual to the experience of the reader. They may record details given in the text; but they do not do so to summarize or convey those details, but to add something of their own."[5]

To this should be added that, in the case of the *Affinity* illustrations as well as the later drawings to accompany the Red Thread edition of Martin Carter's *Selected Poems*, the drawing is also an interpretation of the poem.[6]

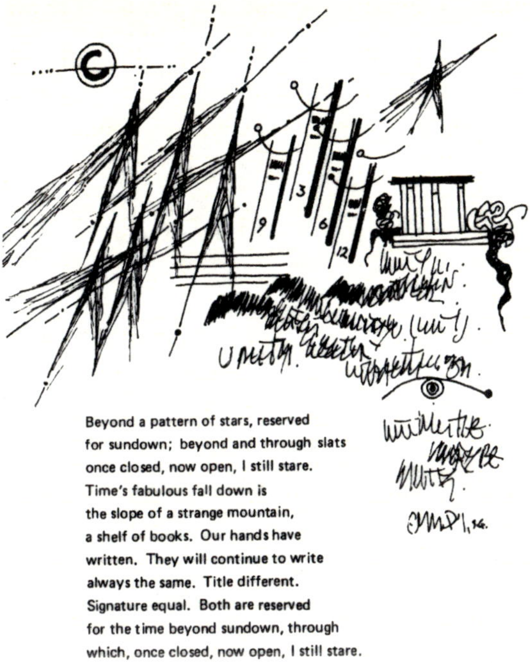

Our hands have written 1980, pen and ink on paper

In *Our hands have written,* he takes his cue from the act of writing that is at the centre of the poem: a word is written, over-written, rewritten over and below a staring eye, a curved line ending in a dot, one circle enclosing another with a dot in the centre. The word is ***unity.*** The compact cluster of "hieroglyphic" marks in the bottom right is counterbalanced by the intersecting straight lines of the pattern of stars. The lines running from bottom left to top right converge into a single line punctuated by dots and in their thrust upwards and outwards suggest infinity: "Time's fabulous fall down is/ the slope of a strange mountain." Four parallel horizontal lines to represent "slats once closed, now open".

In the *Affinity* drawings, the printed text of the poem plays its part in the composition of the page. Text and drawing form a visual whole.

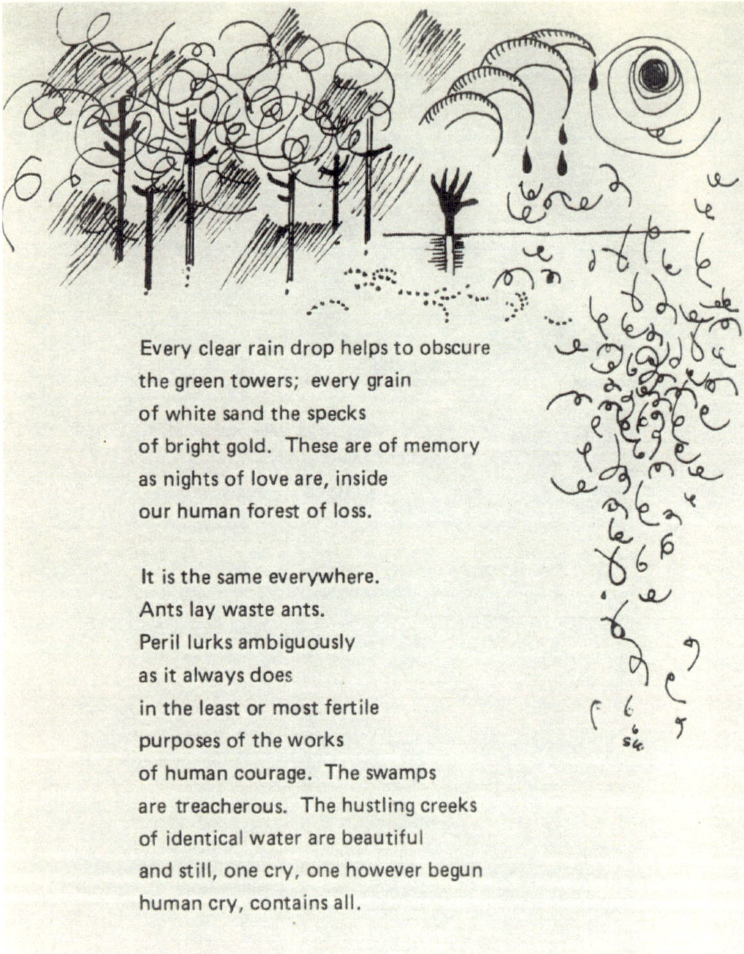

Every clear raindrop, 1980, pen & ink on paper

In *Every clear raindrop*, the peril that "lurks ambiguously as it always does" is a black hand silhouetted on the horizon, emerging from the "treacherous swamps". The clear raindrops that obscure the "green towers" of tall trees are teardrops in "our human forest of loss". Free of story-telling, the domain of the poem itself, the *Affinity* drawings led Greaves into considerations of the line and the blot, of the inter-play between the marks and their organisation into a system. "Perhaps the most important key, both to understanding drawings and judging them is this," writes Rawson. "Drawing is the creating of relationships which are themselves a function of the whole. A good drawing does not present a collection of separated items, it presents the unified whole: *not the units but the system of connection.*"[7] (Italics mine).

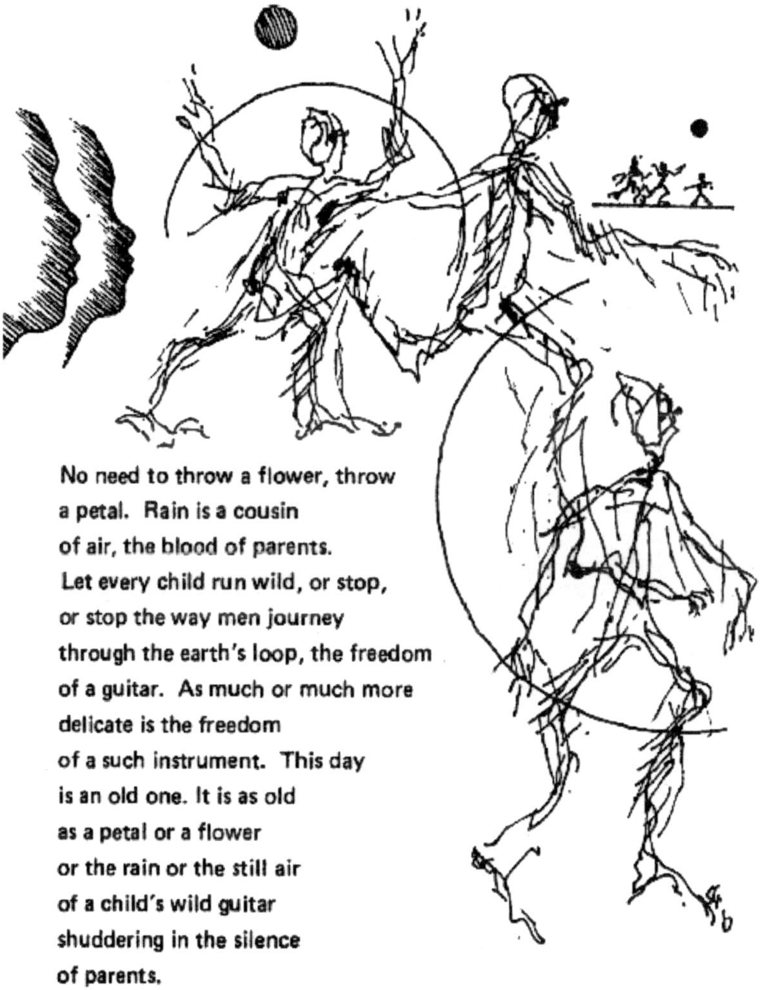

No need to throw a flower. 1980, pen & ink on paper

In *No need to throw a flower* the "system of connection" is the graphic correlative of the connection of family, "the blood of parents", and of the eternal oneness of all things: petal, flowers, rain, the "cousin of air". The *Affinity* drawings, in their simplicity and immediacy, achieve a coherence and consistency of style that had so far eluded Greaves in the paintings where he was yet to settle on a single mode of presentation and expression. The drawings to come – the *Birds of Black*, the Red Thread Carter poems, and the drawings to accompany his own poems – are so many stages in the search for a coherent language. It would be useful to identify the basic units that go to make up the syntax of the drawings. First, the line. Lines can be straight or curved. Rawson: "Straightness implies a fixed sense of direction, *ab initio*, which cannot be deflected. It also establishes a claim to an absolute and necessary rightness and validity...It establishes too a kind of certainty in art..."[8] The curved stroke, on the other hand, in all its immense variety, "is based on the concept of change; for a curve is drawn by an instrument that is continuously changing its direction across the ground." Rawson sees in the curved lines "one of the most important sources of artistic vitality, for they extend the meaning of the drawn forms via the suggestion of change into the dimension of time." In contrast to the "inorganic, lifeless and crystalline immobility of the straight, the flat, and the equally faceted," curved lines are "symbolic of life, suggesting the contours of fruit, flesh, organic substances which are full of sap, juice, blood..." If the line is the mark of order, fixed or changing, the blob is the mark where chance dominates. It is an important element in what Rawson figuratively calls the "graphic principle of indeterminacy". "First comes the mere fact that it is allowed to be there, emblematic of chance, of the unrepeatable event in the unrepeatable instant of time, the product of converging processes in the tissue of reality."[9] In the most successful drawings, the line and the blot establish a dialectical interplay between fixity and change, between order and disorder.

In the *Birds of Black* drawings of the late 1980s, Greaves goes one step further in the elaboration of a language of drawing. For these exercises, he chooses the motif of the bird. "Fascinating if for no other reason than mastery of the sky," Greaves wrote in the Exhibition Statement, birds are "symbols of the life of inner spirit of freedom, of peace, of power, — the Ka of ancient Egypt, the hawk, the dove, the eagle respectively." They can be "harbingers of danger, dire portents and primal power."[10]

The initial inspiration for the series was the ubiquitous Barbadian blackbird, the Caribbean grackle, crossing the street, perched on an electrical wire, flying in and out of a tree, whirling and joyful in flight. The advantage of a single motif is that it frees the draughtsman to follow the momentum and rhythm of the marks. In addition, this serial approach produces a tension between the recurrent motif and its variations from drawing to drawing. The pen and ink drawings are first and foremost *about pen and ink drawing*. Unlike the paintings, which are never about painting. "The theme of this series of drawings," writes Greaves, "is a direct reference to the medium chosen – black ink, and to the activity of drawing."[11]

Greaves's long affinity with the neutral black made the transition to ink easier. A keen observer of Chinese and Islamic calligraphy, Greaves would have made contact with the traditions of the East, where black ink was associated in the minds of the artists and calligraphers with "the root of all colours, the root of all forms, the undifferentiated substance of which the world consists. In drawing with ink they felt they were engaging in an activity that brought them close to the ground of visible being."[12]

Palm Tree Birds, No. 3 in the *Birds of Black* series, contains, in a carefully patterned design, all the elements that were brought into play in the drawings to follow: leaf pods, seeds, branches, feathers. The upper column of the palm-tree is framed on its two sides by the thin parallel lines on the left, branches sprouting from the tree, and dots on the right, seeds scattered by the activity of the birds. Between lines and dots are the intricately patterned pods and leaves. The tonal use of line in the drawing of the birds, the finely controlled hatching that shades from grey to dense black, is a technique to which Greaves returns in several of the *Birds of Black* drawings. The line loses its directional identity and becomes a tonal mark.

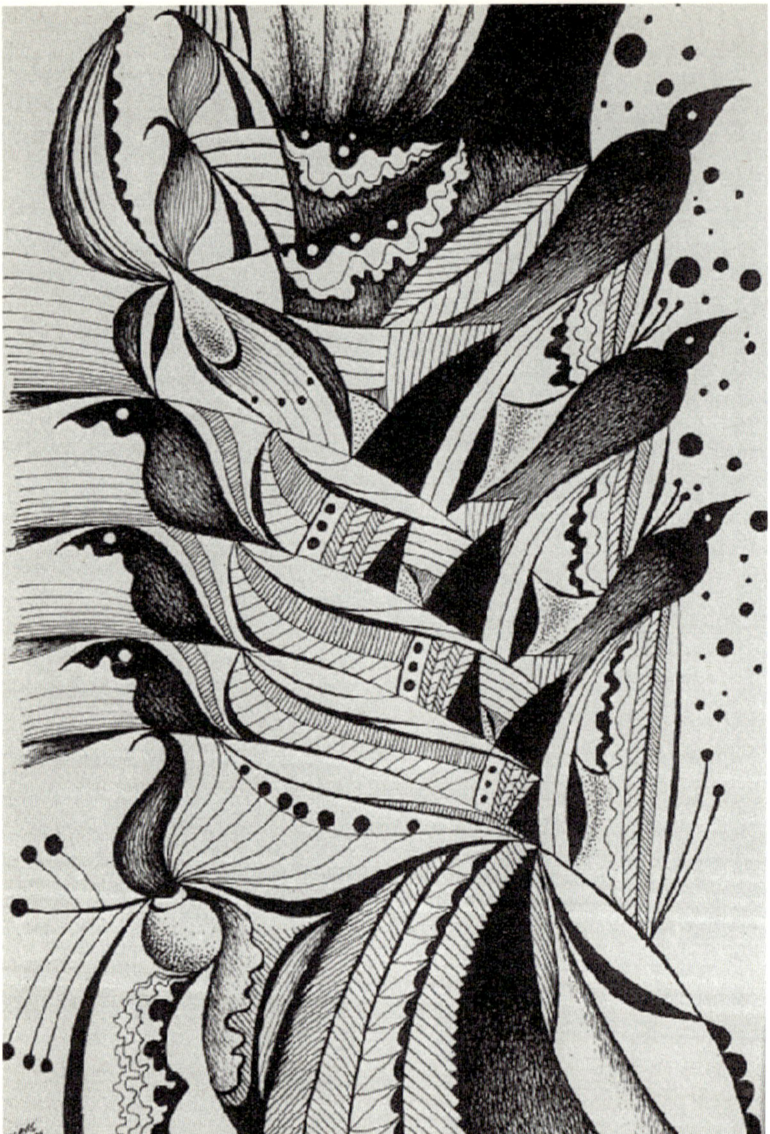

Palm Tree Birds, 1988, pen & ink on rag paper, 26 x 18 cm.

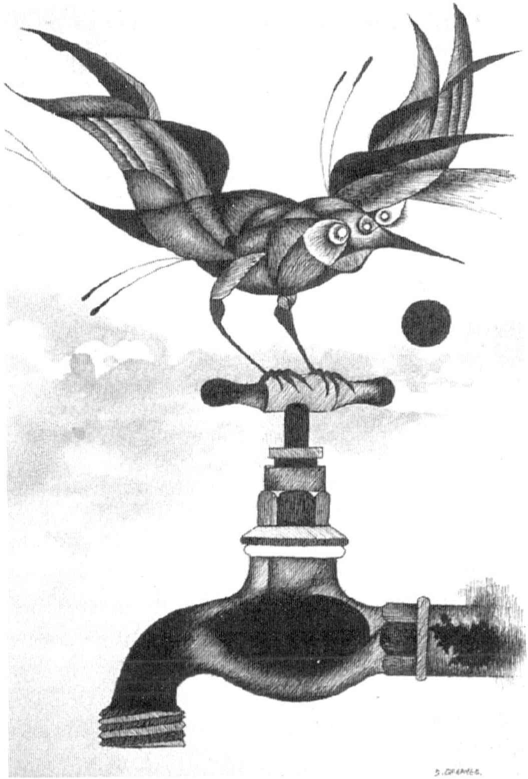

Bird on Tap, 1988, pen & ink on rag paper, 26 x 18 cm

In one of the finest and most self-contained drawings of the series, *Bird on Tap, No. 13,* the tonal hatching technique is employed to achieve an effect of volume in the body of bird and tap that is almost sculptural. Precise and tightly controlled, *Bird on Tap* shows no evidence of the expressionist flourishes and freedom of mark that are to be found in the later drawings of the series.

Pattern and design are paramount in *Chattel House Birds, No.14,* where the strict parallels and right angles of the roofs contrast with the swirling, free-flying birds. The intricately designed fretwork of the eaves are played off against the austere straight lines that meet at the apex of the roof. The fine parallel lines of the mapping pen favoured by Greaves create the sense

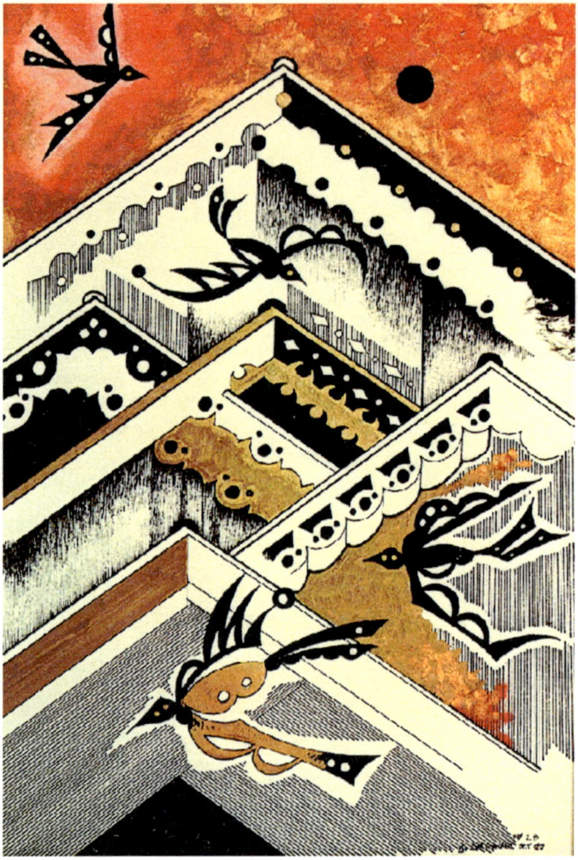

Chattel House Birds, pen, black & gold inks, acrylics

of depth over which the black and gold bird in the foreground wings its way.

It is true to say that in drawings like *Chattel House Birds* Greaves brings the pen under the strictest control. It is as deliberate as his use of the brush in painting which is as different as can be from his use of the brush as a drawing instrument. In *Joy Flight* the brush is used in a calligraphic manner, the body of each bird drawn with one bold stroke of the brush.

If the marks of the pen are an expression of certainty and control, as in the fine lines of the wing and tail feathers streaming in the wind, the calligraphic brush is the instrument of liberation, creating marks that speak to immediacy and risk. The *Birds of*

Black drawings, with their attention to design and composition, in the mastery of the intricacies and inter-play of line and blot and in the calligraphic use of the brush, establish a vocabulary and syntax around their single theme/motif, which Greaves is to further extend in the drawings to accompany the Red Thread edition of Martin Carter's *Selected Poems*.

These later Carter drawings, in their realistic rendering, differ from the *Affinity* drawings of the late seventies that were more abstract, more direct, suggesting a kind of spontaneity of gesture, the sense of the "liberated hand".

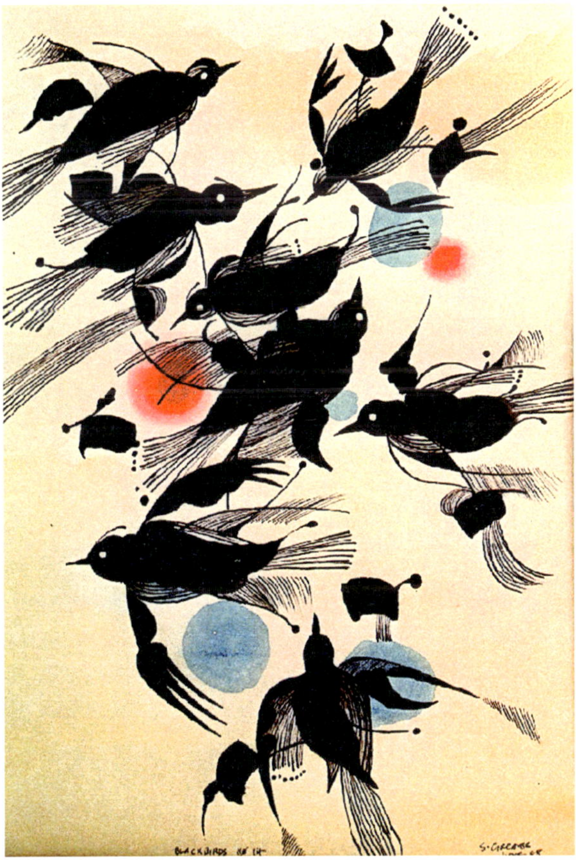

Joy Flight, 1988, pen, ink, acrylics on rag paper, 26 x 18cm

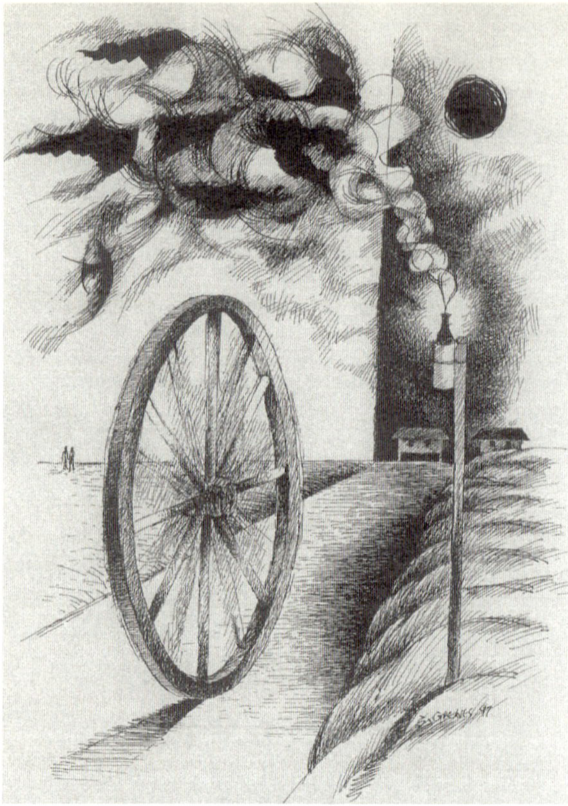

Iron cartwheel rumbling in the night, (pen & ink on rag paper)[13]

Iron Cartwheel is remarkable first for its severity of composition. Straight lines converge at a point on the horizon directly in the path of the wheel, rumbling along the road and the "broken land ripped like a piece of cloth". The wheel centres the drawing, establishing a rhythmic relation to the geometry of straight lines. The curve of the wheel's rim and the straight lines of its spokes are at the very heart of the drawing, radiating out to the horizon. Two tiny figures in the far distance, silhouetted against the horizon, suggest the wide open space of sky and shore at the edge of a continent. Dayclean (the break of day) is marked by a vertical line that runs parallel to the lamp-pole and divides night from day. The tonal use of lines to define the broken land and the curling smoke and clouds is to be a consistent feature of this group of drawings.

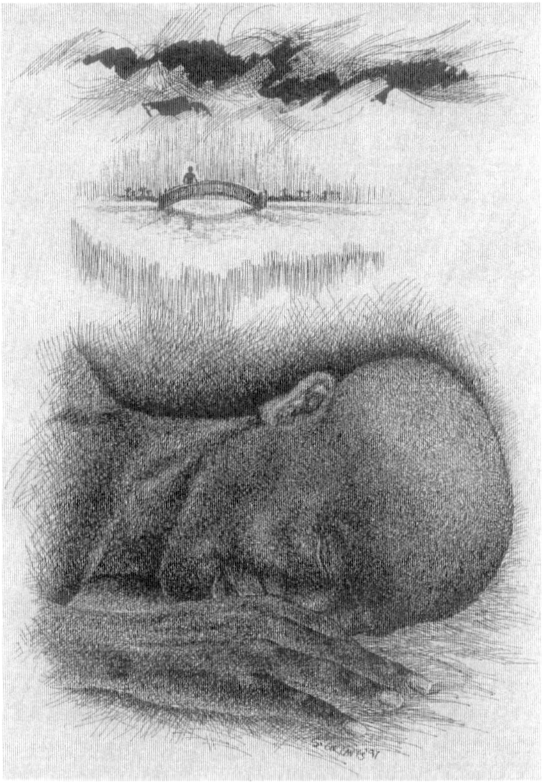

Listening to the land, 1997, pen, brush, ink on rag paper

In *Listening to the Land*, the line "That night when I left you on the bridge" opens the poem and supplies the image on the distant horizon deep into the drawing, the curved bridge of the sugar estates with the silhouette of the friend left behind. The realistic modelling of the head, neck and hand is created by the finest of cross-hatching, producing the graphic effect of an engraving. There is something like reverence in the touch of that hand on the face of the land, as is fitting for an earth that holds in its bosom the voice of the ancestor: "...and all I heard was tongueless whispering/as if some buried slave wanted to speak again."[14]

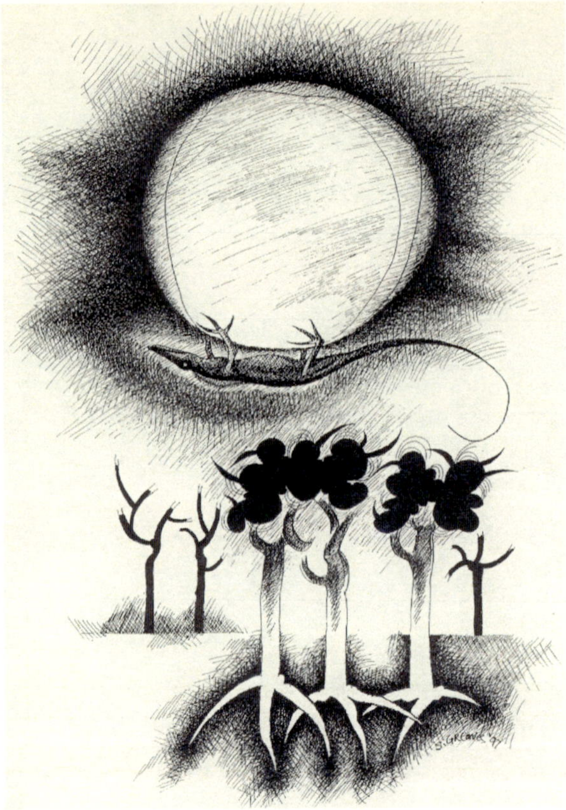

And a lizard upside down walks on the moon,
1997, pen, ink, brush on rag paper

The drawing above restricts itself to the image that is conjured in the first three lines and triggers the philosophical meditation that is the rest of the poem:

> *Trees are arranged like mourners by a sadness.*
> *Root, stem, and wreath, and high above, the crown.*
> *And a lizard upside down walks on the moon.*[15]

Trees and lizard thrust upwards in the vertical movement of the composition, the downward curves of the roots rhyming with the curvature of the moon. For all that, the composition is discreet and does not detract attention from that lizard walk and those "trees arranged like mourners by a sadness."

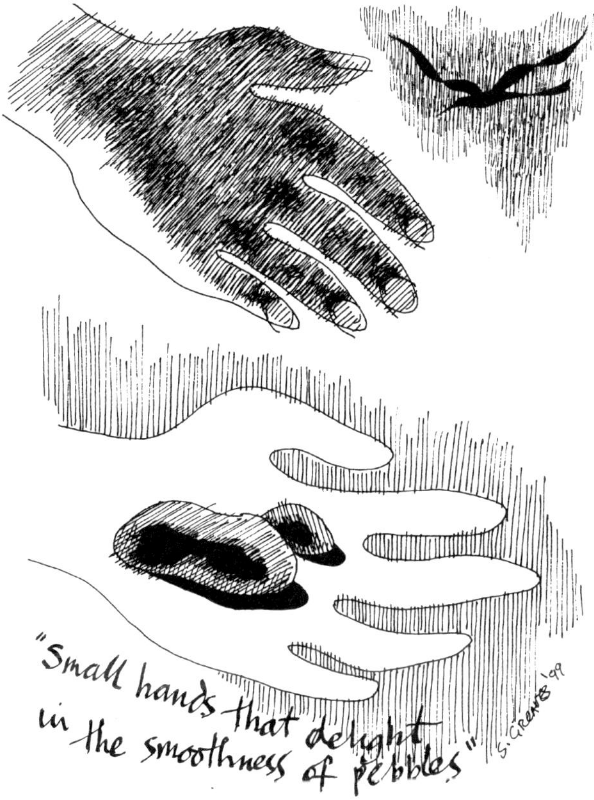

Small hands that delight, 1999, pen, ink, brush on rag paper[16]

In the drawings to accompany his own poems Greaves leaves behind the preoccupation with composition and design that distinguished the *Birds of Black* and the Red Thread Carter drawings. Released, too, from the control demanded by the tonal marks used for the realistic renderings, such as in the modelling of the face and hand of *Listening to the land,* the pen enjoys a freedom of movement not exercised since the early *Affinity* drawings. Illustrative of the line of poetry that is written in an informal hand, the drawings are executed with a minimum of strokes and composed in a manner that does not draw attention to itself, a kind of discreet informality of presentation.

We are far from the sculptural imagery of the Red Thread Carter drawings. Instead, Greaves makes use of flattened graphic effects pure and simple. It is here, in these most recent of drawings, that Greaves achieves a final resolution of a pen and ink language: a directness of stroke and simplicity of design in drawings that narrow the gap between feeling and expression.

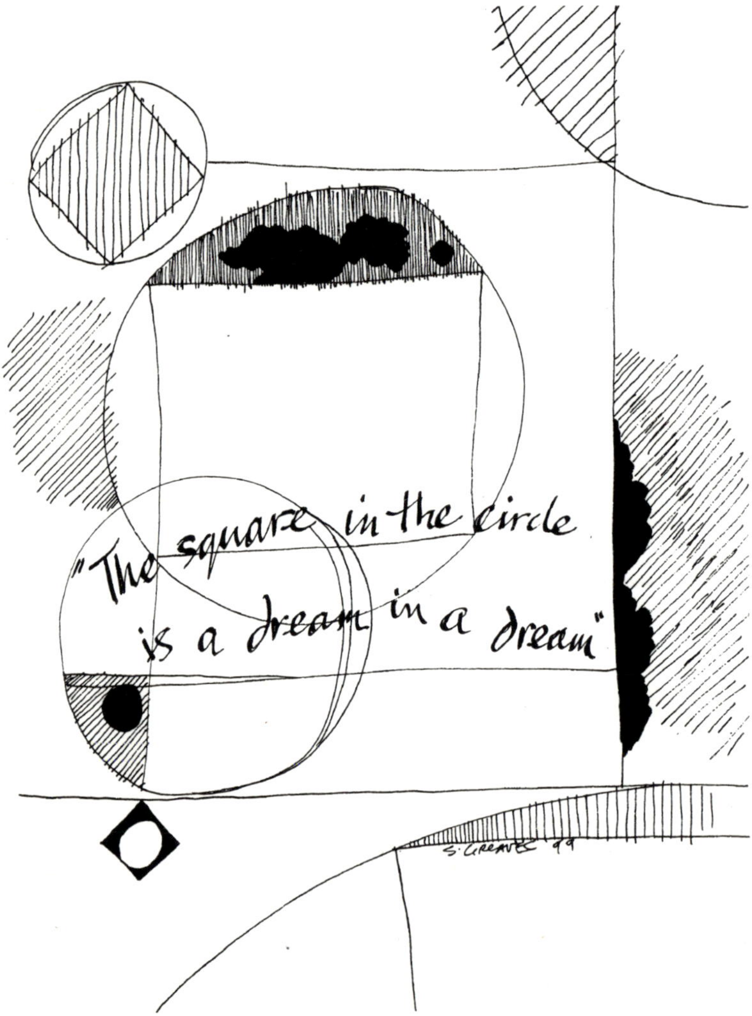

The square in the circle, 1999, pen, ink, brush on rag paper [17]

Where better to end this consideration of the work in pen and ink than in the celebration of our "tree-tall friend of a thousand conversations", Martin Carter, most vertical of men, soul-brother, walking a pavement, caught in a shower of words?

This night is me
I walk the wall of life:
This wall is stone and iron heels of anger
kick sparks into my husk and shell of darkness
till flesh ignite and burn in black and red.[18]

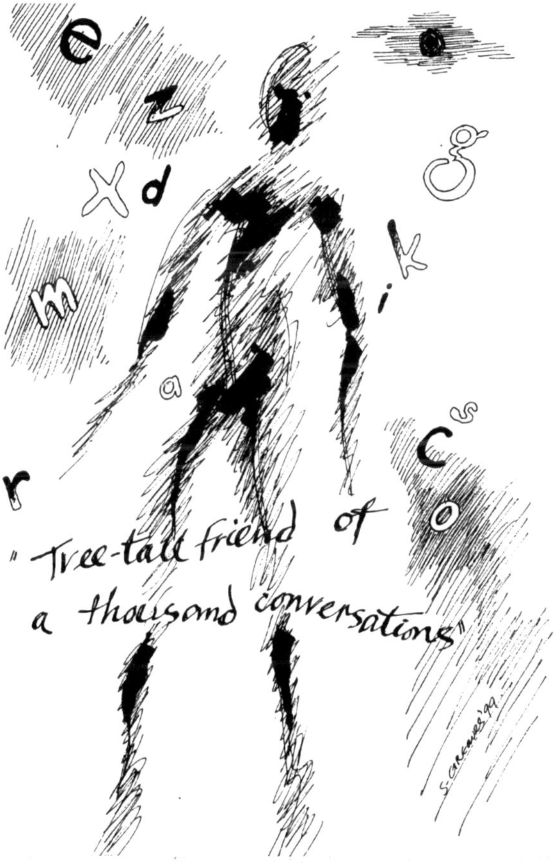

Tree-tall friend of a thousand conversations,
1999, pen, ink, brush on rag paper[19]

ENDNOTES TO CHAPTER SEVEN

1. Saul Steinberg, *Drawing into Being*.
2. SG, journal.
3. *Poems of Affinity 1978-1980*, Georgetown, Guyana, Release Pubications, 1980.
4. Philip Rawson, *Drawing*, London: Oxford University Press.
5. Philip Rawson, op. cit., p. 310
6. *Selected Poems* (Revised 2nd Edition), Georgetown, Red Thread Women's Press, 1997.
7. Philip Rawson, ibid.
8. Philip Rawson, ibid.
9. Philip Rawson, ibid.
10. SG, journal.
11. SG, ibid.
12. SG, ibid.
13. Martin Carter, 'Cartman of Dayclean', *Selected Poems*, p. 50.
14. Martin Carter, 'Listening to the Land', *Selected Poems*, p. 42.
15. Martin Carter, *Selected Poems*, p. 215 ('One' from 'Four Poems and Demerara Nigger', 1984).
16. Stanley Greaves, *Horizons: Selected Poems 1969-1998*, Leeds, Peepal Tree Press, 2002, p. 26.
17. *Horizons*, p. 34.
18. Martin Carter, 'Sunday Night', *Selected Poems*, p. 51.
19. *Horizons*, p. 14.

CHAPTER EIGHT

THE FRONTIERS OF CONSCIOUSNESS: EXPLORATIONS IN SCALE

It is justifiable to consider surrealism as a phenomenon of great importance in the history of modern art, but its importance was precisely that it encouraged the diversity and upheld the validity of all individual attempts to explore the frontiers of consciousness.

Herbert Read [1]

Surrealism is the exaltation of freedom, revolt, imagination and love... [It] is above all a revolutionary movement. Its basic aim is to lessen and eventually to completely resolve the contradiction between everyday life and our wildest dreams.

Chicago Surrealist Group (1976)[2]

More than his work of any other period, Greaves's paintings of the 80s and 90s are consciously aligned with major streams of the international movement in art and thought. Speaking specifically of the mini-paintings about to be considered, he writes: "I am saying that dialogue can be entertained between the most apparently incompatible things and ideas. My works are therefore making the proposition that we must take the line of direct action by integrating the conditions of the past into the regional psyche and propel ourselves forward by the energy or dynamic of our imagination – the world of the artist – to remove us from a marginalised existence in contemporary history ... if this is at all possible." This from his *Artist's Comment* in the Catalogue to the exhibition of mini-paintings in 1993.[3]

These propositions are explored in some three dozen pieces, each 9" x 10", paintings in which we find ourselves in territory that is both strange and familiar. They were painted between 1989 and 1994 and exhibited, most of them, in Barbados in 1993 under the title *Caribbean Metaphysic – Another Reality*. Familiar because we are in the presence, in painting after painting, of those every-day objects we take so much for granted that we no longer see them. It is not for nothing that they are called commonplace. The more familiar the object, the more invisible. And strange – because these invisible every-day objects, when brought together in combination, startle us with their bright new presence. They are estranged into being, rehabilitated, far from common. Unused to each other's company, they come to vivid life in their very dislocation and enjoy a new visibility. While these newly visible familiar things maintain their aspect of resemblance to the world, their combination gives rise to the unfamiliar and can, when successful, reveal unforeseen affinities between unrelated objects, Baudelaire's "intimate and secret connections between things, correspondences and analogies."

Greaves has frequently spoken of his indebtedness to the surrealists and has paid them homage over the years: Giorgio De Chirico and René Magritte, Max Ernst and Salvador Dalí. And in our own hemisphere, the Chilean Roberto Matta and the Cuban Wifredo Lam, thanks mainly to whom the myth was created that twentieth-century Latin American art was essentially surrealist. In the Caribbean, surrealism led a handful of artists to voyage into the realm of the subconscious from which they created imaginary worlds, inherently mysterious, containing their own logic and realities and making use of a recognisable Caribbean iconography of everyday objects, people and their beliefs. Greaves had worked in this mode in the 1950s and 1960s. *Evolution* and *Big Bread* (see pp. 19, 32) come to mind. In the mini-paintings he has returned to it. The paintings of Wifredo Lam, whom we claim as Caribbean, of Hector Hyppolite of Haiti, John Dunkley and Colin Garland, both of Jamaica, as well as that of the Surinamese Ron Flu, when taken together, comprise a body of work which can be considered the Caribbean surrealist achievement, a link in an international movement that emanated from Paris and stretched across continents for most of the twentieth century. Greaves's surrealist paintings belong to and add to this body of Caribbean work.[4]

Even the most cursory treatment of the surrealist encounter with the Caribbean must make mention of its extraordinary impact in the Francophone Caribbean, where a generation of Martinican and Haitian intellectuals embraced and enriched its principles and practice. Their writings are an important part of the development of a poetics of anti-colonialism in the Caribbean. For Robin Kelley, the Martinican writings "reveal the evolution of a sophisticated anticolonial stance as well as a vision of a postcolonial future": "Theirs was a conception of freedom that drew on modernism and a deep appreciation for precolonial African modes of thought and practice; it drew on surrealism as a strategy of revolution of the mind and Marxism as revolution of the productive forces."[5] Suzanne Cesaire was in the forefront of those who refused to confine surrealism to a narrow aesthetic tendency alongside futurism and cubism. "Surrealism, she argued, was not an ideology but a state of mind, 'a permanent readiness for the Marvellous.'"[6] While the rich encounter between surrealism and the anti-colonial movement did not at first reach beyond the Francophone territories, the seeds of revolt it planted in the realm of the imagination bore fruit everywhere.

Greaves, as we have seen, has displayed from the outset a philosophical temperament most at home when in the throes of an investigation. Increasingly, as he has mastered his medium, be it painting, sculpture or ceramics, and acquired a fluent command of technique, his style has simplified into an instrument of pure revelation, drawing no attention to itself, a virtual transparency that permits the clearest play of ideas, expressed through images, to emerge without hindrance. The mini-paintings are executed in the classic *trompe l'oeil* mode, "veristic", with every object meticulously drawn and painted. Robert Hughes has said of Magritte that he realized that his contribution to the surrealist movement might lie "not in the exploitation of chance and random effects, as with Masson or Ernst, still less in exoticism and neurosis, as with Dalí, but in hallucinatory ordinariness." It is the combination of these ordinary things – "so ordinary that they might have come from a phrase-book" – that Magritte achieved his arresting effects. "His poetry was inconceivable without the banality it worked on and worked through: it subverted ordinary meaning."[7]

Of the great European surrealist masters, the Italian De Chirico and the Belgian Magritte are the guiding spirits, theoretically and technically, of the mini-paintings. Greaves's title is not idly chosen: *Caribbean Metaphysic.* Metaphysic because, to speak first of its art-historical meaning, the paintings declare their alignment with the work and more particularly the theories of the *Scuola Metafísica* founded by de Chirico and Carlo Carra in 1917, a supersession of Cubism and Futurism which was to become a main pillar of the Surrealist movement and an essential element in its canon. André Breton referred to De Chirico as a "sentry" along surrealism's route. De Chirico was the first to translate into painting the Symbolist principle of *dépaysement* in Lautréamont's celebrated paradigm of "the chance encounter of a sewing machine and an umbrella on an operating table." For the Surrealists, De Chirico's poetic image of incongruity, like Lautréamont's, became a focal point.

As important as the objects themselves was the space that separated and surrounded them. De Chirico employed certain techniques of linear perspective not to create a rational space, as it was devised to do in the Renaissance, but to distort space in a variety of ways, at times foreshortening and tilting his planes to produce a seesaw perspective. De Chirico's early paintings exercised an immense influence on artists working in the illusionist mode of the Surrealist movement, such as Yves Tanguy, Magritte, Dalí and Ernst.

"My interest in Surrealism and the Metaphysical School," writes Greaves, "has a long history. I was attracted first to Surrealism and its exploration of the power of intuition, imagination and dreams. Early interest focussed on Dalí and then on Ernst. In recent years more attention has been paid to the works of Magritte and De Chirico as being more compatible to the problems I encountered in articulating my ideas. My focus is on a kind of allegorical story-telling as opposed to painterly effects. I am therefore interested in the use of paint in its potential for description which is the first position in metaphysics as I understand it."[8] He could have been echoing Dalí who once famously declared: "Artistic painting does not do a thing for me." In the same essay in 1927 Dalí stressed that his paintings were "anti-artistic and direct. They move and are understood instantaneously, without the slightest technical training (artistic training is what prevents people from understanding them."[9] Because of the freedom from purely painterly concerns, the mini-paintings engage us in their labour of investigation and speak to us of the complex structures of our being in the world and the ever-recurring paradoxes of human existence. It should be added that Greaves did not share, as Matta undoubtedly did, the enthusiasm of the fathers of Surrealism for psychoanalysis or automatic writing, Breton's "pure psychic automatism." For all that, his explorations objectively connect with this surrealist practice, in that automatic writing led to the recognition that entire cultures possessed methods of thought and articulation that transcended the conscious. "Surrealist automation," writes Robin Kelley, "was neither 'stream of consciousness writing' nor an experimental writing strategy but a state of mind – a plunge below the surface of consciousness. Related more to shamanism and trance states than to 'modernity' as it was understood in the West, automatism was a struggle against the slavery of rationalism, a means to allow the imagination to run free."[10]

Greaves calls them mini-paintings to distinguish them from the earliest miniatures that enjoyed a vogue in Europe from the 16th to the 18th century, portraits for the most part, which, painted on ivory and porcelain, sometimes on vellum, and replete with arcane symbolism and allegory, proclaim their derivation from medieval manuscript illumination. At times small enough to hold in the hand, the traditional miniature is simply a tiny painting, a miracle of reduction down to the minutest detail. Size as such is unproblematic. Smallness is all. Not so the mini-paintings where the question of size, or more, of scale, becomes the actual point of departure for Greaves's newest investigations. "The format of the work is small," Greaves has written, "because it sets out to explore the view that ideas can determine the most efficient format or use of scale needed to give them full expression."[11]

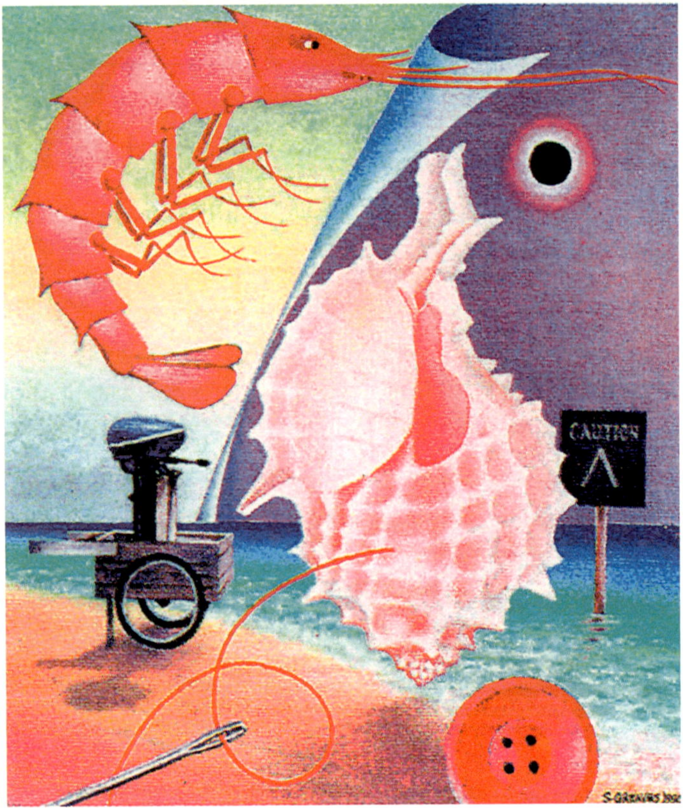

The Birth of Venus, 1990, Oils, 23 x 23 cm

The main technical exploration which Greaves embarked upon, after beginning the series with the *Birth of Venus* in 1989/90, centres around the relation between scale and theme. Searching through his notebooks for paintings which did not require a large format – it is his method of work – he selected all those which could be realised in the 25 x 23.5 cm. format he had settled on. He then discovered, as he worked, that some of the objects described in these paintings were painted at their natural size. Limes, nails, ants, needle and thread, pencils, buttons, an egg, a cherry – all could fit into the composition at their natural size.

"I noticed," he wrote in the exhibition catalogue, "that the use of objects more or less in their natural scale created a force that would have been destroyed if the scale was larger. A natural scale makes the paintings very accessible to the viewer. Moving away from natural scale creates a totally different feeling. It is left to the artist to determine the specific effect desired."[12]

What the paintings show is that he used scale in a very deliberate and provocative manner, placing certain objects next to other objects that made them obviously out of scale. And it is precisely this *out-of-scaleness* that helps to create the atmosphere, the particular conditions, the emotion ("feeling") and the drama of the paintings. It is a strategic distortion of scale. This distortion is at times a compositional imperative. But size and scale are also traditional determinants of meaning, with things of importance painted big and things of less importance painted small. "My approach was to use two or three objects at natural scale and manipulate the scale of others according to the demands of my intuition and interpretation of the rules of pictorial composition."[13]

He had to ensure as he proceeded that this flouting of the conventions of scale and proportion did not result in ungainliness. The boardwalk of *Guitar Bird*, the checkerboards of *Alison's Cups* and *Plantation Boots*, the floorboards of *Red Eye*, the checkerboard roadway of *Game Plan*, with their horizons and geometrical precisions, ensure containment and measure. The chattel-house at the end of the roadway in *Game Plan* is either a miniature house covered by a natural-sized leaf or a natural sized-house covered by a gigantic leaf.

There can be no mistaking the Greaves world, teeming with the signs and obsessions that have emerged over the years of painstaking enquiry, such as the ubiquitous points and edges which Martin Carter, in a happy choice of word, called "acuities", zones of maximum tension and power where objects barely impinge on each other: a cherry on the edge of a razor-blade, just before the slicing of the skin, against an infinite space of sky in *Biscuit Story No 1*. Nor are the objects of this world matters for astonishment: birds, leaves, fruits, nails, keys,

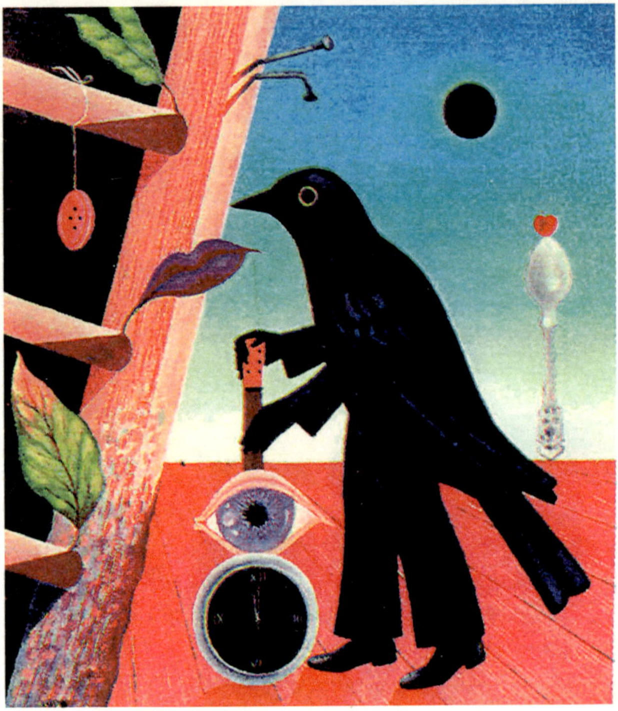

Guitar Bird 1991, oils, 25x23.5 cm

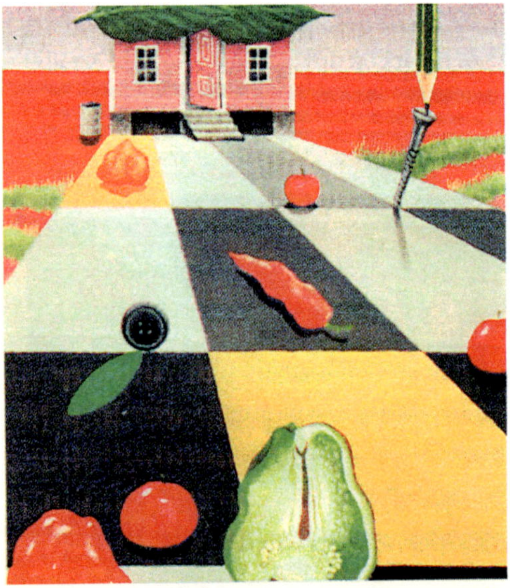

Game Plan 1991, oils, 25x23.5 cm

buttons, fish-hooks, needle and thread, and all the bric-a-brac fetched up from the crowded store-room of memory. The mini-paintings are among the most autobiographical of Greaves's works, a celebration of his childhood in working-class Georgetown of the 1930s and 40s. *The Tap* recalls the great municipal tank outside St. George's Cathedral where the little boys from the neighbourhood, among them the boy Greaves, gathered to buy the family's water from the Municipality at one penny a gallon during the dry season. The contents of a small-boy's pockets are everywhere: a forbidden razor-blade in lieu of the forbidden penknife, buttons for trading, a fish-hook, bent nails left over from the last rainy day when the boy Greaves had to take hold of the hammer and straighten bent nails for his father, a rainy day chore in the work-shop, a place of pure magic. Allusions to 'Sweetie' Greaves and his myriad manual professions abound: rope-mender and master of splicing and knots, dice maintenance specialist who would take in dice that had become unreliable from the gambling men from the racecourse, and sand and

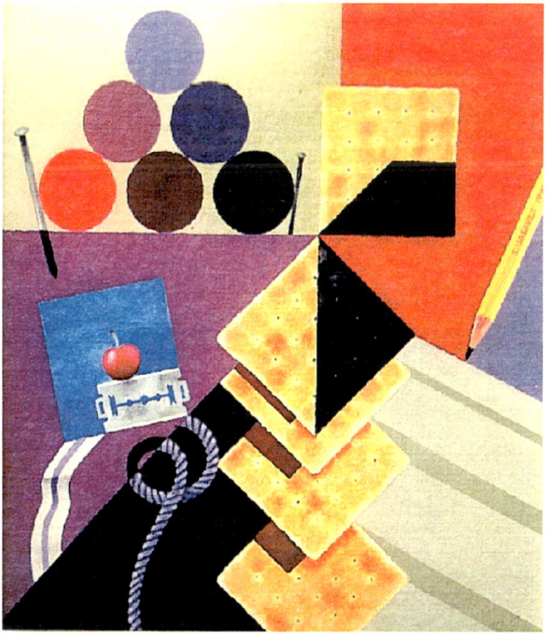

Biscuit Story No 1, 1991, oils, 25 x 23.5 cm

balance them until they were true. His mother Lydia's needles and threads have their place, as do the tastes of childhood: Weiting and Richter Edge-a-Boy biscuits, the point of departure for the finest of the pieces, *Biscuit Story No. 1.*

No vulgarities here of so-called Caribbean colour. On the contrary: a yearning after the close-harmonied, monochromatic palette achieved here in *Tap No 2* and *Alison's Cups No. 3.* Greaves is no colourist, in the sense of colour being an end in itself, the sense in which his fellow-Guyanese Aubrey Williams or James Boodhoo of Trinidad were colourists. Greaves's whole approach to the use of paint also distinguishes him from these contemporaries. He has written of Williams's "expressions revealing the spiritual aspect of colour that stressed a contemplative approach to the act of painting."[14]

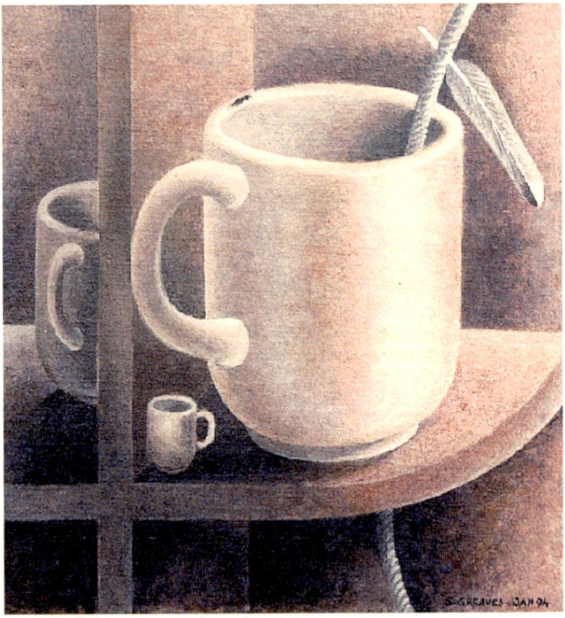

Alison's Cups, 1991, oils, 25 x 23.5 cm

Distinguishing Boodhoo's "perceptual" approach from Williams's "internalised position", he sees them both as impassioned colourists, with Boodhoo working "to establish areas of textured colour reacting together with the degree of harmonic subtlety... directed to the investigation of the way in which nature reveals herself through colour." To say that Greaves is no colourist is not to deny the long years of labouring in colour and testing its possibilities of revelation, as in the *Hearts and Diamond* series of 1985, with its methodical explorations into the uses and functions of colour. Colour in the mini-paintings is entirely functional, used like other techniques to make the paintings clear.

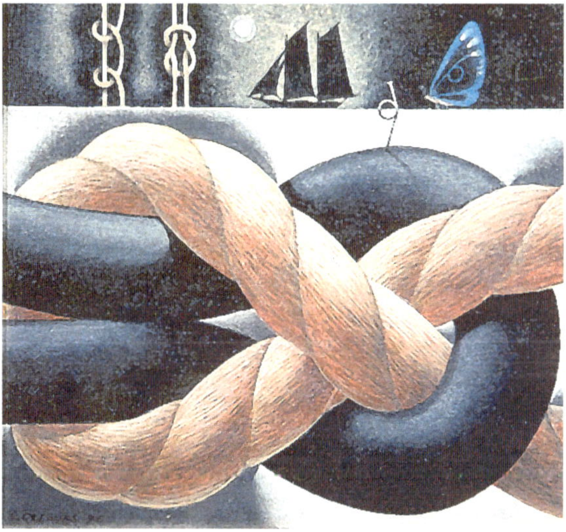

Knot No. 2, 1991, acrylics, 25 x 23.5 cm

Except for *Knot Nos 1 & 2, Tap No 2, Alison's Cup No 3*, and *Hooked Sandwich,* limited palette and monochromatic paintings where paint is carefully worked and manipulated, colour is no more and no less a function of composition and meaning.

It is a *Caribbean* metaphysic distinguished not only in Greaves's choice of objects native to the region, but in his exploration, below the level of consciousness, of dream states and beliefs that flow from the Caribbean folk imagination, as in the mysterious *Visitor* and the two obeah paintings, *The Doll* and *Jaguar Table*. The paintings, Greaves has pointed out, "are composed of two categories of objects, those native to the region and those that are not, and refer to the somewhat gratuitous nature of our existence."[15]

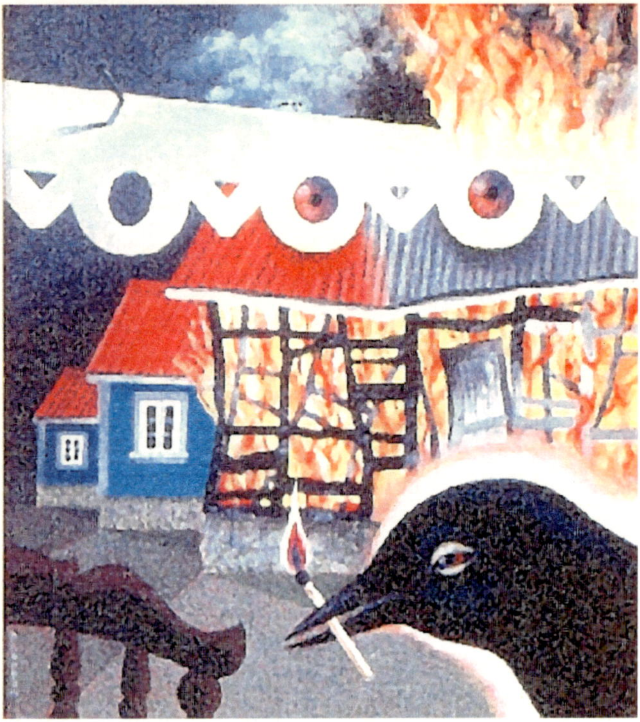

Dalkeith Village, 1991, oils, 25 x 23.5 cm

It is Caribbean in the celebration of our birds and leaves and shrimps and ants. These latter are Greaves's favourite insects, these minute survivors from forever, crawling over the surprisingly human face of *Tap No 2*, on the rim of the cup in *Alison's Cups No 3* and on the burning fretwork in the foreground of *Dalkeith Village*, (the name of a village in Barbados, where mysterious fires burned down chattel houses), where a blackbird, magically haloed, holds a lighted match in his beak. Caribbean especially in the abundance of the fruits of the region: the Barbadian cherry, the grapefruit, (invented in Jamaica from the shaddock and other citrus brought to the West Indies by Captain Shaddock), green peppers, pigeon peas and the poised, elegant, feminine okra of *The Visitor*, complete with her ruffled collar.

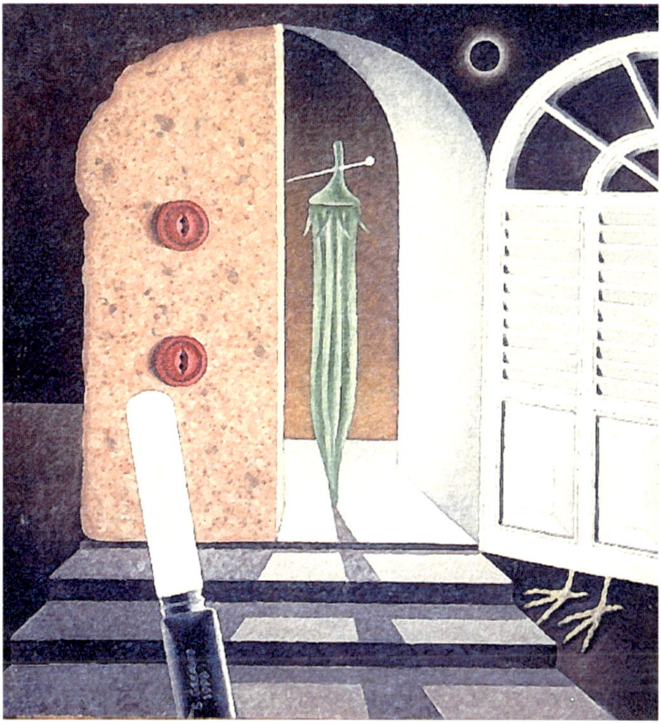

The Visitor, 1991, acrylics, 25 x 23.5 cm

There is the mild political satire on the great Caribbean "Circumlocution Office" where officials meet and meet and talk and talk and achieve nothing very much.

Who, of the Caribbean, does not know that rooster set to crow into the microphone, its stand a boy's slingshot fork, as befits an instrument of violence? The nut with no bolt? And the paper-clip, essential tool of the paper trade, fore-shortened to draw you into the space of the painting? The spoon of *Bird Bread*, the knife come to visit in the *Visitor*, the nail of *Plantation Boots*, the scissors of *The Doll*, and the umbrella of *Red Eye* all have the same function. Utterly Caribbean in the two "obeah" paintings where the connection to the African belief systems is most explicit: *The Doll* and *Jaguar Table*, where buttons have turned into celestial objects caught in the eyes of the doll and the well-dressed macaw is in a space that is either room or landscape. Separated by a white picket fence from the field of flowers and

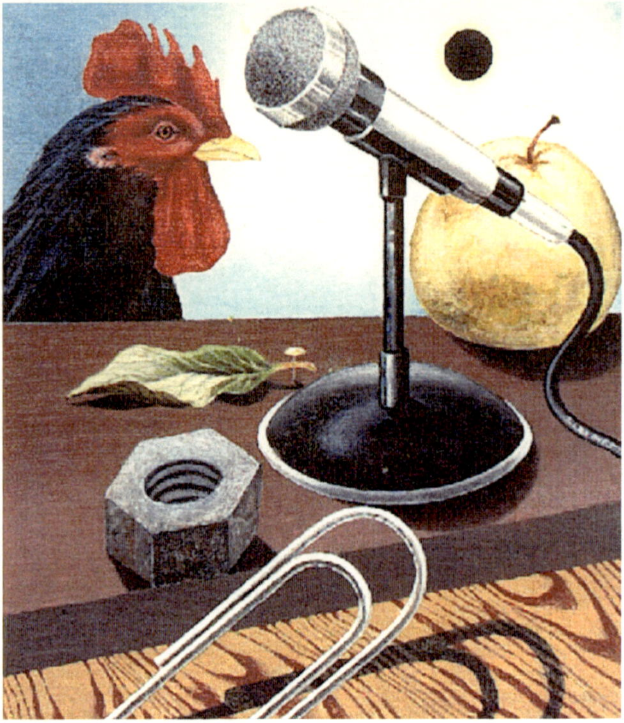

Caribbean Committee

the further fields stretching out to the whitened horizon, a celebrant jaguar presides over his "wuk" table. The lighted candle, with its thin plume of smoke, reel of thread, nail and purple onion are ceremonial objects awaiting deployment. The officiating jaguar, exactly spotted, stares out of eyes of an arctic blue, cold European eyes in the head of a tropical beast.

In presenting this Caribbean metaphysic as another reality, Greaves is reflecting on the absence of a Caribbean philosophy and what flows and does not flow from that absence. In the mini-paintings he is putting forward certain propositions of his own. It is necessary to begin by asking for a greater awareness of "the manner in which languages not indigenous to the region influence the way we view ourselves, the region and the world." The task before Caribbean artists is to define "the fundamentals of a Caribbean experience that cuts through or transcends the history of colonialism."[16] Martin Carter liked to say that

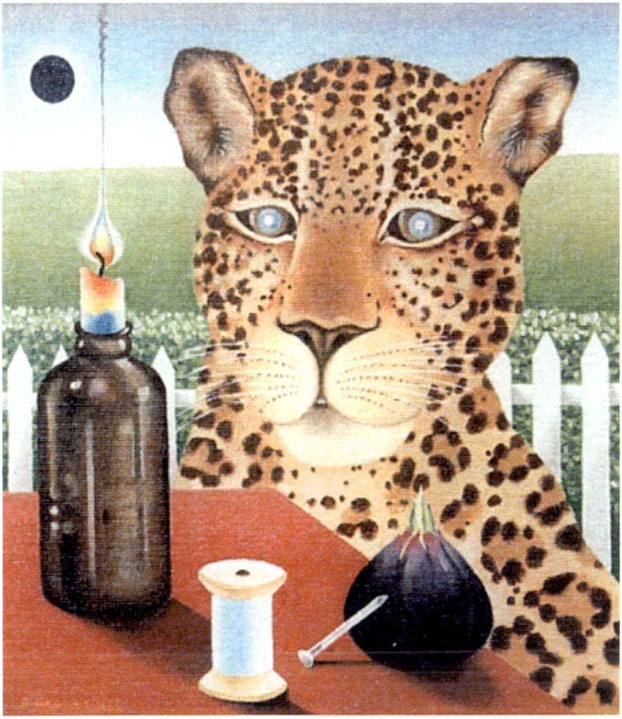

Jaguar Table, 1989, oils, 23 x 23 cm

the solutions to these problems of identity that were of such great concern to Caribbean peoples could be found "right under our own feet." Greaves is of like mind. It is a question to which he will return in the series of paintings on Caribbean folklore.

ENDNOTES TO CHAPTER EIGHT

1. Herbert Read, *Icon and Idea, (Faber & Faber, London, 1955), p.118.*

2 Quoted in Robin D. G. Kelley, *Freedom Dreams – the Black Radical Imagination* (Beacon Press, Boston, 2002.

3. *Caribbean Metaphysic – Another Reality,* Exhibition Catalogue, Queen's Park Gallery, 1993.

4. COLIN GARLAND b.1935 Australia.
Trained in National School of Art, Sydney, and Central School of Art London. Arrived in Jamaica in 1962, achieving recognition by the mid 1970s. Style is narrative descriptive, with surrealist or fantastic overtones often difficult to decipher. Imagery sometimes combines tropical elements with overtones of Early Italian art, and early Renaissance. Frequently visited Haiti. He has exhibited in London, Melbourne Adelaide, Kingston, New York, Havana.

JOHN DUNKLEY 1891-1947. b. Jamaica.
Of a poor rural family, as a teenager went to work on the Panama Canal and banana plantations and had early informal lessons in painting. Became a sailor. In 1926 he returned to Jamaica, set up as a barber and decorated everything in his shop. His work was promoted by H.D. Molesworth, director of the Jamaica Institute in 1937-8. He declined to join classes organized by the Institute on the grounds that his vision was unique. His paintings feature mystical landscapes, sometimes with figures. His output was small and he wanted it to be kept together as a museum.

His work was classified by David Boxer, head of the Jamaican National Gallery, as belonging to the "intuitive school"...(auto-didact visionary might be more appropriate, I feel. All artists are intuitive to some degree or other.) Exhibited mainly in Jamaica.

RON FLU
Born in Singapore, Ron Flu has been exhibiting since 1965. He was self-taught. His early work, highly stylized, was heavily influenced by Cubism. During the 1980s he developed a new style marked by an unusual form of realism with a sure architectural manner of depiction, sharp tonal contrast, evoking an other-worldly, almost magical atmosphere. His later paintings, many of them inspired by the lives of the prostitutes in Paramaribo, present a critical commentary on social injustices in the community.

5 Robin D. G. Kelley, *Freedom Dreams,* p. 169

6. Suzanne Cesaire, "The Domain of the Marvellous", 1941, in *Manifesto: A Century of Isms*, University of Nebraska Press, 2000.

7. Robert Hughes, *Nothing if not Critical* (London: Penguin, 1992), pp. 155-158.

8. SG, journal.

9. Quoted by Arthur Danto in an essay on Salvador Dalí, 1994. In *The Madonna of the Future* (New York: Farrar, Straus and Giroux, 2000, p.75.

10. Robin D. G. Kelley, *Freedom Dreams*, p. 160

11. Artist's Comment, Exhibition Catalogue, *Caribbean Metaphysic – Another Reality.*

12. Ibid.

13. SG, in conversation.

14. Stanley Greaves, "Art in Progress – Wifredo Lam, Leroy Clarke, Aubrey Williams, James Boodhoo, Hector Hyppolite", in *Trinidad & Tobago Review*, September 1993.

15. Exhibition Catalogue, *Caribbean Metaphysic – Another Reality.*

16. Stanley Greaves, "Art in Progress – Wifredo Lam, Leroy Clarke, Aubrey Williams, James Boodhoo, Hector Hyppolite", op. cit..

CHAPTER NINE

CARIBBEAN FOLKLORE, CARIBBEAN IKONS

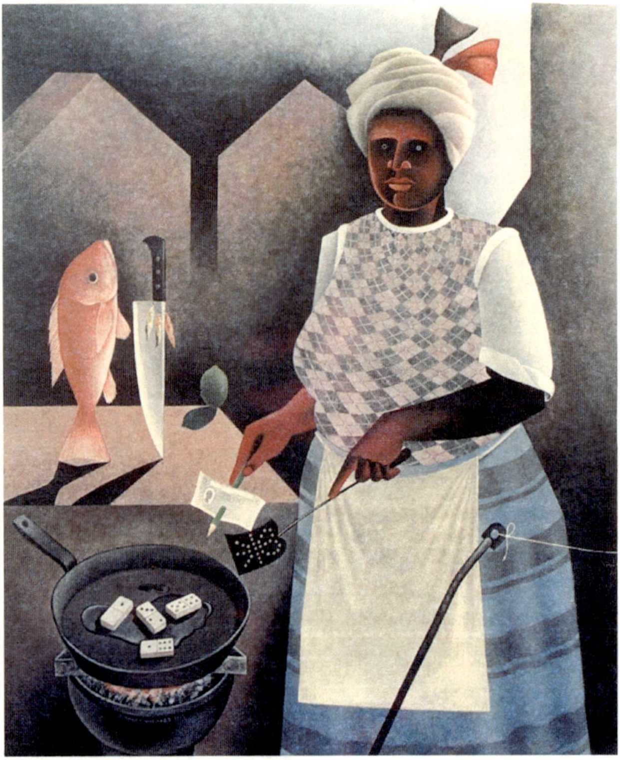

Mrs Baxter, 1992, acrylics, 113 x 96 cm

It was only after the detour through the symmetries of the *Hearts and Diamonds* sequence of the eighties and the essays on scale and space of the mini-paintings that Greaves returned to figure paintings.

He had discovered, coming out of the experience of the mini-paintings, that while he stuck to a realistic modality for the presentation of objects, the space inhabited by the objects took on different aspects. There was a certain flattening in some areas, where space was really shape implying space; in other areas, space took on a kind of cosmic aspect, hinting at infinity. Space was no longer the representation of an actual space, but an almost purely pictorial space. As he moved into the earliest of the new figure paintings, he sensed the need to locate the figure in a certain kind of space. In the case of the first one, *Mrs Baxter* – named after the street of fried-fish vendors in Bridgetown – he firmly anchors her in a particular place with its silhouettes of houses in the background and in a space defined by the table on which she does her frying. Mrs Baxter is set firmly in volumetric space. Brought over from the mini-paintings are the objects mysteriously deployed: knife, fish, a dollar bill speared by a pencil, domino pieces in the frying pan, a lemon balancing on the table's edge, peppers adorning the knife. The veve-like pattern on her spatula establishes a whimsical connection with the world of Voudon. The objects are realistically depicted while the houses are reduced to shapes, no more than prismatic figures representing houses. A certain tension is created by the juxtaposition within the same painting of realistic and abstract modalities. This contradiction is carried over into the treatment of the figure itself which is partly realistic and at the same time flattened and idealistic, especially in the treatment of the face and hands which are little more than ideas about faces and hands. Contrast this to the painting of the dress that, while somewhat flattened, clearly clothes a real body. The contradiction persists in *Hat Man* where his face and hands and well tailored shirt are treated in a stylised manner, while his hat, as well as the hats he holds, the leaf, cup, eggs and stalk of sugar-cane are all rendered realistically. The hat magically balancing on its rim on top of the stack of hats, the two eggs in a space beyond, one resting on top of

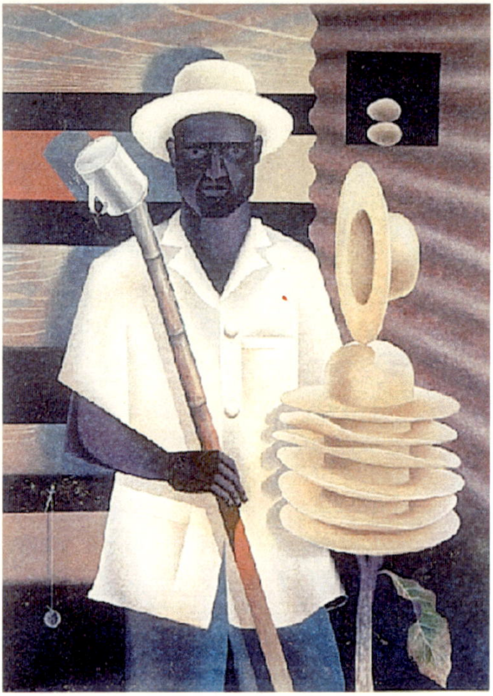

Hat Man, 1992, acrylics, 112 x 82 cm

the other, and the button at the end of a piece of string suspended from a nail have their place in the orchestration of the objects that make for the rhythmic composition of the picture. The *vanitas* leaf drooping from the stalk crowned by the stack of hats signifies mortality and the passing of time; the upturned enamel cup that is the "hat" of the sugar-cane speaks to the condition of need that turned a worker into a seller of hats, while the button and eggs hint at the magic world of folk belief.

In the later *Magus with Reversed Bananas, Banana Manna* and *Madonna,* however, the unity of language has been maintained in the single object and figure. The tension has shifted from the pictorial and compositional aspects to the psychological. As in the *Caribbean Folklore Invented* series, the later figure paintings are concerned less with pictorial problems and more with issues and ideas and how to present them, storytelling in a sense. The more insistent the symbolic and narrative

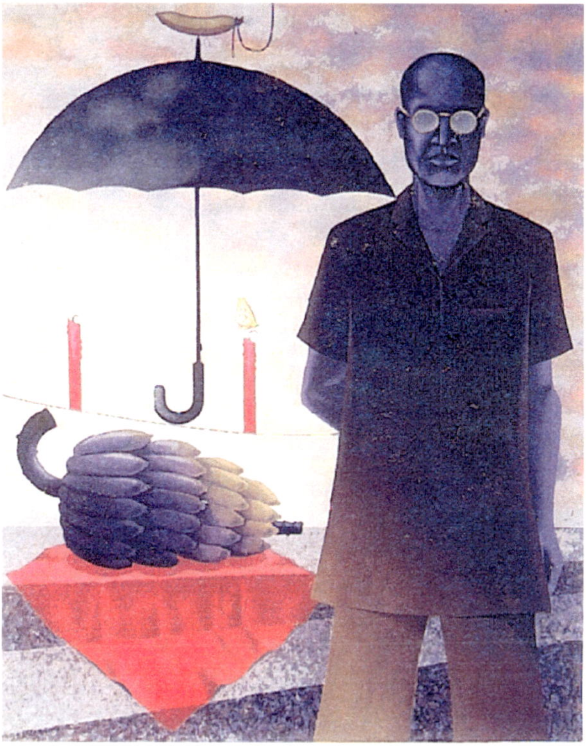

Magus with Reversed Bananas. 1995, acrylics, 110 x 90 cm

content, the more metaphor intrudes in the painting, the more realistic the treatment. The emphasis now falls on the figures and the activities they are engaged in. The space surrounding the figures acquires a greater significance and grows emptier and more vast. The board and zinc fence of *Hat Man* and the silhouettes of houses in *Mrs Baxter,* reduced to a high degree of abstraction, give way altogether to the stark, cosmic landscape of *Magus* and *Banana Manna*. Space has become a subject in its own right and is no longer just a space in which things happen.

The space of *The Magus* is sacred space, made votive by the red altar cloth and the red candles, one with a *vanitas* butterfly for flame, balancing on a string that the Magus may or may not be holding behind his back. Visual rhymes connect the disparate objects: the umbrella handle, the curving banana stalk, the curl of the drooped string from above. A similar function

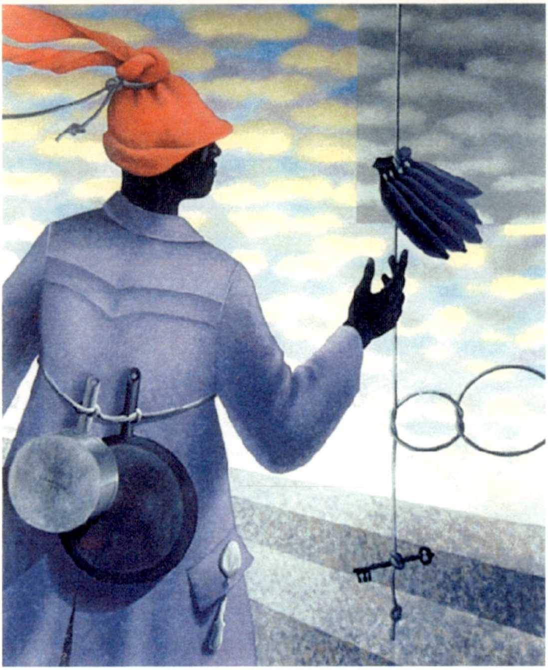

Banana Manna, 1995, acrylics, 110 x 90 cm

is served by the ropes and knots of *Banana Manna* where a hermaphroditic figure reaches for the manna come down on a rope whose loops open to another dimension, which may be the dimension from which the rope descended.

The two banana paintings derive from the ongoing banana war which involves the continents of Europe and the Americas and the Caribbean archipelago. In *Banana Manna,* the step-like wall, a reference to the seawall in Guyana, represents non-specific territory. Through the double circle in the cord, the mathematical symbol of infinity, we look into another dimension represented by the grey monochromatic area in the top right of the picture. The manna comes down from this other world of heaven on the looped cord. Therein lies salvation. The somewhat enigmatic and sexually indeterminate figure is dressed in what appears to be a winter coat, an incongruity in the Caribbean. The figure seems to stand for all of humanity with all its longings. The strange hat and cord tied to it is perhaps linked to the cord with bananas, establishing man's link to heaven. The harsh reality of life on earth is represented by the cooking pot and pan tied to the waist of the figure and by the spoon in the pocket. The key, universal symbol of protection, is tied to the end of the cord from above and promises the accessibility of material and spiritual goods. The painting presents in a universal sense an allegory of humanity's wishful thinking: specifically, of the Caribbean hope that salvation will descend from above like manna from heaven. Given the harshness of things, belief in the higher power is consolation; where else are the powerless to exercise power but in the domain of the spirit? It is a yearning as old as humanity.

Magus with Reversed Bananas carries on the subject matter of the banana wars, elaborating the theme of wishful thinking in a more specific way. Here the religious is presented not as an importation from or imposition by the metropolitan powers, but as an indigenous movement cultivated and instituted by the folk throughout the Caribbean under different names – Winte, Santeria, Pocomania and Vodun – to satisfy a basic human need: the engagement with a power above and beyond the self. In his trim bureaucrat's uniform, the figure is less enigmatic and more recognisable as a figure of authority. He has come from the office to carry out a "wuk". His real office as a celebrant is indicated by the paraphernalia behind him. We are in the world of ritual and magic. As Magus he is the recipient of extraordinary powers. He can cause an umbrella to balance on a string with candles, a string he is perhaps holding behind his back, keeping his manipulations hidden from the common gaze and revealing only the results of his actions. The other string leading out of the picture might be his connection to another dimension. At once priest and politician, he exhibits his powers and proposes that magic and ritual are the way out of this world of need and oppression. Both paintings reflect on the powerlessness pervading the Caribbean and the acts of imagination and spirituality the working people have devised to conjure an alternative world of solidarity and fulfilment. Buffeted by mighty impersonal forces emanating from outside the region, the folk create their own separate, parallel world out of the reach of earthly authority, the only available zone for the reclaiming of the truly human.

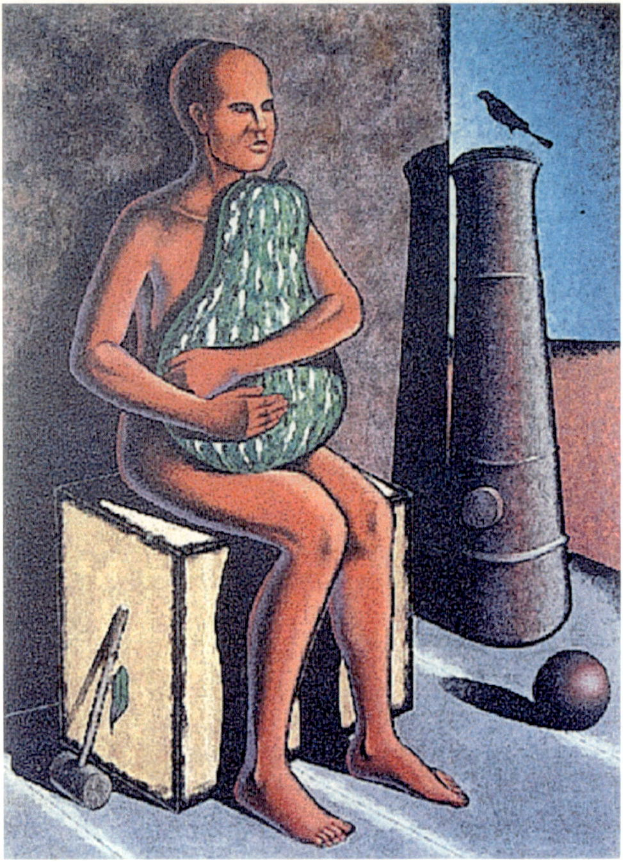

Madonna With Pumpkin, 1998, acrylics, 80 x 61.5cm

In *Madonna with Pumpkin*, the hope/salvation theme linking these figure paintings is deepened. A direct reference to a central Roman Catholic icon, the Virgin Mary, is overlaid with allusions to the Egyptian goddess Isis. The painting presents the principles of protective motherhood and unassailable virtue in an hieratical figure, the earth and spirit mother found in all cultures. Through a kind of transliteration, the hieratical is rendered through the use of the strictly commonplace: the ubiquitous vendor of fruit and vegetables found everywhere in the Caribbean represents the Mother. The cannon against the wall is a feature of the district of St. Michael, the parish in Barbados where Greaves lives and the site of the second largest garrison for British forces during colonisation of the Caribbean. The cannon was de-militarised by the Barbadian authorities and put to practical civilian use as a protection for walls against vehicular traffic, an ironic end. In the symbolic language of the painting, the cannon and ball represent the male principle, an oblique reference to Joseph, the stepfather of the Christ. The pumpkin is Osiris/Christ, the principle of resurrection and growth. And to draw our attention to the transient nature of all things, a *vanitas* statement: the leaf growing from the handle of the mallet.

Caribbean Folklore Invented

> *All of this talk in the Caribbean about identity is for me inextricably linked with a mythology. With a mythology as a base line, one can then go on to create other structures in social dimensions. In my own way, to assuage the pain of not having a mythology that can really sustain me, I began to do these paintings, taking material from wherever I could find it, from my own consciousness, my sub-consciousness, from things I read, bringing it to bear on the issues. The principle that runs through all mythology is the principle of universality; certain concepts are universal: the creation of man and the creation of woman, how plants and animals came into being.*
>
> **Stanley Greaves**[1]

Greaves has had a life-long interest in mythology. Enticed by the stories from Greek and Egyptian mythology he had read as a boy, his fascination with mythology has persisted and deepened over the years. In his continuous explorations in South American and Egyptian mythology he has come to set great store by the sense of psychological, intellectual and imaginative wholeness that a cosmology provides: all is one. He has found no such coherence in the Caribbean: instead, a hodgepodge of folktales from different cultural and ethnic groupings cobbled together. "Mythology is a whole," he writes, "it contains universals that underpin the mythology. So one can extract folkloric tales about particular events that are part of the whole mythology. In the absence of a total mythology, which I cannot propose, I can make statements at this level, inventing particular events based on universal themes, and giving them a Caribbean dimension."[2]

Four paintings, executed in 1993-94, are his mythological statements: *Venus-Ymanja*, *Caribbean Chimera*, *The Visitation,* and *The Tree of Life*.

The first painting in the series, *Venus-Ymanja,* has a long history reaching back to the 1950s. The story begins with the young artist's encounter with Botticcelli's *Primavera* and *Birth of Venus.* The technician in him was struck by the mural-type flatness and edged quality of the Botticelli paintings and by their fine draughtsmanship. The *Venus*, in particular, left a lasting impression – the woman emerging from a shell, with winds blowing about her, the flowers and sea waves. In the mid 1950s, as he was collecting shells on the Georgetown sea-shore, he came upon the brown and white striped shell which was to replace the classical clam shell in the first *Birth of Venus* he painted. Woman, water, moon and shell were brought together in a single dramatic situation. The shell was rendered completely realistically. Emerging from the shell a flat, stylised shrimp in pinks and reds, against a stark background. The second Venus painting (*The Birth of Venus*,1990) was in the mini-painting series. It was in fact the first of the mini-paintings (see p.122)

Here the imagined shrimp is rendered somewhat more realistically. Great attention has gone into the rendering of the shell, poised on the tip of the volute, balanced and self-sustaining. In keeping with the *ostranenie* (making strange) technique of the mini-paintings, there is a signpost stuck in the sea. "Caution" written above an upturned "V". The sky is two-layered, creating a palimpsest effect of layered meanings. Behind the peeled back sky, another sky. Behind that, perhaps

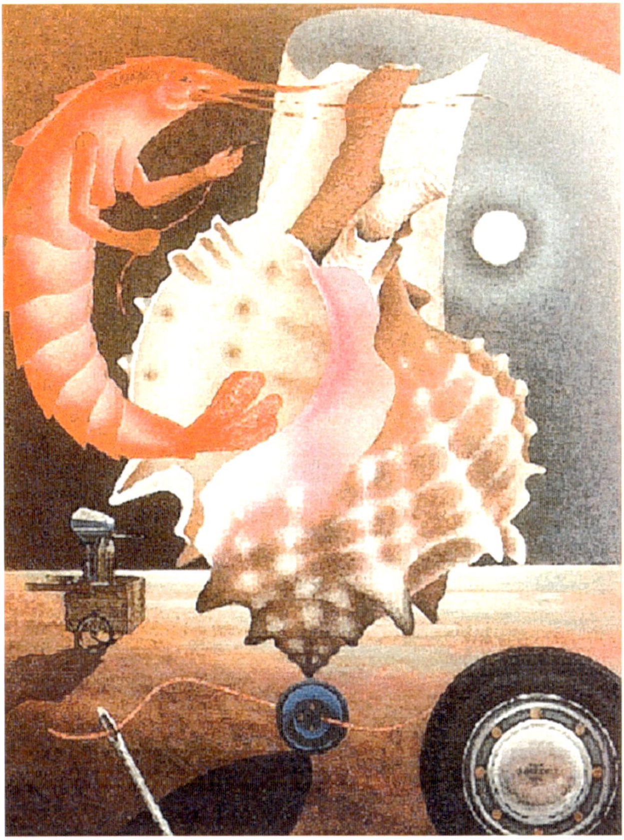

Birth of Venus-Ymanja, 1994, acrylics, 80 x 61.5 cm

another, and another. Through the infinite skies, the black sun or a black hole, the space beyond. The hand-cart used by Barbadian fishermen to transport their outboard engines is at the water's edge, an enigmatic object from the real world, linking man and sea. A sewing needle with looped red thread and a red button frame the foreground and participate in the interplay of objects. In the environment of the mini-paintings, the needle, looped thread, button, cart, engine and sign-post are objects that realise their individual identity in and through their active inter-relationship with one another. Their primary function is compositional and rhythmic.

Many of the pictorial elements recur in the *Venus-Ymanja* of the *Caribbean Folklore* series: the needle, thread and button, the handcart with its outboard engine, the peeled-back sky, and at the centre of the drama, the shrimp and shell. The large, prawn-like creature is turned into an anthropomorphic figure, an elegant female form with breasts. In the realm of mythology, the needle and thread, associated with women's activity, bring to mind both Penelope, weaving by day and unravelling by night, and Ariadne's thread to navigate the maze. Venus is yoked with *Ymanja*, Orisha Goddess of the Sea from the Yoruba, a powerful retention still active in Brazil and Haiti, and Trinidad where Ymanja is an Orisha associated with healing and corresponding to the Guyanese Water-Mamma, (though this is perhaps more a Congolese than a Yoruba retention). In *Venus-Ymanja* Greaves succeeds in bringing together European and African mythologies and traditions with the everyday objects

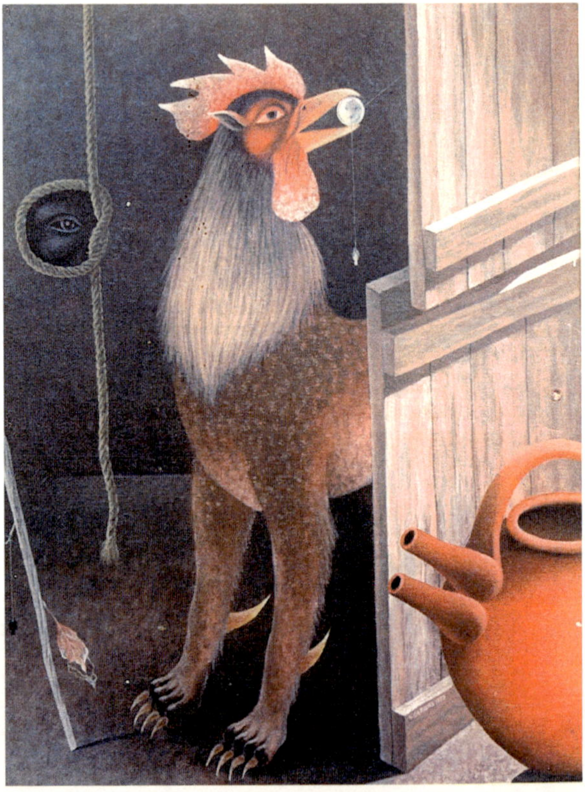

Caribbean Chimera, 1993, acrylics, 80 x 60.5 cm

of the Caribbean, combining them into a resonant synthesis that is an authentic, lived Caribbean experience.

No mythology is without its fearsome beast, the beast of beasts. The Caribbean Chimera is such a beast. A composite creature, it has the head and spurs of the ubiquitous cockerel, the furry mane of a red howler monkey (the Guyanese "baboon"), the spotted coat and claws of the jaguar. The figure is shown only partially, a kind of bust. The other half of its body, concealed by the bottom half of the Dutch door, a feature of Guyanese architecture, is left to be imagined. Outside the door, a terracotta pot establishes a continuity with the pots common to all cultures in a variety of forms. Called a monkey pot in Barbados, it is a traditional water cooler with a spout and a lid and a handle coming off the top. In the painting, Greaves has given the pot two spouts to mark it as a mythic/magical object, as magical as the 3-holed button through which the spider has spun his thread. Within the mythic space of the painting, set off from the actual space of the viewer, the Dutch door opens onto a space occupied by the beast. The rope descending from the heavens, a leitmotif in Greaves' work, is looped. Within the loop, an eye looks out from another dimension, alluding to the infinity of dimensions and the continuity of things. The *vanitas* object leans against a wall, a branch with a single dry and browning leaf. Hanging by a thread from a twig of the branch, there is a three-spotted spider, rhyming with the 3-holed button held in the cockerel beak of the beast. Thus, Greaves' rendering of the universal theme of the mythic beast.

The mythological essays continue with *The Visitation*. The event is common enough, the spirit-being that appears before the hero or heroine, giving instructions or issuing warnings.Here Greaves is drawing on the power that dreams and visions exercise on the lives of the people. In the painting, the cactus is such a spirit-being, with its branches and flowers for arms and hands, its wings marked by assorted feathers, with bees for eyes and a moth for a mouth. Before the apparition, the heroine, holds a slim rod of grass. To enhance the magical powers of the rod, twelve black ants crawl upwards. A thirteenth ant, red, crawls downwards. The twelve black ants, like the apostles, follow their red leader. Allusions to Christian and specifically

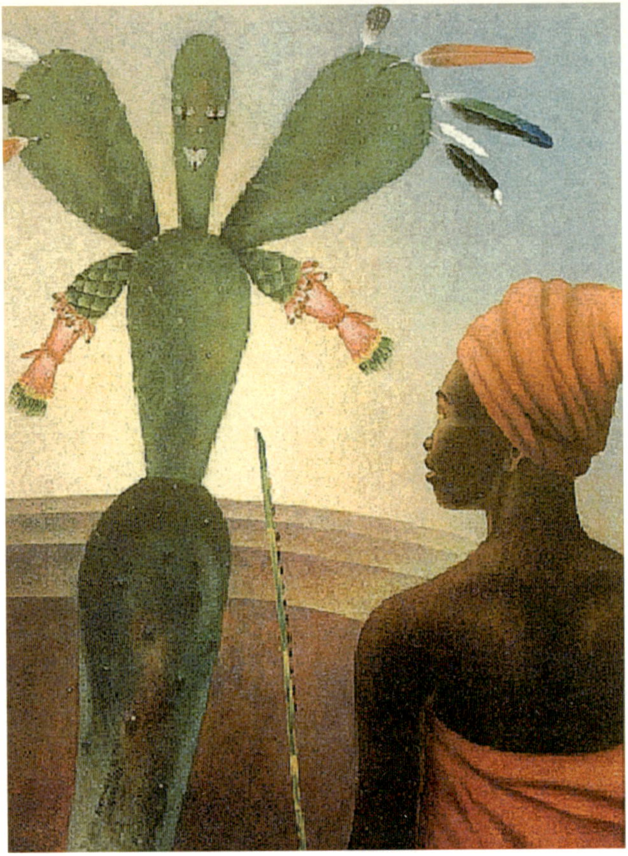

The Visitation, 1993, acrylics, 80 x 60.5 cm

Catholic mythology are frequently just below the surface in many of the paintings, vestiges of Greaves' upbringing at the hands of the Jesuits in Guyana. The curvature of the earth and the horizon describes and defines the mythic space.

The stand-pipe that was at the heart of the social life of the tenement yard of his childhood has found its way into many of the paintings across the years. Here in *The Tree of Life*, the humble taps from the humblest of yards are elevated into mythic status.

The world-tree connecting the three regions of man, heaven and the underworld is common to many cultures. In Norse mythology, the giant ash tree, Yggdrasil, links and shelters all

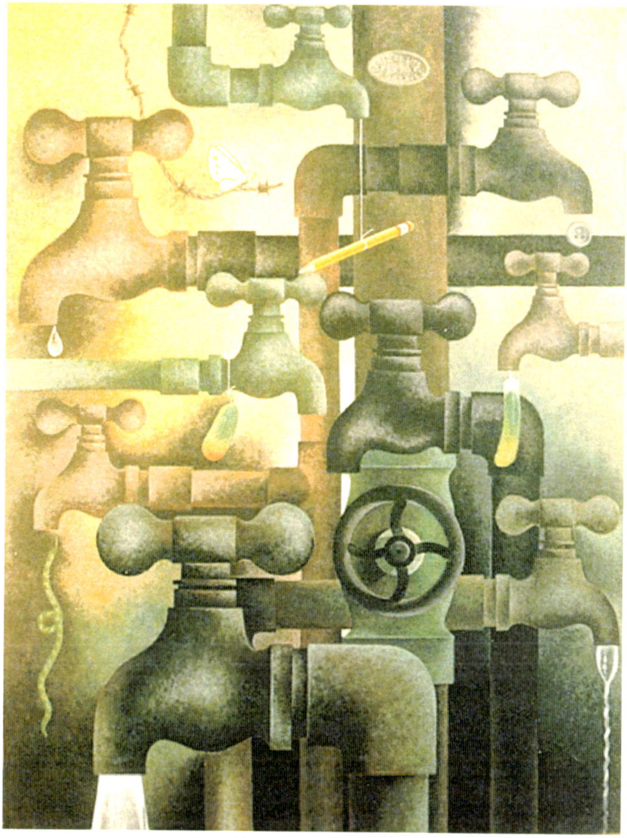

The Tree of Life, 1994, acrylics, 80 x 60.5 cm

the worlds. By now familiar objects issue from the mouths of the taps: another 3-holed button, a feather, a string bean, looped, a pencil hanging by a thread. A white moth has alighted on a strand of barbed wire descending from on high. The main tap in the foreground releases a full flow of water, unlike the single drop and air-bubble of the other two taps from which water issues. A tree of Georgetown tenement yard pipes to express the power of the mythological Tree of Life, to connect the everyday Caribbean experience to a universal symbol.

The four paintings that comprise the Caribbean family – *Mr. Fixxe, Mrs. Plaits* and their children, *Miss Girl* and *Bro' Boy* – are a new thematic departure. Since Mr. Fixxe and Mrs. Plaits are nothing if not typical, it is safe to assume that theirs is a common-law marriage. (It may be of interest to note that at the time of the 1990 census in Barbados, only 30 percent of mothers between the ages of 15 and 49 were married.) It is a truth first pronounced by William DuBois as early as 1908 in his *The Negro American Family* and re-affirmed by recent scholarship that the family was among the major casualties of slavery.[3] While the varied consequences and residues of this legacy of slavery are all around, the subject has not, until Greaves's series attracted the interest of the visual artists of the region.

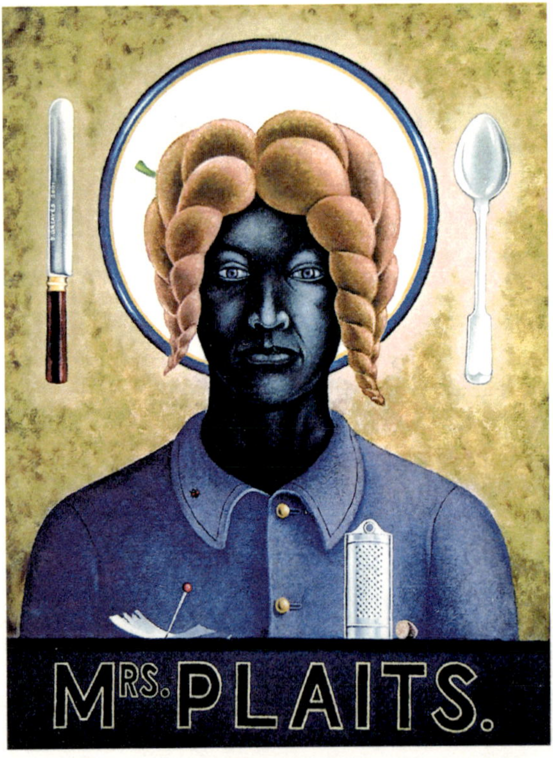

2001, oils, 60.5 x 47 cm

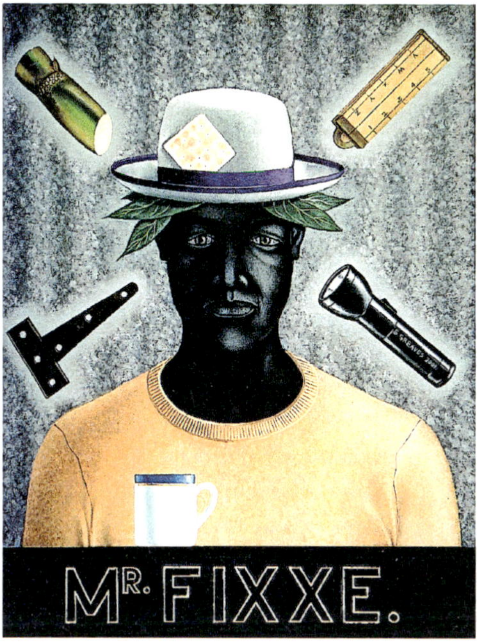

2001, oils, 60.5 x 47 cm

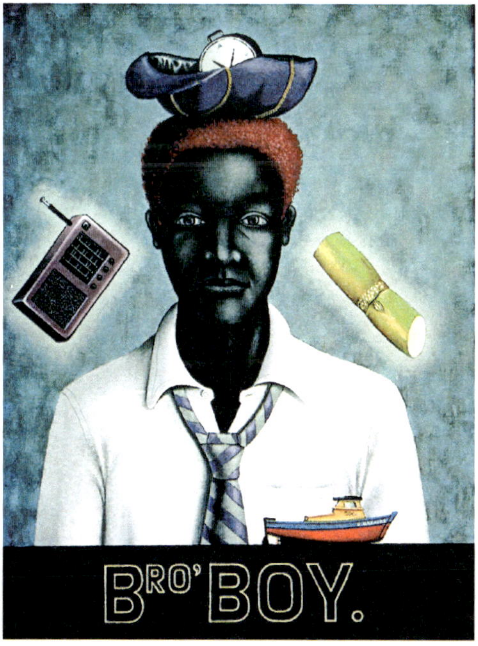

2001, oils, 60.5 x 47 cm

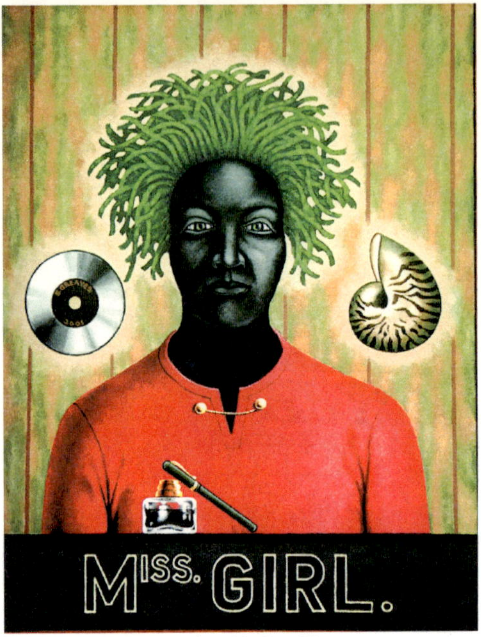

2001, oils, 60.5 x 47 cm

The portraits of the Fixxe-Plaits family, with their surrounding haloes of objects, have their art historical reference in the Byzantine and early Italian paintings of saints that were an accompaniment of the boy Greaves's Catholic education in Guyana.

Mrs. Plaits's hair of plaited bread, surrounded by the halo of a plate with knife and spoon as well as the grater and nutmeg in the foreground, marks her as the mother. The fraying scrap of paper pinned to the table, a market list perhaps, is a *Vanitas* object telling of mortality and the passage of time. Mr. Fixxe is surrounded by his tools, a carpenter's folding rule, a flashlight, hasp and, to signify the birth of the Caribbean as an economic power and the dominant role of sugar, a piece of sugar cane. Bro' Boy continues the legacy, his piece of cane riper. The leaves under Mr. Fixxe's elegant hat are for cooling, an old folk practice. His blue-rimmed mug rhymes with Mrs. Plaits's plate, establishing their bond.

The children, Miss Girl and Bro' Boy, that is everygirl and everyboy, are surrounded by the objects of their age: CD disc and transistor radio. Miss Girl's Rasta locks of string beans suggest she is a country girl with the ambition to move on to higher things signalled by the fancy pen and ink bottle. The shell is an ancient symbol for sexuality.

Bro' Boy, younger than his sister, is in school cap, tie and shirt. The tug in the forefront signifies both his boy's attachment to the model boat and a feeling for adventure. The clock in his rebelliously upturned cap represents the passage of time as he approaches adulthood.

The clock faces that recur in Greaves's work have their source in a childhood practice. The boy Greaves was in charge of setting the house clock and his father's pocket watch when the church bell rang at 6 in the morning and again in the evening. The incorporation of the titles as part of the paintings is a direct homage to his father the sign-painter. "Sweetie" Greaves could not have known of the effect that his brushes and pencils and cans of paint were having on the little boy as he cleaned the brushes and was even permitted to paint the pencilled-in letters marked on sign-boards in progress.

The four faces are carefully modelled and deliberately expressionless. They are archetypical, this black working class family of the Caribbean: they are Caribbean ikons. As with their Byzantine predecessors, they are clearly recognizable – Mother, Father, Daughter, Son: ease of recognition was a requirement of the Byzantine icon, the figure facing out of the picture, "ready to receive the prayers of the worshipper".[4] To fulfil its mystic function as a doorway to the saint it depicted, the icon had to adhere to a set of stylistic criteria: "Clarity and the repetition of recognized types were for long characteristics of Byzantine painting."[5] To this might be added the absence of conscious experimentation. Contrasting the religious art of pre-eighteenth Russia to that of Ancient China, which "is full of references to the world as perceived through the senses," John Berger writes: "In the Russian ikon, neither space nor time exists. It addresses the eye, but the eye which then shuts in prayer so that the image – now in the mind's eye – is isolated and spiritualized."[6] In his Caribbean ikons, Greaves is testing the boundaries between the secular and religious in painting. It is a theme that is to receive deeper elaboration in the next major body of paintings, *There is a Meeting Here Tonight.*

ENDNOTES TO CHAPTER NINE

1. SG, journal.

2. Ibid.

3. James Q. Wilson, "Slavery & the Black Family" in *The Marriage Problem* (New York: Harper Collins, 2002).

4. *The Oxford Companion to Art,* Harold Bloom, Editor, (Oxford: Clarendon, 1970).

5. Ibid.

6. John Berger, *Art and Revolution, Ernst Neizvestny and the Role of the Artist in the USSR*, (London: Penguin, 1969), p. 19.

CHAPTER TEN

THE POLITICS OF DESOLATION

If an artist doesn't educate the public, what will become of mankind?

Alfred Brendel, the pianist
(A quotation entered in Stanley Greaves's journal, November 1993).

Over the years Greaves grew increasingly disillusioned with conditions in the Caribbean and despaired at the blight that had settled over his native Guyana. The bright promise of the early post-independence years, ringing with confident assertions of sovereignty and selfhood, had lost its bloom. Degradation was the order of the day. As Martin Carter liked to intone, "Where have all the flowers gone?" And nowhere was this degradation more alarming than in the political arena.

To give expression to this sense of waste, the old student of the Working People's Art Class turned to a painting he had seen in the exhibition of 1951 and never forgotten, Burrowes's *Guyana, Land of the Dolorous Guard*.

A waste land of ruination under an angry, blue-black sky; scudding clouds, a full moon, and a stretch of stagnant water reflecting the sky. Next to the water's edge, the remnant of a building reduced to a sloping roof, a supporting wall with a doorway through which figures scramble simian-like on hands and knees, following the leader. No *homo erectus* here. On the branch of a leafless tree, the mere stump of a trunk and broken branches, a carrion-crow "practises to wait", presiding over all. Against the trunk of the tree, a woman leans, cradling a child, Mother Guyana, the future in her arms. On a rope strung tight from the trunk two figures in suits totter, tightrope walkers struggling to master balance. A third has made it to the end and is dismounting the rope, awkwardly. In the left foreground, a huddled shape wrapped in a shroud, has burrowed into the ground. In the centre, another figure, torso bare, buries his head in the sand. For complement, a broken cart wheel in the right foreground, half buried in the sand. A limited palette to enforce the austere sense of dread.

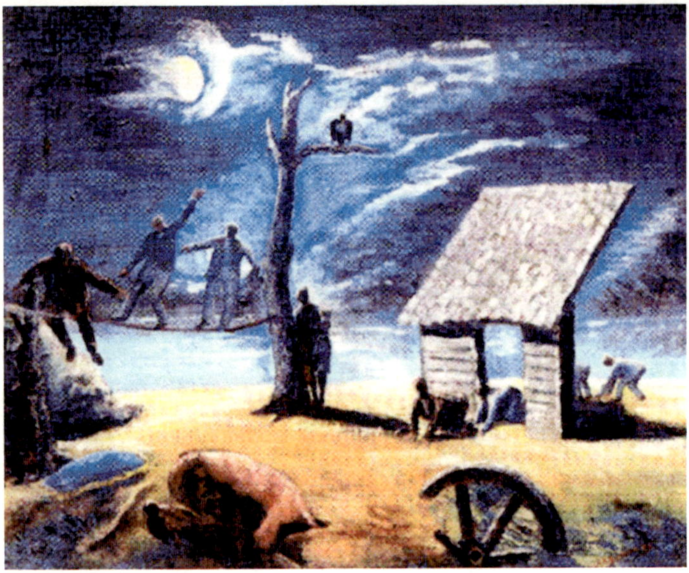

E.R. Burrowes, *Guyana, Land of the Dolorous Guard*,
1951, oils, 46 x 57 cm

Guyana, Land of the Dolorous Guard was painted in 1951, the year that Martin Carter's first collection of poems, *The Hill of Fire Glows Red,* was published in A.J. Seymour's pioneering Miniature Poets series. In April of that year the painting was shown at the Working People's Art Class Exhibition at St Andrews School in Georgetown. Included in the show was a painting by the seventeen-year-old Greaves, his first to be exhibited, *Tropical Lights.*[1]

Burrowes's painting is as fine an image of the colonial waste as any, Fanon's "motionless Manicheanistic world" made vivid. It is the nightmare of oppression. Its bleakness is cosmic: the Guyanese condition is the human condition. It is at one in eloquence, potency of image and starkness of vision with the lines of Martin Carter, written a decade later when Guyana was in the throes of the agony bequeathed by the violence and ruptures of 1953.

For is only one way, one path, one road.
And nothing downward bends, but upward goes,
like leaves to sunlight, trees to the sun itself.
All, all who are human fail,
like bullets aimed at life,
or the dead who shoot
and think themselves alive!

Behind a wall of stone beside this city,
mud is blue-grey when ocean waves are gone,
in the mid-day sun!
And I have seen some creatures rise from holes
and claw a triumph like a citizen,
and reign until the tide!

Atop the iron roof tops of this city,
I see the vultures practising to wait.
And everytime and anytime,
in sleep or sudden wake, nightmare, dream,
always for me the same vision of cemeteries, slow funerals
broken tombs, and death designing all.[2]

(From 'Black Friday 1962')

For the progressive artists and intellectuals of the time, particularly those of an activist bent – whether politically, like Carter, or culturally, like Burrowes – the anti-colonial upsurge of the early 1950s was a time of hope and awakening, of thrilling and seemingly boundless possibilities. The rebellion gathered momentum after the murder of five striking sugar-workers, and the wounding of fourteen, by the colonial police at Enmore estate in 1948 and was spreading through the towns and villages. The descendants of bondspeople, emerging upright out of slavery and indentureship, were on the march. It was a season of new teachings, calling into question the right of Empire and the right of others to dominate our lives. Heaven, it seemed, was there for the storming.

The euphoria was short lived. British gunboats invaded Guyana in October 1953 to prevent "a dangerous crisis both in public order and in economic affairs." On October 9, the British government announced that it had suspended the constitution because of a communist plot, overthrew the first elected, 135-day-old government, and set in train a period of studied repression. In the words of Eusi Kwayana, one of the "ring-leaders" identified by the Colonial Office: "A State of Emergency, detentions without trial, restrictions on movement, trials and imprisonment affecting leaders and activists, a ban on meetings and assemblies were part of the new democratic process."[3] In the end, the united nationalist movement succumbed to the complex mix of pressures and fragmented, resulting in the African/Indian ethnic polarisation of the country that has blighted its development ever since. Manoeuvre and manipulation replaced the politics of heroism and revolt. It was the beginning of Guyana's "dark time", culminating in the waste and senseless devastation of the sixties. In such an environment, the patriotic imagination was provoked into visions of desolation. Carter and Burrowes before him, each in his own way and according to his own lights, were in the forefront of those who gave expression to that absence of hope and common purpose.

Almost fifty years later, Greaves reflected on the significance of *Guyana, Land of the Dolorous Guard* and its enduring power. "It seems to span time," he writes in 1999, "and has a significance that is still frighteningly relevant to the present political scene in Guyana. It is the most prophetic work on this topic by far in the National Collection, and it should be registered as well in the national consciousness. Our political leaders would be well advised to go have a real close look at that work. ...While it is presenting a message of total despair it is paradoxically also saying that one should recognise what is taking place and do something positive about the situation... The recommendation to the political leaders is also extended to the Guyanese people because it is only through 'meaningful dialogue' between the two that a solution will be found for the problems set out by Burrowes forty years ago." He sees the Burrowes painting as "based on a sensitive scrutiny" of the society, with a subject matter that was "not about technical prowess or style as is so often the case these days."[4] The previous year, in a journal entry of July 1998, he had written: "The [*Meeting*] series has been fundamentally supported by the painting *Land of the Dolorous*

Guard by E. R. Burrowes which from the time I saw it struck a responsive chord. I am very conscious of its presence every time I look at the series and more so when in the act of painting the individual paintings. It is quite remarkable the way a single painting can develop and sustain such energy over a period of time."[5]

Greaves has explicitly acknowledged the influence of the Burrowes painting on his own work, calling it "the singular motivation" for the *There is a Meeting Here Tonight* series, begun in 1992. *Guyana, Land of the Dolorous Guard* and the *Meeting* series it inspired bring to the fore issues such as the function of art and the responsibility of the artist in our crisis-ridden and riven societies. These in turn give rise to questions of accessibility, how idiom, style and technique are to be mobilised and deployed if paintings are to "register in the national consciousness" and instruct the general public. In a journal entry of January 1985, a period given over to his obsessive explorations of symmetry and to the formal aspects of composition, Greaves poses the problem of accessibility: "The practice of art," he writes, "is mainly self-referential. It has little to offer the general public. If this is to be changed art will have to move towards the exhortational, the didactic, or the propagandistic. It will have to become more 'readable', not necessarily literary. The danger here is the linking of art to an ideology of a non aesthetic basis bringing the concepts of moral action into consideration."[6] With the *Hearts and Diamonds* series behind him, Greaves returns to the subject. In a journal entry of April 1992, he comes to the conclusion that the dichotomy he had posed seven years earlier needed to be revised: "For the longest while," he notes, "I read and I thought that the art which was produced based on religious or political or any other theme was done in the service of those themes. I was wrong: it is all really done in the service of art."[7]

Not since his *People of the Pavement* paintings of the 1950s has Greaves's work been as explicitly political as in the *Meeting* series. More than merely political in that they address political themes and subjects, the *Meeting* series is a conscious intervention in a political conjuncture. In the notes he drafted for the exhibition of the series, he writes: "It is a savage irony that the institution of politics which should be the instrument of protection of the people (and the development of their strength across a range of activities) and contain the potential for significant action should be the instrument of the destruction of the same values... Herein lies the irony which is the fundamental message of this body of work which poses questions whose answers lie in the manner the will of the nation is expressed – self damnation or self salvation. The choice is clear."[8]

II

It is now that, for the first time in the history of the country, we have a chance to initiate things, and to fashion them to our own purpose. And without in the least condoning the tragic events of February 16 and their unhappy consequences, it may be, after all is said and done, that what happened on that day is certainly not the worst that could have happened to us in this time and age. For now at the very least we know what can happen. And also that the old days have gone forever.

The new days are for us to make. Are we good enough?

Martin Carter, March 23, 1962[9]

While it is true to say that the theme, content, manner of execution, and iconography of *Guyana, Land of the Dolorous Guard* provide the starting point and inspiration for the *Meeting* series, of even greater significance is the stand-point adopted by these works, separated by some fifty years in time, vis-à-vis their respective social, cultural and political contexts. Over those fifty years, the West Indian colonies were granted their independence from Britain, hoisted their bright new flags amid high ceremony and much jubilation and expectation, and set about the management of their own affairs. It is beyond the scope of this chapter to trace the particular degenerations which have seen the promise and exuberance of the immediate post-independence years turn to so much ashes. There can be little doubt that the desolate landscapes of the *Meeting* paintings speak to dashed hopes and broken dreams. Because Greaves thinks and imagines out of his experience of Guyana in particular, the paintings focus on elections, that Guyanese torment. In Guyana all elections, both fair and unfair, following the fragmentation of the national movement between 1953 and 1957, have unfailingly left in their wake seething discontent and at times convulsions. After three consecutive elections of 1992, 1997 and 2001, there was urban conflict, including African Guyanese attacks on Indian Guyanese individuals, property and businesses, which after the 2001 elections, spread to the region of the country closest to the capital and on the coast. In Guyana, the persistence, forty years on, of the crisis addressed by Martin Carter after the February 1962 conflagration resides in the reluctance of the old political elite to dismantle the system of governance inherited from the "mother country", the so-called Westminster system – in spite of the growing evidence of its unsuitability for societies far from Westminster. It is the most enduring and saddest of our colonial inheritances, this attachment to the institutions and habits of the old power. The political posture of colonialism had been to disregard all who were not caught up in its machinery and treat them as subjects and serfs. The post-colonial leadership mastered the art of mimicking the worst aspects of colonialism while denouncing it. This mimicking may be very refined and subtle, and may continue amidst grand exhibitions of national cultural expression and rhetoric about the national ethos. But the national culture and ethos in the ex-colonies seldom inspires a search for relevant forms of national or local government. Even when new constitutional designs have been attempted, they have more often than not been aimed at a concentration of power in the old way. Pompous structures have been set up only to keep the masses and, in a special way, the loser group in particular of the population at bay. In such conditions, elections are less about changing a government than asserting and re-asserting the domination of one ethnic group over another.

To answer Martin Carter's question of 1962, "Are we good enough?", let the recurrent trauma in post-independence Guyana instruct us.

It is to this reality that the *Meeting* series addresses itself. "Not being a writer, nor political activist," Greaves writes in his Notes for the exhibition of the *Meeting* series, "I have had to use what is appropriate to my personal existence – the ability to create images that give expression to one area of living that involves all of us. I refer to the expectations alive in all our hearts that a political system as an institution of change is here to serve our social need."[10]

III

> *'...the imagination never allows a perception to remain in its raw, direct state, if indeed there is such a thing. It is plastic, infinitely mobile, and its tendency is to allegorize.' (Dore Ashton): This is certainly the principle behind my recent figure paintings where the formal aspects of composition – line, balance, complex colour harmonies taken to some degree of abstraction – have been relegated to a minor role.*
>
> **Stanley Greaves**, journal entry, December 1994

Executed between 1992 and 2001, the *Meeting* series comprises a sequence of 14 paintings: 4 trilogies bracketed by a Prologue and an Epilogue. While Greaves's method of work over the years has involved the production of clusters of paintings devoted to explorations of a technical or philosophical nature – we need only think of the *Mazaruni* paintings with their elaborations of the lattice effect, or the *Hearts and Diamonds* series and its ventures into the mathematical domain of symmetry, or the *Metaphysical Mini-Paintings*, those meticulous surrealist essays in scale – the *Meeting* series is the first body of work where a grand architecture is suggested. Greaves did not begin with such an architecture in mind. The series did not set out to be a series, but proceeded in the form of discrete trilogies where the themes illustrated sprang from the available imagery, rather than the imagery being created to fit a linear narrative logic. Were he following the logic of the narrative, *Electoral Boundary* would have preceded even the presentation of candidates and the opening of the campaign. As it stands, *Electoral Boundary* forms part of the final trilogy. These precisions aside, we may usefully consider the series a dramatic structure in four Acts, each consisting of three Scenes, preceded by a Prologue and concluded by an Epilogue. Or even a kind of epic narration, a single story with beginning, middle and end, structured episodically. But tragedy and epic are heroic forms issuing from heroic ages. Much of the force of the *Meeting* series proceeds from this initial irony.

Greaves takes up the theme of heroism in an explicit way in the second painting of the final trilogy, *Political Hero* (see p. 184). The hero is swathed in the black plastic of the garbage bag, mounted on a pedestal inscribed with the words: *In hoc loco, Aeternitas.* Bound by ropes from which assorted silhouetted objects are suspended, the hero faces an empty horizon. The square hypothetical space cut into the sky may be the place of eternity which he is constrained from entering. Earth-bound, wrapped in plastic, attracting the curiosity of a black dog, the hero is of our unheroic time, a Prometheus writ small. The painting was inspired, as is so often the case with Greaves, by a real object/event, in this instance the Broodhagen statue of Grantley Adams in Barbados which, before it was ceremonially unveiled, was wrapped in black plastic[11]. In a journal entry of September 1992, Greaves reflected on the possibility or rather the impossibility of the heroic in the modern Caribbean: "The use of themes of the vernacular is characteristic of my work, but the matter does not rest in reportage. I always seek to establish a sense of hieratic values. In a sense I am perhaps seeking aspects of the heroic in a society where the heroic with its concomitant glory or disaster on a grand or tragedic scale does not exist in the present or immediate past of the psyche of the people."[12] In another journal entry of September 1997, we find the following impatient remark: "L'Ouverture, Martí, Castro. Heroes of/in the Caribbean are really too few. What we have in abundance are parodies – any number of individuals passing for heroes."[13] While not intending it in its aesthetic and formal sense, that "parody" is instructive. Not tragic, nor epic, but parodic, or more strictly, a form of burlesque: the incongruity achieved by the adoption of a high form to express a low content.

The story as such of the *Meeting* series is quickly told: it is the story of an election, from the announcement and introduction of the candidates to the declaration of the results and the aftermath, moving through the launching of the campaign, the presentation of the party manifesto, the political meetings, the demarcation of electoral boundaries, the casting of the ballot and the fate of the ballot papers, the announcement of the results, the enthronement of the victor, the protests, and in the *Epilogue,* the judgement of the court, a final judgement of sorts. The episodes are mainly though not exclusively drawn from Guyana's elections, especially the elections of 1997 and 2001. The specific reference of the second trilogy, *The Candidate, The Manifesto* and *Party Supporters*, is to the Dominican Republic elections of 1996.

The *Prologue* (see p. 173) establishes the setting, the actors and the emotional tone of what is to follow: the ruined facades, one sacred/religious, the other profane/secular, both crumbled and decrepit, define a square where the black dogs gather. Burrowes's tightrope walker has become a black dog silhouetted against a sunset sky. In a mysterious space behind the secular façade, a room with a verandah, a wooden floor, one plank broken loose, and an elegant bed with brass knobs on its four corners. In the distance, a schooner drifts, its sails reflected on the face of a still sea. Other iconographic elements which will recur throughout: the stone steps in the foreground, descending into some mysterious underground space, the rows of houses, the black sun which may be a black hole in the sky, opening into infinite space. The cross formed by the lamppost reinforces the religious dimension, inviting us to consider not only the exploitation of religious imagery and idiom in the utterances of the politicians, but, more significantly, the accelerating dissolution of faith in the politicians as original spiritual beliefs gain more and more ground. *Political Protest* (see p. 185), one of the final paintings in the series, strongly suggests that this faith has been abandoned in favour of the older beliefs.

The religious theme predominates in the titles, pictorial representation and subject matter of the paintings of the first trilogy: *The Annunciation, The Presentation* and *The Apotheosis.* The slick, smartly dressed politician stands in a garbage bin as elegant as himself, pushed along in a trolley by the woman who is in the work-clothes of the cane-field worker. It is she who is the figure of authority, looking boldly out of the picture at the viewer. One of the lenses of his dark glasses is missing, this one-eyed king in blind man's country. Ominously, hanging from the skirt worn over her corduroy work trousers, is a box of matches, the sugar-worker's traditional weapon of war. The politician holds two microphones in his hands, like a maracas player, primed and ready for his next performance. The star and stripes of his cap tell us that he is a normal Caribbean politician in his allegiance, not to say subservience to the United States. We are as far as can be from the sublimity of Donatello's *Annunciation* in Santa Croce, where the Virgin Mary is receiving from the spiritual messenger information, in the words of Kenneth Clark, "fraught with doom and glory". It is of no small significance that here, in the first painting of the first Trilogy, the overwhelming sense is one of a twice fallen, degraded world. Contrast the treatment of the religious in *Madonna with Pumpkin* (see p. 140), where the Virgin Mary/ Isis figure, represents the pure essence of redemptive motherhood. Here too, through a kind of transliteration, the hieratic is rendered through the use of the strictly commonplace, with the Mother represented by the fruit and vegetable vendor of every Caribbean market. But there is no sense of degradation. The dog being made god in a monstrous elevation in *The Apotheosis* (see p. 176) deepens the theme of degradation: behold the Lord thy God. The silhouette of the celebrant holding aloft the deity is projected, as by a magic lantern, on to the distant clouds, adding to the eerie other-worldliness of the scene.

The religious imagery is explicitly invoked in the second painting of the third trilogy, *Election Results*(see p. 181), where the loaf of bread and the fish descended from on high are for the feeding of the hungry multitudes, manna from heaven in a degradation of the miracle of Christ. (Kwame Dawes's narrative poem *Prophets* has the stanza: "Two angels with brief cases/ and diplomatic immunity/ landed in Kingston from heaven// on American Airlines..."[14] which points to where this degraded "heaven" might lie in the Caribbean imagination.) The two "obeah" paintings, *The Manifesto* (see p. 178) and *Political Protest* (see p. 185), invite us into the dark spiritual dimension, the symbolic inversion of Catholicism. In *The Manifesto*, a festive table is mounted on the upturned bin, invoking cult practices with its altar laden with offerings to the various spirits. The offerings of the political altar include a cake, one wedge removed, goodies for the electorate; blue candles to summon help from the spirits, the columns of smoke rising from the two lit candles, solemnly, as from a pyre; the bell, perhaps a party election symbol, to summon voters and spirits alike. The broken book at the foot of the altar is full of the broken promises to the electorate. The blue egg, key and schnapps glass are "obeah" objects. (I am indebted to my friend Ras Akyem for the observation that the egg can fit into the empty glass, a play on space and volume). It is the most symmetrical of the paintings, its objects studiously deployed as if to contain the swirling dark energies in the most elaborately formalised of structures. Magic and knowledge of the arcane are the key to electoral success. The power of the leader over the led resides in the unseen, the unspoken, the irrational. Greaves has in mind the late ruler of Guyana, President Burnham, who was known to be a keen student of the "science". Greaves has returned to this theme which he had previously elaborated in one of the figure paintings executed in 1995, *Magus with Reversed Bananas* (see p. 137), where the religious was presented as the indigenous folk movement cultivated throughout the Caribbean under different names: Winte, Santeria, Pocomania or Orisha and Vodun. At once priest and politician, the Magus too had proposed that ritual and magic were the way to salvation. In *Political Protest*, the final painting of the fourth trilogy, the votive table is illuminated by a beam of light from above. The red egg and blue candles surround the doll, all hemmed in by the spikes being driven into the table. As in *The Annunciation*, it is the woman, eyes hidden under the brim of her hat, who is the figure of authority. There is more menace in her hammer, upturned and at rest, than in the hammer being wielded by the male figure. She is the officiant, he the acolyte, her striped skirt rhyming with the stripes of the upturned cable spool that forms the work table. *Political Protest* was triggered by the street activity of protesters outside the courts in Georgetown following the 1997 elections. With their candles and other paraphernalia, they were ceremonially beating white dolls with the cry "We gun wuk pon she!", referring to the then President of Guyana, Mrs. Janet Jagan, a white American-born Guyanese citizen, the object of their wrath.

The issue of race is the central theme of the paintings of the second trilogy, *The Candidate* (see p. 177), *The Manifesto* and *Party Supporters.* The new arrivals on the scene, whites and blacks, are drawn into the political process. *The Candidate* has as its specific reference a recent episode in the electoral politics of the Dominican Republic. In 1996, when the trilogy was exhibited in the Santo Domingo III Bienale, the white president of the Republic, with the backing of the octogenarian Balaguér, had defeated the black hopeful born of Haitian parents, Peña Gómez, who would have won the presidency of the republic had the white ruling class not concocted a reconciliation of convenience among themselves, closing ranks against the upstart from below.

The white dog as leader has nothing to offer but the contents of a rubbish bin and the trappings of political ambitions, his microphones. He wears a dour, forlorn air. The looped tail, which he shares with his mulatto colleague in *Party Political Broadcast* (see p. 180), signals duplicity and deviousness, cardinal election virtues. The imperialist whites who enslaved the peoples of the Caribbean are now presenting themselves as the leaders in the new post-emancipation dispensation that still sees blacks politically and economically enslaved. *Plus ça change...*

Deformations and perversity abound. In *Party Supporters* (p. 179), those who should be fighting the white candidate are his henchmen. Two fingers protruding from a barrel hold a blue feather, an obeah object to invoke the power of the irrational.

At the heart of Greaves's critique of political behaviour is the politician-trickster, the wily one. His friend and colleague, the late Martin Carter, called them "the loud men who cry freedom and are so full of lies." Carter went further and as was his habit when faced with a curious phenomenon, sought to explain the behaviour of our politicians. In an article written for *Thunder*, organ of the People's Progressive Party, in 1955, when the politics of manoeuvre and slipperiness was the order of the day, he notes: "One very popular idea in this country, as in other countries, is that to be successful, a politician must be dishonest, must be tricky, smart, slick, must know to say one thing and mean something else, and do something absolutely different from what is said or meant. No one can deny, of course, that politicians by their words and deeds have done everything to create such an attitude of suspicion among the people." He poses the question: "Now what is it that causes politicians in particular to acquire such unpleasant reputations?" A materialist by instinct and persuasion, he finds the answer in history: "With the arrival of slavery, the first form in which class society appeared in history, the human grouping is broken into two classes, master class and slave class. And it is here that politics as we know it begins." As one of the manifestations of the class struggle, politics gives rise to politicians who are themselves only the symbols of the manifestation. "Politicians then," he concludes, "are symbols of the class struggle." And because we live in class society, "our political outlook is determined by our class interest." This for him is "the key to open the door of understanding why people as politicians behave as they do. For just as at Christmas time masqueraders put on painted masks, so too in politics politicians put on false faces to hide their real motives, to fool the lookers-on, to pass in the same way as well made counterfeit coins are passed. How can people not be suspicious of politicians?" As an Amerindian sister in a Patamona mountain village put it to me at a recent election campaign meeting: "Politicians are like parrots. They only come to the tree when the mangoes are ripe." Carter's analysis leads him to conclude that such ideas about politics "emerge from the bowels of capitalistic and colonial society where the binding tie of human relations is the profit motive, the exploitation of man by man in economic, moral and social life." With all the bitterness of the 1953 defeat at the back of his throat, he makes his assessment: "In such surroundings moral principles are as stray dogs in a butcher shop."[15]

The theme of chicanery is explicitly addressed in the paintings of the third trilogy, *Party Political Broadcast, Election Results* and *Ballot Boxes.* The mulatto dog steps on to the stage. His old school tie tells the electorate that he is a respectable member of society, what George Lamming calls "a chosen one". The general demeanour is that of a charlatan willing to take risks, like walking on electrical wires, for personal advancement. He exudes self-confidence, presenting himself as someone in control of the situation. He thrives on the false optimism he inspires. Promises and more promises: shoes for the masses, albeit worn-out shoes, but then what would the barefoot masses do with new shoes? He dangles fruits of bright promise, like apples of temptation, here the Caribbean starapple, exotic in its colours of green and purple. The sky is dark and menacing, hinting at convulsions to come. His microphones come down from another space, a dimension ruled over by a black moon. In *Ballot Boxes* (p. 182), the mulatto dog is keeping an eye on developments from a discreet distance on the horizon's edge, ready to disappear into a world of his own making, the rectangle of other space in which he is standing, if things go badly. The irony is explicit. Ballot papers float down from the sky. What need for human voters? Ballots by divine dispensation, surely. Elections are a not so elaborate game of noughts and crosses. Along with the ballot papers come the less unusual inhabitants of the rubbish bin – rotten fruit, discarded vegetables, banana skin, tin can. The bins themselves emerge from some source underground, a provenance as mysterious as that of the ballot papers. The painting speaks to the false hope, the leitmotif of the entire series, that elections would bring justice and prosperity for all. Instead, in *Election Results*, the party activist bears the results and the victor's gifts to the electorate: Christ's miraculous feast

– a loaf of bread and a fish come down from heaven. His eyes have a furtive look, hinting that all may not be as well as it appears even for the victor. Contrast his shiftiness with the bold and knowing look of the woman in control of the action in *The Annunciation.* A kind of board-walk has replaced the earth as elections have turned the world into a vast stage where the farce is played out. The politician is the supreme *farceur.*

Barrels, microphones, fruits, eggs, old shoes, cords, ropes and strings, candles, a key, a pair of scissors, a glass, stalks of sugar cane, a jug, an empty plate, books, a feather, a spanner, a cup, a single leaf. Across the fourteen paintings of the series, an array of disparate objects. While certain of these objects are of symbolic significance within and across particular paintings, others fulfill a primarily compositional function, while yet others belong to the realm of private reference. The most recurrent are the barrel and the microphone, the main elements in Greaves's iconographic scheme. Both the politician of *The Annunciation* and the white dog of *The Candidate* stand inside the barrel which, in both these instances, signifies the rubbish bin from which their political exhortations arise – similarly, the barrels of *Ballot Boxes* where the scraps of garbage float skywards along with the ballot papers. Barrels support the votive tables of both obeah paintings, *The Manifesto* and *Political Protest.* In *Party Supporters*, two fingers protrude from a barrel, holding a blue feather. For Guyanese who lived through the long night of the Burnham dictatorship, barrels brought in not only votes from overseas to rig the elections but also essential food items the government had banned from the shelves and kitchens of the people.

The microphones that amplify and broadcast the lies and empty promises are everywhere, the primary instrument of mobilisation and inducement, the essential tool of the contenders for power. They too can stand inside rubbish bins, or have their wires issuing from a sewerage pipe. It is eerie, this proliferation of microphones in these silent, menacing spaces. The defeated one lying bare-backed on the stones of the *Epilogue*, his head pillowed on a book with no title but in the purple of authority, grips a microphone aloft. It is cordless, fallen silent in the face of the final judgement.

Certain objects, as noted elsewhere, are inscriptions within the *Vanitas* tradition of still-life painting that developed after the Reformation and consisting of a collection of objects chosen and arranged to remind the spectator of the transience of mortal life: *vanitas vanitatum* of Ecclesiastes. The unlit and broken flambeaux in the left foreground of *The Annunciation*, the spectacles at the top of the steps in *The Apotheosis*, the discarded worn-out shoes on the concrete steps of *The Presentation*, the single leaf sprouting from the twig at the foot of the altar of *The Manifesto* are all *vanitas* objects. Greaves had once before, in the *Caribbean Metaphysic* series of mini-paintings, mined this early European tradition to give expression to his existential concerns with the passage of time and the finality of things of this world. It is also an act of appropriation that establishes an art-historical connection. It is an important gesture for Greaves, this setting down the marks of a tradition and entering into a dialogue with it, locating his art at the conjoining between a Caribbean iconography and experience and the art-historical tradition.

The eggs, key and candles of *The Manifesto* and *Political Protest* are "obeah" objects, standard paraphernalia for the performance of the dark ceremonies. We encountered these objects before, notably in the two obeah paintings of the mini-painting series, *The Doll* and *Jaguar Table*; and later, in *Magus with Reversed Bananas*. They are the stock-in-trade of the celebrants throughout the Caribbean. The leitmotif of the stalk of sugar cane, synecdoche for the plantation of slavery and indentureship, recurs in *The Annunciation, The Candidate, Party Supporters* and *Electoral Boundary*. The fruits and vegetables, like the star-apple of *Party Political Broadcast* and the okra of *Ballot Boxes* belong to a category of objects of private reference, intuitive marks to fulfil an almost purely compositional function while celebrating the things that grow among us in the Caribbean. The same is the case with the ropes, cords and string, sometimes looped and knotted, from which objects, like the fish of *Election Results* and the microphone of *Party Political Broadcast* are suspended. Greaves has had a life-long fascination with the ropes and knots of his childhood as the son of a waterfront worker and jack-of-all-trades who included rope-working and sign-painting among his activities.

What may at first appear a random array of objects is in fact a carefully controlled iconographic scheme which unifies the fourteen paintings of the series. Recurring motifs establish a pattern of visual rhymes and function as a mechanism of regulation, a rhythmic device within the iconographic system. The story may be simple enough. Not so the plot, the artistic rendition of the story through the organisation and modulation of themes and the strategic deployment of images.

Rigorous in the pursuit of its themes and in the distribution of its objects, in the end it is the emotional impact of the setting within which the episodes unfold that generates the haunting power of the *Meeting* series. And it is here, I believe, that the Burrowes painting, *Guyana, Land of the Dolorous Guard*, exercises its greatest influence. It is everywhere, that lowering sky with its broken colours and its ruffling clouds, heavy as a pall over the land, nowhere more sombre and laden with omen than in the skies of the second trilogy, *The Candidate, The Manifesto* and *Party Supporters.* In contrast, the skies of the *Prologue* and *The Epilogue* are less confining, less portentous, though their relative clarity conveys its own bleakness and a certain pitilessness that is no more consoling. Under such skies, the land is dull and flat, unrelieved by vegetation in these mineral places. The only trees in sight, in *The Prologue* and *The Epilogue,* are trapped in walls of stone. The landscapes of the series are de-natured, places of stone and hard edges. In *The Apotheosis*, the eye moves up the sculptural stone steps, follows the line of dogs towards the pyramid top and beyond, out to the horizon and the sky, strangely illuminated by the light emanating from a black moon and throwing shadows in opposite directions. The earth is cast over, as far as the eye can see, with smooth stone. The concrete steps, a feature of Barbadian houses Greaves admires for their sculptural quality, are there in *The Prologue* and are to recur in *The Presentation.* As in *Banana Manna*, the seawall of coastal Guyana inspired the concrete steps in *Electoral Boundary*, the most geometrically designed landscape of them all, where the picture is divided into triangular segments marked by lines that converge at a single point on the horizon.

Horizons are never innocent for Greaves. Nor are they limited to the line where land meets sky. In a journal entry of

December 1993 we find the following thought: "That which splits a thing from an image of itself – the 'line' between the bank of a river and the image of the bank seen in the water. Also the reflecting surface of a mirror. A horizon is really an expression – a visible one – of infinity."[16] Four years later, during the time of painting the *Meeting* series, he returns to the subject, more philosophically: "The macro-horizon we see – and cannot reach – between the ocean and the sky. There is a micro-horizon between river and bank – closer to us and still inaccessible. At a kind of quantum level we have the horizon between our feet and our shadow. The ultimate horizon of course is between the life of the body and that of the soul. The ultimate horizon is death itself made accessible through death."[16]

The literary element is dominant in the *Meeting* series. The pictorial and compositional concerns of the early figure paintings have been displaced by narrative and symbolic elements. Painterliness is at a minimum. Paint is applied thinly in glazes with brush-strokes used in a modelling technique as opposed to the slash and verve of the painterly expressionist technique. Working with a greyed palette, chromatic values are lowered as everything is imbued with a grey tonality. Virtually monochromatic, the paintings of each trilogy are distinguishably of a single palette, unifying each trilogy within the larger unity of the series. The impulse into the exploration of form we find in the figure paintings, like *Madonna with Pumpkin*, has been restrained. There is no lack of attention to composition, but it does not draw attention to itself, even in *Electoral Boundary*, where the play of lines achieves a hypnotic, almost vertiginous effect. There could be no better place for this play of lines than the sea wall of the Guyana coast, the line that separates the ocean of water from the ocean of land. Lines, edges, shapes, colours and textures are precisely controlled, entirely in the service of the story to be told and the mood to be conveyed.

In the end, is it all bleakness and desolation? Or can we take hope from the leaves surprisingly sprouting from a branch that has broken free of the crumbling wall of the *Epilogue*?

Recall Greaves's assessment of *Guyana, Land of the Dolorous Guard*: "While it is presenting a message of total despair it is paradoxically also saying that one should recognise what is taking place and do something positive about the situation." And did not Martin Carter himself, on the very edge of the abyss, dare to hope and dream of renewal?

> In a great silence I hear approaching rain:
> There is a sound of conflict in the sky.
> The frightened lizard darts behind a stone.
> First was the wind, now is the wild assault.
>
> I wish this world would sink and drown again
> So that we build another Noah's ark
> And send another little dove to find
> What we have lost in floods of misery.[17]

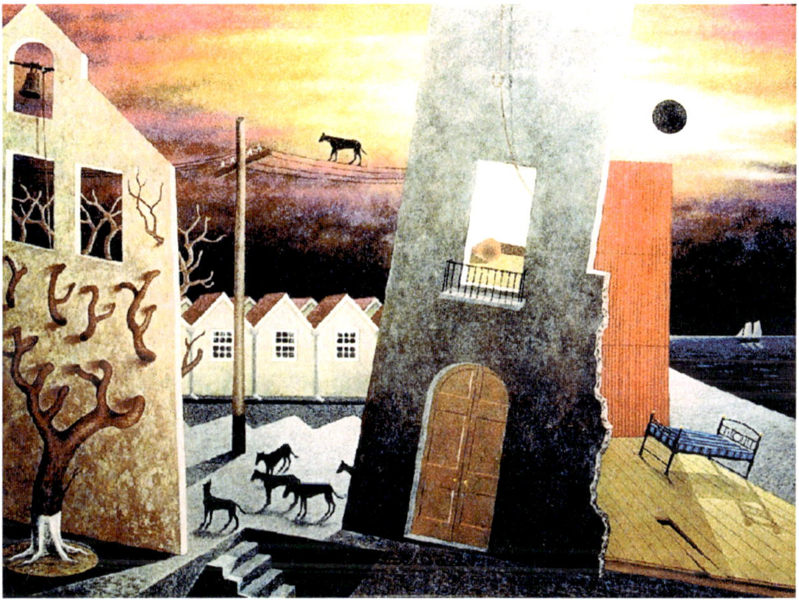

Prologue: There is a Meeting Here Tonight

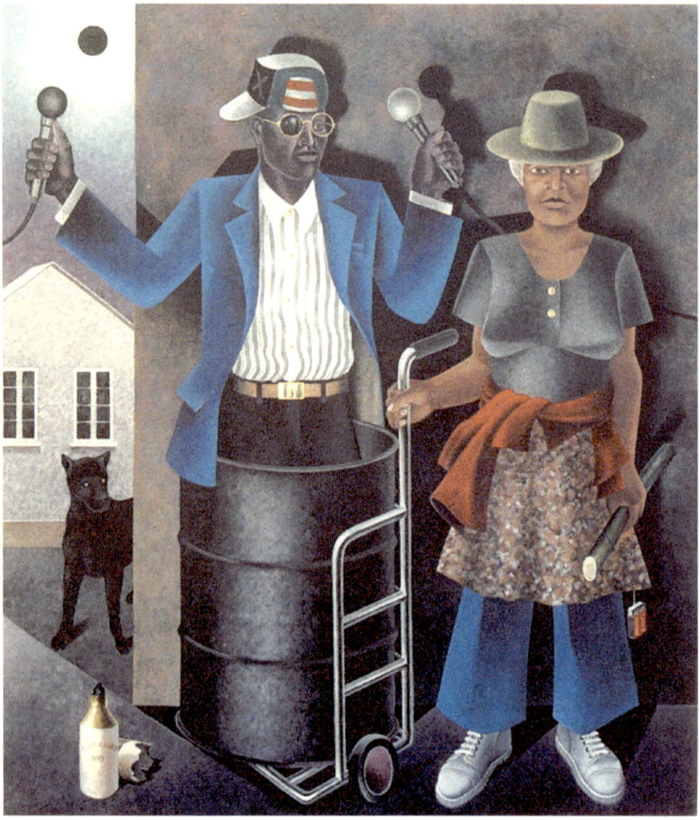

The Annunciation

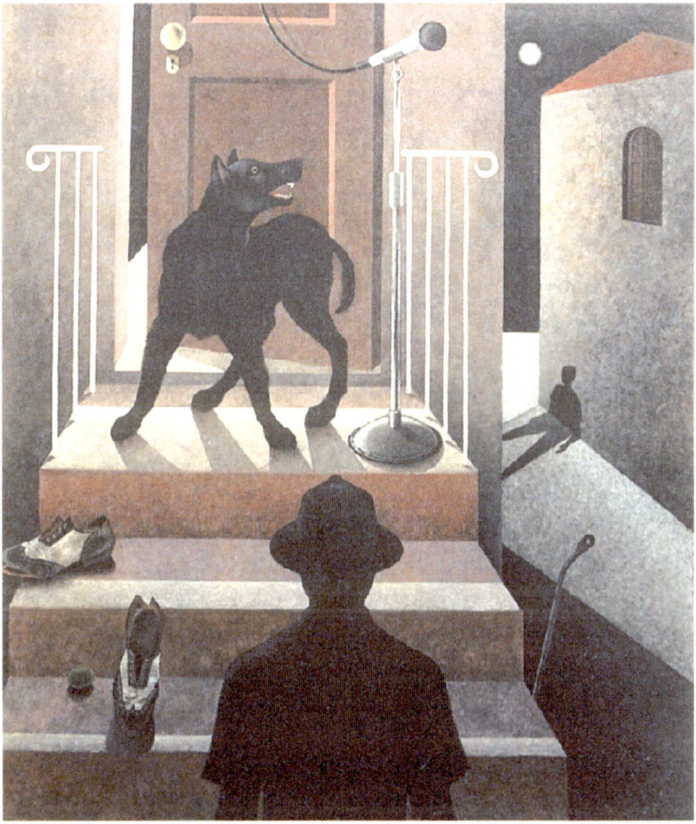

The Presentation

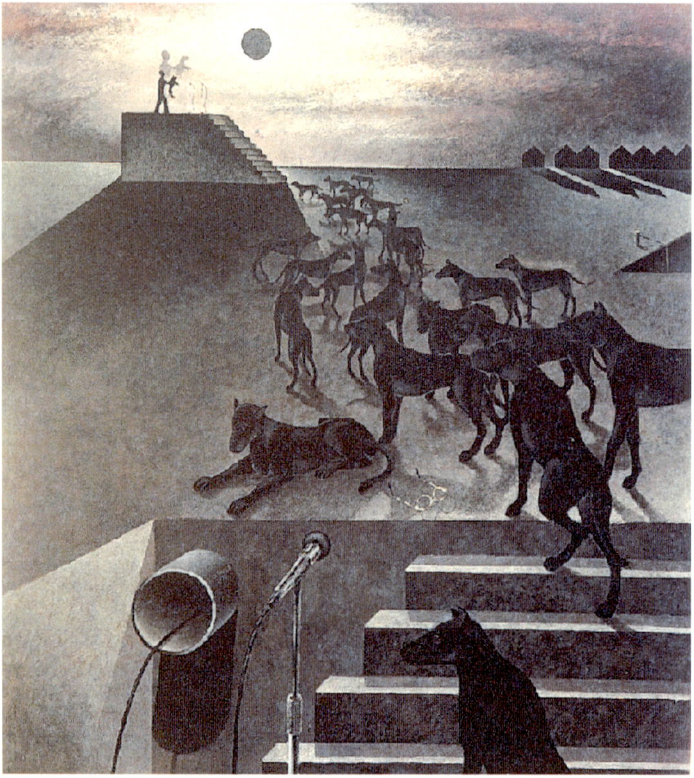

The Apotheosis

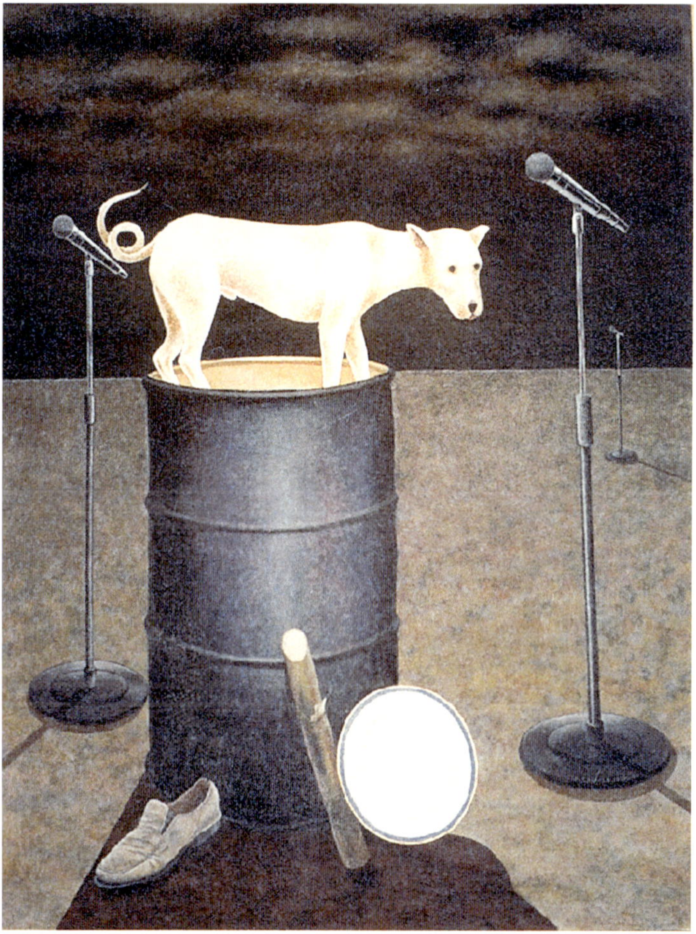

The Candidate

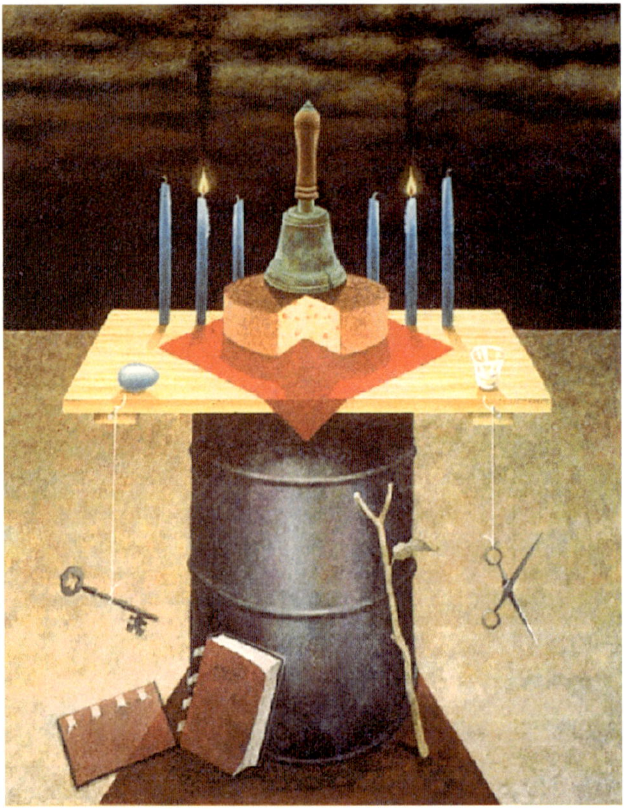

The Manifesto

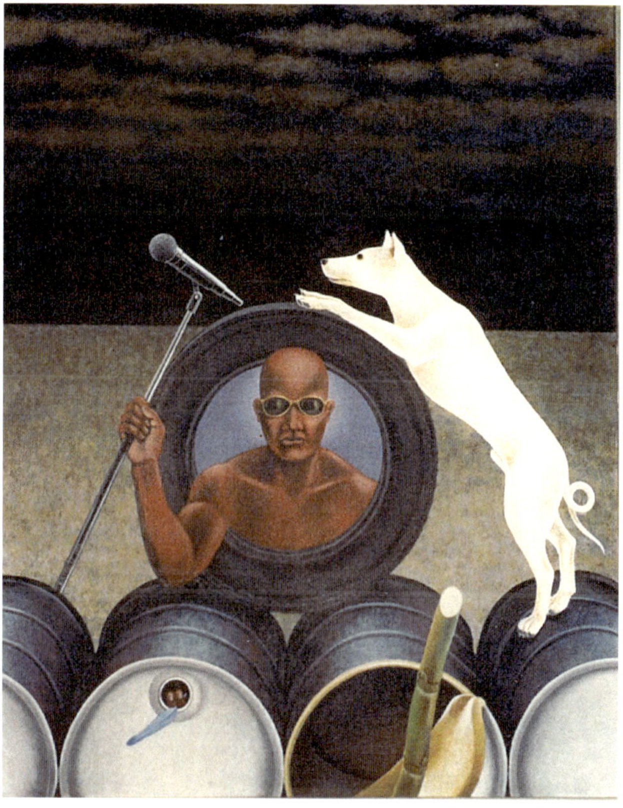

Party Supporters

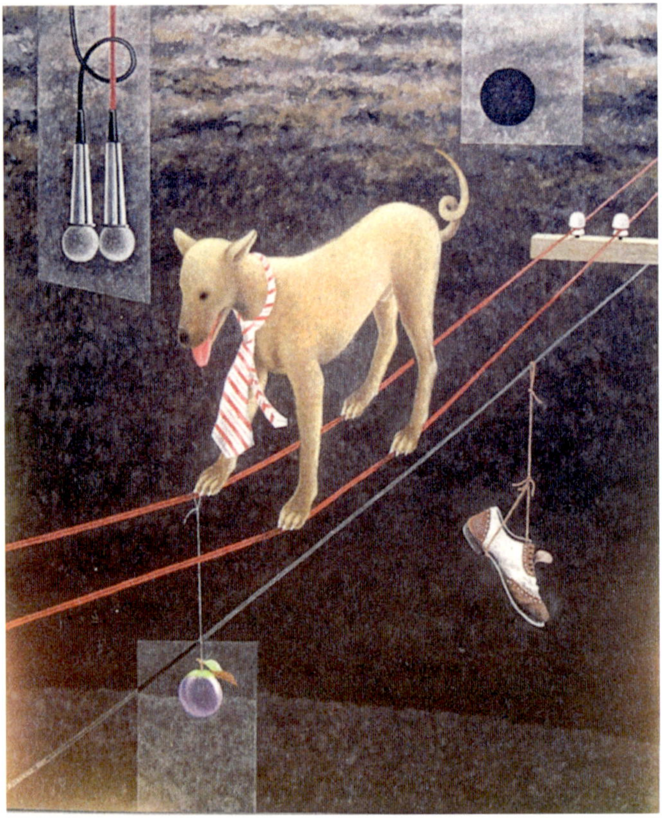

Party Political Broadcast

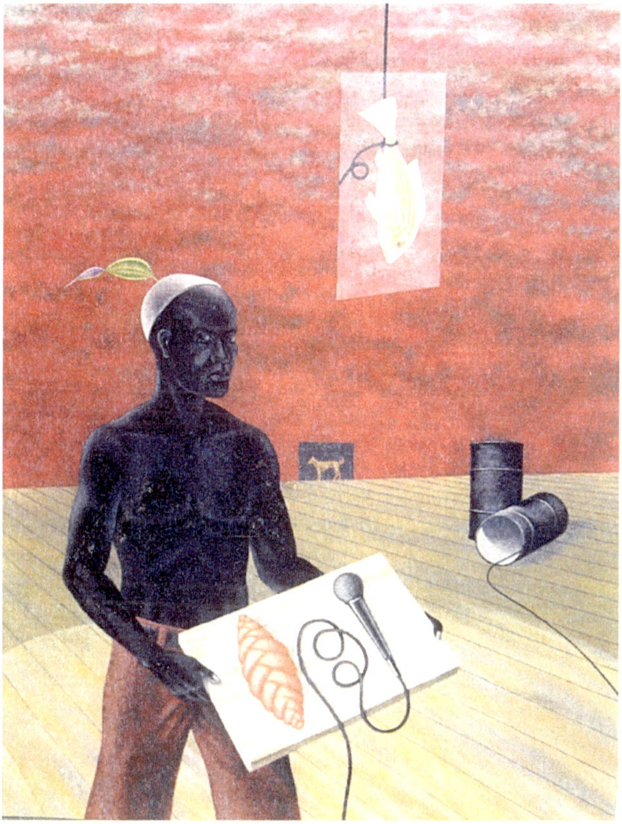

Election Results

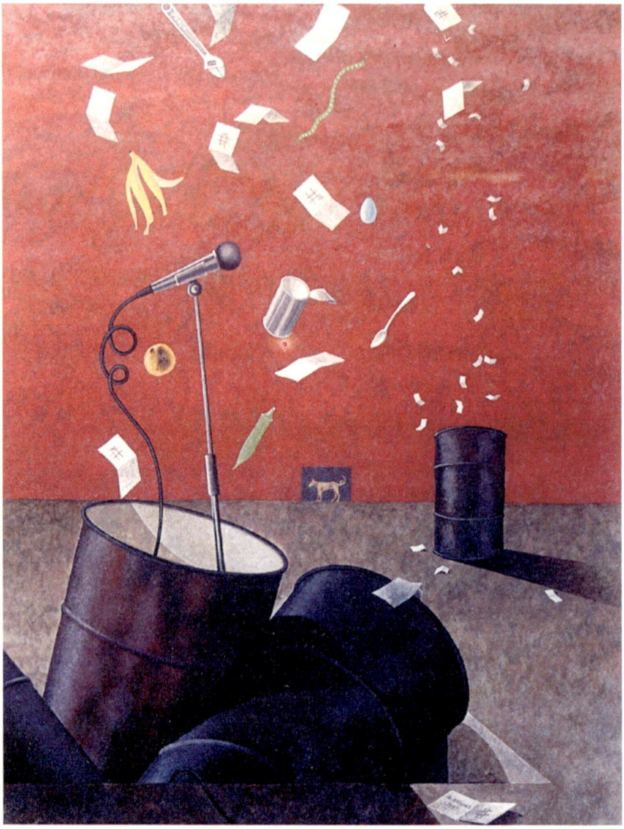

Ballot Boxes

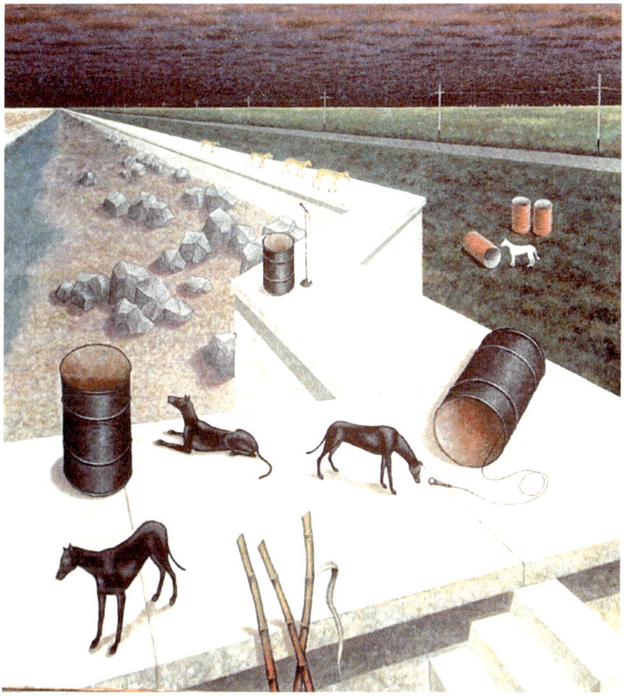

Electoral Boundary

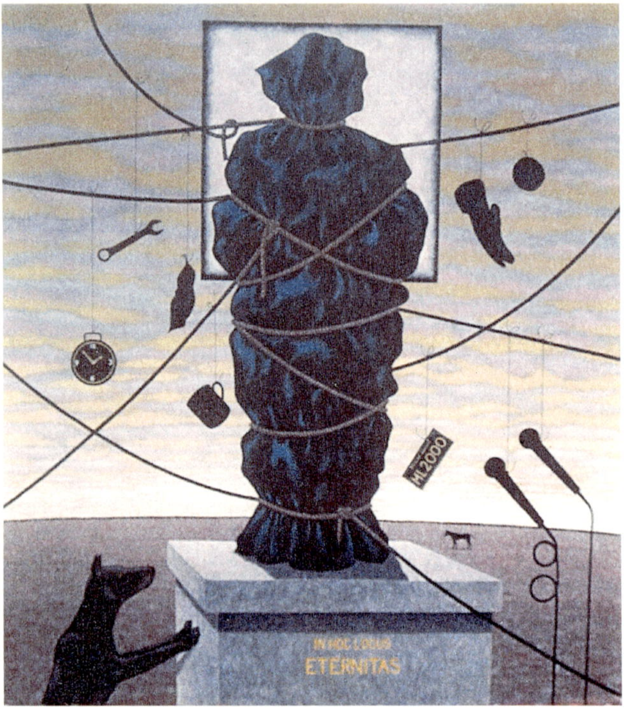

Political Hero

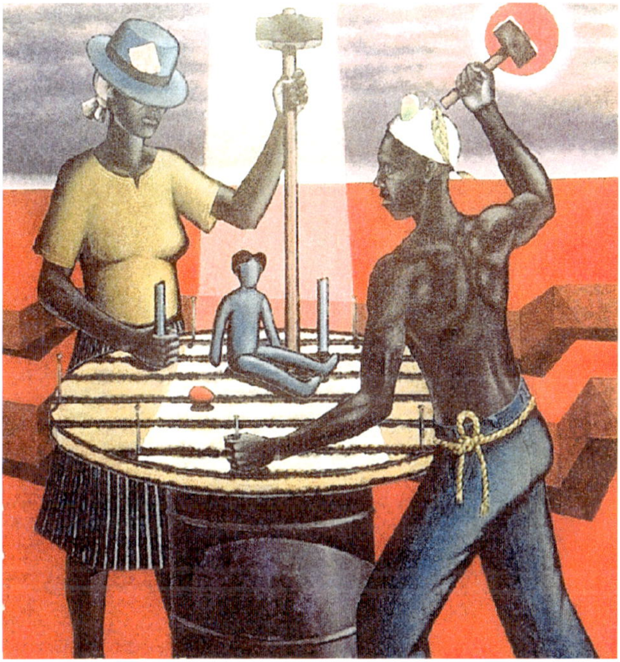

Political Protest

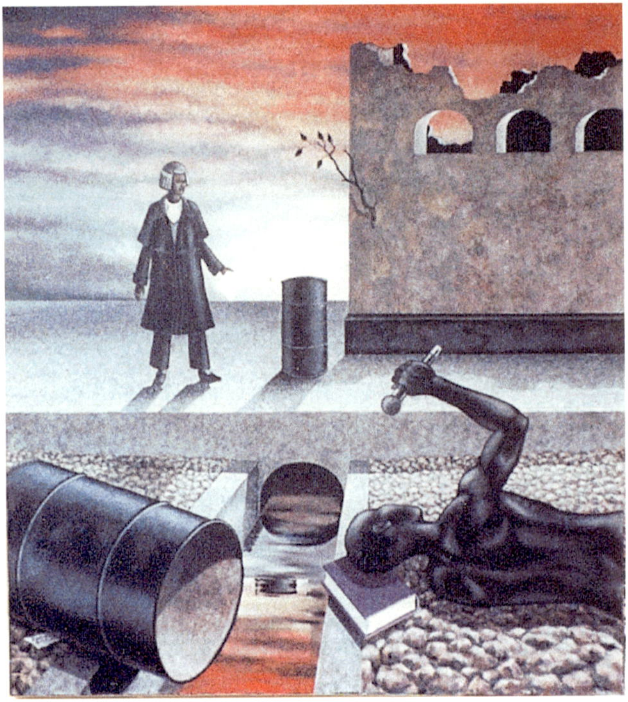

Epilogue

ENDNOTES TO CHAPTER TEN

1. *El Dorado, Magazine Catalogue of the Working People's Art Class, British Guiana, Exhibition:14 April 1951.* The catalogue, priced at three shillings, contained short stories and poems by members and illustrations, wood-engravings (not woodcuts) by Burrowes that had been shown at the Royal College Annual exhibition as part of the four submissions from the Brighton School of Art where he was on a British Council scholarship, 1948-1950.

2. Martin Carter, "Black Friday", *Selected Poems* (Georgetown: Red Thread Women's Press, 1997), p. 117.

3. Eusi Kwayana, "Guyana in the 20th Century: The Fifties", *Guyana Review,* Georgetown. May 1999, No. 77.

4. Stanley Greaves, "The Sustainable in Art", *Sunday Stabroek,* Georgetown. 9 May 1999.

5. SG, journal entry of July 1998.

6. SG, journal entry of January 1985.

7. SG, journal entry of April 1992.

8. SG, journal entry of March 2001.

9. Martin Carter, "Recent Events Spring from Social Undercurrents", *Kyk-over-Al*, Georgetown, Special Issue 44, May 1993, p. 82-83.

10. SG, journal entry of March 2001.

11. Karl Broodhagen (1909-2002 b. Guyana) arrived aged 15 in Barbados in 1924. Apprenticed to a tailor. Then set up his own shop. Studied art on his own with a special liking for portraiture. Played soccer, boxed and did "physical culture". Taught in Trinidad 1946. Around 1947 taught Art at Combermere School until he was 80 years old. Was awarded a British Council Scholarship 1952-3 studied at Goldsmiths College of Art. Worked almost exclusively in modeled portraiture in sculpture, also in other media. Late years produced work cast in bronze for public monuments – Slave leader Bussa, Prime Minister Grantley Adams, Cricketer Garfield Sobers.

12. SG, journal entry of September 1992.

13. SG, journal entry of September 1997.

14. Kwame Dawes, *Prophets*, Leeds, Peepal Tree Press, 1995, p.72.

15. Martin Carter, "What is a Politician", *Kyk-over-Al*, Georgetown, Special Issue 44, May 1993, p. 52-54.

16. SG, journal entry of December 1993.

17. Martin Carter, "So that we build", *Selected Poems*, p. 113.

LIST OF WORKS REPRODUCED IN TEXT

COVER

Knot Eye Left, 1996, oils 25 x 24.5cm.
Collection Natasha Greaves

FRONTISPIECE

Alison Chapman-Andrews, *Imitation of Birds* (Portrait of Stanley).
Collection Barbados Gallery of Art

ONE: THE GREAVES WORLD

1. *Evolution*. Collection Dr. Frank Williams, Guyana
2. *Askari*. Collection Aubrey Williams, USA
3. *Preacher.* National Collection, Guyana
4. *Old Time String Band.* Collection Alim Greaves, USA
5. *Weeding Gang.* Collection Noah Greeen, USA
6. *People of the Garden City.* Collection Isabella Ponder
7. *Magic Pepper Tree.* Casa de las Americas Collection, Cuba
8. *Beggar and Urchin.* National Collection, Guyana
9. *Beggars.* Collection the late President Forbes Burnham
10. *Big Bread.* National Collection, Guyana

TWO: EXTENDING INTO THREE DIMENSIONS I

11. *Amatuk*. Collection Dr. Terry Roopnaraine, Guyana
12. *Slave Stock*. National Collection, Guyana
13. *Diamond Box.* Dorothy Taitt Foundation, Guyana
14. *Twin Towers of the Martyrs.* Collection not known
15. *Sonya*. Collection Sonya Greaves-Ponder, USA.
16. *Orisha.* Collection Fiona Greaves, USA
17. *Ancestral Figures.* Dorothy Taitt Foundation, Guyana
18. *Flayed Culture God, Xipe-Toltec.* Dorothy Taitt Foundation, Guyana

THREE: CRISIS AND RENEWAL: THE MAZARUNI PAINTINGS

19. *Mazaruni.* National Collection, Guyana
20. *Canecutters.* Collection Dr. Terry Roopnaraine, Guyana
21. *Channaman.* Collection Dr. Terry Roopnaraine
22. *Black Sunflowers.* Collection Dr. Terry Roopnaraine
23. *Caribbean Man No. 2.* Artist's Collection
24. *Swamp Birds.* National Collection, Guyana
25. *Traffic Lights and Banana Trees.* National Collection, Guyana

FOUR: EXTENDING INTO THREE DIMENSIONS II

26. *Stone Flower.* Collection Andre Greaves, USA
27. *Two-Eared Jaguar.* Collection Andre Greaves, USA
28. *Man and Bird.* Collection Natasha Greaves, USA
29. *Black Ant.* Collection Aubrey Williams, USA
30. *Heliconia.* Collection Natasha Greaves, USA
31. *Ancestral Figures.* Collection Sonya Greaves, USA
32. *Peas for El Dorado.* Artist's Collection

FIVE: TRADITION AND TECHNIQUE IN CERAMICS

33. *Orchid Pot 2.* Collection Bonnie Coles-Wilson, Barbados
34. *Great Pot.* Collection Andre Greaves, USA
35. *Dry Leaf Dish.* Artist's Collection
36. *Mycerinus 2.* Collection Jocelyn Dow, Guyana
37. *Orchid Pot 5.* Artist's Collection
38. *Yam Pot.* Sonya Greaves-Ponder, USA
39. *Cocktail Vase.* Coolection not known
40. *Banyan Pot*, Artist's Collection
41. *Susa Pot.* Collection Bonnie Coles-Wilson, Barbados
42. *Jenne Jenno.* Collection Bonnie Coles-Wilson, Barbados
43. *Arawak.* Collection Neisha Haniff-Rainsford, USA
44. *Raindrops.* Artist's Collection
45. *Vines and Frogs Legs.* Artist's Collection
46. *Benab.* Artist's Collection

SIX: GRIDS OF ORDER: EXPLORATIONS IN SYMMETRY

47. *Tantric Landscape.* Collection Lakshmi Kallicharran, Guyana
48. *Mountain of Hearts and Diamonds.* Dorothy Taitt Foundation, Guyana
49. *Yellow Hearts, White Diamonds.* Collection Dr. Terry Roopnaraine
50. *Pyramid of the Heart.* Artist's Collection

SEVEN: BETWEEN THE BLOT AND THE LINE: PEN AND INK DRAWINGS

Martin Carter Affinity Drawings

51. Our hands have written
52. Every clear raindrop
53. No need to throw a flower

Birds of Black Drawings

54. Palm Tree Birds
55. Bird on Tap
56. Chattel House Birds
57. Blackbirds

Martin Carter Red Thread Drawings

58. Iron cartwheel rumbling in the night
59. Listening to thc land
60. And a lizard upside down walks on the moon

SG Poems Drawings

61. Small hands that delight in the smoothness of pebbles
62. The square in the circle
63. Tree-tall friend of a thousand conversations

EIGHT: FRONTIERS OF CONSCIOUSNESS: EXPLORATIONS IN SCALE

64. *The Doll.* Collection Fiona Greaves, USA
65. *Birth of Venus.* Collection Fiona Greaves
66. *Guitar Bird.* Collection John Seale, Sydney, Australia
67. *Game Plan.* Collection Audrey Williams, NY, USA
68. *Biscuit Story No. 1.* Artist's Collection
69. *Alison's Cups, No. 1.* Collection Jocelyn Dow
70. *Knot No. 2.* Collection Dr. Clive Cave, Barbados

71. *Dalkeith Village.* Collection Andy Toppin, Barbados
72. *The Visitor.* Collection Sonya Greaves-Ponder
73. *Caribbean Committee.* Collection Dr. Rupert Roopnaraine
74. *Jaguar Table.* Collection Alissandra Cummings, Barbados

NINE: CARIBBEAN FOLKLORE, CARIBBEAN IKONS

75. *Mrs Baxter.* Collection Bonnie Coles-Wilson
76. *Hat Man.* Collection Andy Toppin
77. *Magus with Reversed Bananas.* Collection Dr. Michael McGrath, Canada
78. *Banana Manna.* Artist's Collection
79. *Madonna with Pumpkin.* Collection Andy Toppin
80. *Birth of Venus.* Collection not known
81. *Birth of Venus-Ymanja.* Collection John Seale, Australia
82. *Caribbean Chimera.* Collection Andy Toppin
83. *The Visitation.* Collection Sir Henry Forde, Barbados
84. *Tree of Life.* Collection Dr. Mark McWatt, Barbados
85. *Mrs Plaits.* Collection Isabella Ponder
86. *Mr Fixxe.* Collection Noah Greene
87. *Miss Girl.* Collection Natasha Greaves
88. *Bro Boy.* Collection Alim Greaves

TEN: THE POLITICS OF DESOLATION

89. *E. R. Burrowes, Guyana, Land of the Dolorous Guard.* National Collection, Guyana
90. *Prologue.* Collection Bonnie Coles-Wilson
91. *The Annunciation.* Collection Mervyn Awon, Barbados
92. *The Presentation.* Collection Bonnie Coles-Wilson
93. *The Apotheosis.* Collection Mervyn Awon
94. *The Candidate.* Collection Mervyn Awon
95. *The Manifesto.* Collection Mervyn Awon
96. *Party Supporters.* Collection Mervyn Awon
97. *Party Political Broadcast.* Artist's Collection
98. *Election Results.* Artist's Collection
99. *Ballot Boxes.* Artist's Collection
100. *Electoral Boundary.* Artist's Collection
101. *Political Hero.* Artist's Collection
102. *Political Protest.* Artist's Collection
103. *Epilogue.* Artist's Collection

CHRONOLOGY

1934-45

Stanley Greaves was born to Priscilla and John Greaves at 6 am on November 23, 1934 at the Public Hospital Georgetown. Priscilla knew the exact time because the 6 o'clock gun went off. (Daybreak in the colony was announced by a gunshot fired from the seawall near to the lighthouse). As a boy, Stanley's father John had run away from school and, perhaps to persuade him onto the straight and narrow, was sent by his own father, Joseph Greaves, to be the traveling companion and factotum to Rev. John Smith, SJ, whose missionary forays took him to the Amerindian villages deep in the North West District of British Guiana. Back in Georgetown, John served as a choirboy at the Cathedral of the Immaculate Conception (Brickdam Cathedral). He later became a waterfront worker and jack-of-all-trades. Work at the waterfront included rope work for making the slings and mooring lines for cargo boats and John became a rope-work specialist. His talents extended to music: he was a guitarist member of a group of part-time musicians who performed professionally at a wide range of social events, a role recorded in Stanley Greaves's 1977 painting, *Old Time Story Band* (see page 27). Stanley's mother, Priscilla *née* Whyte, known as Lydia, hailed from Agricola Village on the East Bank of Demerara. A wife and mother in a disadvantaged working-class home, she did a variety of occasional menial chores to supplement her husband's small, sometimes irregular, income. She never complained when things were hard, which they frequently were. She was especially interested in needlework, which she had learned from Addie Mayers, her Portuguese godmother. Stanley was her only child. Her husband John had two children by a previous marriage, Ivan and Enid. A third child, Gladys, had been adopted. John's father, Joseph Greaves, had been born in Barbados and was part of a stream of migrants from the Caribbean islands who went to settle in BG, as British Guiana was popularly known. A cabinet-maker and upholsterer, Joseph Greaves owned two workshops in central Georgetown. He was very friendly with the Catholic priests of the day and seems to have been a man who loved books. He was married to Mary Fernandes, a woman of Portuguese descent.

Stanley grew up in the heart of the city, in a tenement yard a stone's throw away from the landmark of St. George's Cathedral. Lot 132 Carmichael Street was a yard where working-class tenants lived cheek-by-jowl in single-room ranges. The yard was a little world of its own, with an enforced but genuine sense of community. Marriages, births and deaths were celebrated, but there were no birthday parties, no doubt considered an extravagance of the better-off classes. The standpipe was the social centre of the yard, the hub of every intrigue. Every yard had its characters and its dramas, acted out in deadly earnest. Miss Alda was the matriarch of 132 Carmichael Street. In the yard the children played the games of the time: skipping, rolling wire hoops, marbles, improvised soccer and cricket matches with strict rules and rough and ready equipment, and the ever popular, sadistic "hot bread and butter", a whipping "game". One player, the controller, hid a leather belt that the other players had to find, guided by his directions of "water", "smoke", and "fire" the closer they got to the belt. The finder then chased and whipped anyone caught nearby and became the next controller. A less brutal but no less popular activity with Stanley and his comrades was playing cinema, another small-boys' delight. Strips of film were salvaged from the garbage bins of the nearby Astor cinema: The "cinema" was located under someone's steps, carefully enclosed with cardboard. The projector was a shoebox to which, at one end, a magnifying glass had been fixed with a piece of film in a rectangular opening at the other. The assistant "projectionist" used a mirror to focus sunlight through the lens and the image – including those of such stars as John Wayne, Randolph Scott, Johnny Weismuller and Richard Widmark – was projected on to a borrowed white pillowcase. The films were often supplemented with homemade glass slides. Stanley used his father's paints to create pictures for his stories. The entrance fee was paid in buttons, which was also the currency for marble games.

Stanley Greaves recalls the excitement of Easter, kite-flying time. No self-respecting boy bought a kite and kite-making was another of his father's specialties, along with tree-trimming and sign-painting.

Stanley took great pleasure in the errands he had to run as part of his household chores, choosing routes that took him past workshops where things were being made and past the hardware stores full of tools. Gazing at the elegant inter-island sloops and schooners off Stabroek Market wharf was a favourite Saturday morning activity, linked, of course, to shopping for his mother. Building and sailing model sailboats in the nearby Church Street trench soon became a passion. To build his sloop he copied the rigging from the magazine pictures of the grand sailing yachts competing in the America's Cup races, cast lead to make his keel, sewed the sails from one of his father's discarded old white shirts, and painted the boat.

The young Stanley was an avid reader, devouring the "William" books, G. A. Henty's historical adventure books for boys and Forester's Horatio Hornblower series. One book he read was *Sinuhe the Egyptian,* the start of a life-long interest in historical Egypt. The Henty books transported him to Khandahar and the British battle against the Pathans, to the Malays with the British expeditionary forces up against the Sea Dayaks. It was a special treat to visit his half-sisters, Enid and Gladys, and gain access to their magazines, or visit cousin Leena who had a collection of fairy-tale books. The practice among many working-class people of papering their walls with pages from magazines meant being able to read these "wall-books" when out visiting. The only frustration was wanting to read a page that had subsequently been papered over.

Stanley's primary education began at Sacred Heart Roman Catholic School for boys in Main Street, Georgetown. In 1944, the ten-year-old from the tenement yard at 132 Carmichael Street was admitted to his first "art group": the select circle of boys who made drawings, copying illustrations of famous persons from World War II who had been featured on *TIME* magazine covers. They also copied and circulated among themselves the legendary comic book heroes serialized in the Sunday papers: Superman, Captain Marvel, Batman, the

Phantom, Tarzan, and other figures like L'il Abner. A qualification for joining the group was artistic skill in copying. The Public Children's Library was another matter – at ten he was too young to join – but his teacher "guaranteed" and he was let in. He could wander along the stacks, try out new books with that sharp library smell, read to his heart's content. The picture lessons in his *West Indian Readers*, which dealt with technique, composition and simple critical appreciation of famous paintings in European collections, fueled Stanley's interest in art. The lessons in Books 4 and 5 of the *West Indian Reader* left an indelible impression: reproductions of paintings by Velásquez, Chardin, Rembrandt, Gainsborough, Constable, Turner, accompanied by discussions on composition, on the lines and directions and forces at work in the paintings. In 1946 he was awarded a scholarship to St. Stanislaus College for boys, one of the colony's three major secondary schools. "Saints" was founded by the Jesuit order.

1946-61

At Saints learning became an adventure. Stanley began to relate the new things he was learning to his own life experiences. The world of his imagination was being expanded by the study of literature, geography and science. In class the boys exchanged books and tried to join as many libraries as they could in Georgetown. Books like the *Decameron,* Balzac's *Droll Stories,* and bootleg copies of *Lady Chatterley's Lover* made the rounds. Such reading selections were eventually made known by the Librarian of the Public Library to the Headmaster, Father Scannel, who warned that as young Catholic gentlemen they were forbidden from reading any book listed in the Index *Librorum Prohibitorium* published by the Vatican. A man of the world, Scannel added, "Later in life perhaps; but not now." This led, not unsurprisingly, to increased efforts to locate the forbidden fruits.

There were no art classes at school but Stanley continued to draw on his own. His father, in his occupation as a sign-painter introduced him, to his great delight, to the world of lettering, using real paints and brushes. Before going off to work at the waterfront, his father would paint the outlines of the letters, leaving Stanley to fill in the letters with paint. He also watched his father restoring the regalia of Freemasonry, replete with fascinating symbols that appealed to his imagination. The hours spent among the tools and paints and ropes in his father's workshop were among the happiest of his childhood. He was fascinated by his father's guitar and would pluck and strum at it when he was out. He had visions of owning it one day. His father showed him how to play a wooden banjo. Stanley was most distressed to come home from school one afternoon to find the guitar missing. His mother told him that his father had sold it to buy an electric bulb for the house so that he could prepare for his final school-leaving GCE exams. He was devastated, especially as the kerosene lamp was more efficient than the one bulb hanging from the roof. But he was moved by the sacrifice his father had made; he knew how much the instrument made by one of his friends meant to him.

Both parents were Catholics. Stanley attended church regularly, drawn more by the rituals than by the dogma. His interest in religious doctrine developed at Saints where students had to study the faith and were encouraged to ask "provocative" questions, such as the popular: "If God is good and all-powerful, why does he allow evil things to exist in the world?" They were, of course, always steered in the direction of the articles of the faith. By his late teens, he had become a confirmed agnostic.

It was at Saints that an event occurred that determined the direction of his life: one of his former school friends, Lloyd Bouyea, told him that an artist called Burrowes was conducting free art classes, weekly, on Thursday evenings at a place called the Auditorium, which housed a private secondary school. The Working People's Art Class, for such it was, was founded by E.R. Burrowes in 1948. The Class met twice a week: Thursday evening for drawing and preparing sketches for painting classes on Saturday afternoons. These early years in the WPAC were decisive. Greaves was introduced to painting in gouache as a preliminary to painting in oils, and introduced later to working in different media. This was a great leap forward from the homemade watercolours he used to concoct from crushed crayons and bits of tailors' chalk. His notions about the meaning of art were nurtured through discussions led by Burrowes and his assistant, Donald Locke. On Sundays, a few members would visit Burrowes at his home to listen to his experiences in England as an art student. Other Sundays were spent sketching around Georgetown and especially in the Botanic Gardens. From Burrowes, an extremely erudite man, he borrowed books and magazines on art. Greaves took away from the WPAC, and from Burrowes in particular, a commitment to the sharing of knowledge and an uncompromising attitude to the practice of art. The reading and the lively discussions in the group led Greaves to form the idea of getting to the UK to study art. The British Council at the time offered art scholarships to England. Burrowes was a recipient in 1949, as was Donald Locke. Unfortunately for Greaves the scholarships dried up soon after.

1952-62

After leaving Saints, Greaves wanted to work with plants in the horticultural section of the Ministry of Agriculture. While waiting for a reply to his application, which appears never to have arrived, he was asked to act for a teacher at his old school who was going on study-leave. He went on to do the Teachers' examination and eventually got his Teacher (second class) Untrained. He declined to enter the training college, preferring instead to spend the two years preparing for university entrance. He was appointed to the permanent staff at Sacred Heart School.

In 1956, Greaves started keeping the journals (occasionally diaries) that became a lifelong preoccupation. He regretted having no mementos whatever from his four grandparents, of whom he knew only one as a small child. He felt that at some distant time in the future relatives would be able to read of his interests and his experiences of the times in which he lived. At this point the journals also served as sketchbooks.

The Rev Brian Scannell S.J, the headmaster of Saint Stanislaus, approached him in 1957 to become the first ever Art Master at his *alma mater.* He was drawn to teaching, stimulated by the challenge of getting children to discover things about themselves and their country and to do so through art. How better to engage the eyes and encourage observation? The years at Saints also provided him the opportunity to indulge in a favourite pursuit: camping out in the interior. He and his friend, geography teacher Leslie Cummings (later Professor and Deputy Vice-Chancellor at the University of Guyana), spent their long school holidays leading groups of students on camping trips into "the bush".

At Saints, he became friendly with Fr. Byrne who used to listen to his questions about life and the role of religion and who assured him that there were many ways to serve God. Greaves's conclusion, which he acted upon, was that the way for him to understand spirituality was through art. At this time, in the middle 1950s, a number of books came into his hands that sparked his intellectual awakening: Lewis Mumford's *The Condition of Man*, Hendrik Van Loon's *The Story of Mankind*, and H.G. Wells's *The Outline of History.*

Around this time, Greaves's interest in the guitar was rekindled. He started with some elementary folk-guitar playing but it was not until he heard on the radio a recording of Andres Segovia playing *Recuerdos De La Alhambra* that he turned seriously to the classical guitar. The *Recuerdos* involved a technique that made the instrument sound like a mandolin and guitar playing a duet. On a borrowed Spanish-type guitar, made by a popular maker, Hussein of Lombard Street – (his guitars were glued *and* nailed, designed for the rigours of travel in the hinterland) — and with a simple method book, Greaves began an adventure that has not ended. During the middle to late 50s he met Peter Andersen of England and his Guyanese wife, Pat Evan-Wong. Andersen had served in the RAF, studied art in the UK and played classic guitar, in a fashion. He supplied Greaves with music and a proper manual.

The appointment at Saints also brought him one step closer to getting to the UK, as he would now be supported in his studies for his Advanced Level Certificate, the requirement for entering University. In 1961 he married Barbara Klein. Their first child, Andre, was born in 1962, the same year the family left for the UK. Stanley had obtained his "A" Levels and through begging letters was able to obtain some financial assistance from an unlikely source. Anthony Tasker, an expatriate director of the Booker Group of Companies and art lover, obtained funds from the company and later on from the Government. Later that year he left by ship for London.

1962-63

He spent the year in London awaiting placement at the University of Newcastle-upon-Tyne. He continued his reading on subjects related to art, in particular noting the work of Herbert Read, Carl Jung and Basil Davidson's writings on Africa. He was a regular visitor to London's museums and galleries, and was particularly interested in general purpose museums like the British Museum and the Victoria and Albert. Their historical collections of artifacts from all cultures gave an added dimension to his readings in history. While in London he met Aubrey Williams, his fellow Guyanese artist, and through discussions and observation gained some idea of what it was like to be a practicing Caribbean artist in London. The conclusions were not appealing: either join the mainstream or remain marginalized. Greaves had also begun to read about the Black Power Movement and Negritude and attempted to see what relationship existed between the work of Black artists and those concepts. He found much to sympathize with in the movement but did not feel that one's artistic themes had to come from there.

That first year in London he bought his first real Spanish guitar for 12 guineas. He continued his self-instruction. Two years later, he was able to treat himself to concerts given by Andres Segovia and Julian Breem.

1963-68

At the University of Newcastle, his Director of Studies was Richard Hamilton, the doyen of the Pop Art movement in Britain. Stanley Greaves was the only non-British student in the Art department. He felt no connection with Pop Art and came to feel so isolated he was ready to return to Guyana at the end of the first year. His ability to work in different media saved the day. He decided to do sculpture instead; painting would have to await his return home. Greaves's particular temperament made the expression of reduced form in sculpture extremely attractive to him. He found the work of Brancusi, Marini and Noguchi very instructive. He wrote his Honours thesis on Brancusi. He was disappointed, though, that Eduardo Paolozzi, a sculptor whose work he admired, had just left the institution.His work at the University attracted some attention and earned him two awards.

He spent time during one of the summers he was in England visiting museums in Rome, Florence and Venice to look at the achievements of the Renaissance. Another trip took him to Paris, to the Louvre and the Musée de l'Homme. A special visit was made to see the work of Constantin Brancusi to collect material for his dissertation in the final year. He traveled to Amsterdam to see the important works of the masters Rembrandt, Vermeer, Rubens. He was overwhelmed by the still-life paintings.

At Newcastle he was struck by the interest some students took in the *Scientific American* magazine: the images produced by scientific instruments had a highly attractive visual content which a number of students further manipulated in an effort to produce something "original". Greaves's interest in pure form in sculpture satisfied the academic conditions and his name was proposed by his sculpture tutor to be employed as a "studio demonstrator" working with first year students. However, Richard Hamilton (the Pop art painter) was in charge of that group and seemed to feel that Greaves would be of no use to him. Instead, Greaves spent the year doing the diploma in Art Education paid for by a student loan from the Ministry of Education in Guyana after Anthony Tasker took his case to them. His twin daughters, Sonya and Fiona, were born in December of 1967.

1968

On his return to Guyana, Greaves worked as Art Master at two leading secondary schools, the Berbice High School and Queen's College, to which he was transferred in 1971, replacing Donald Locke who had left to seek his fortune as an artist in

London. His last child, Natasha, was born that year. He continued to work in painting and sculpture, and contributed to several exhibitions. He worked on a small series of abstract paintings called the *Heartland Series* after the novel (*Heartland*, Faber, 1964) by Wilson Harris. He was having problems however resuming his figure painting from the point where he had left it in 1962.

1975

Greaves was appointed Head of the newly formed Division of Creative Arts at the University of Guyana, where efforts to establish extensive programmes were defeated due to the sudden decline of the economy. He also received a travel fellowship from the Cultural Affairs Department of the US State Department, which he used to visit collections of art from Ancient Egypt and tropical Africa. He was keen to further explore his interest in things Egyptian and also to examine the relationship between "African Art" and the appropriations of artists like Picasso and Brancusi. Both areas of interest were then related to the ideological premises of the Black Power Movement.

In a rare victory over the university bureaucrats, Greaves did manage, after a struggle, to have Martin Carter appointed as poet-in-residence. This allowed him even more contact with Carter, whom he had first met in the 1950s at the WPAC exhibitions. Along with Professor William Carr, Rayman Mandal and Michael Aarons, Greaves and Carter made up an informal group that met on and off campus to discuss a wide range of topics and read their poems to each other. They attempted, with little success, to encourage others to join their sessions on campus. Greaves also formed the habit of reconstructing private conversations he had had with Martin Carter, finding support for his own work in Carter's flashes of insight and his elaborate explanations of things. The poet provided Greaves with the means to develop a very critical response to his work in art as well as in poetry. Carter taught him precision in the use of language and drew connections – between art and morality, poetry and politics, intention and execution, the private and the public – that resonated with his own concerns.

1977

In 1977 he went into the hinterland with his photographer friend, Bobby Fernandes, who was photographing little known waterfalls. Greaves always had a special feeling for the forest and on this particular trip he experienced an epiphany that had a profound effect on him. He felt that some vital aspect of his psyche had at last returned to Guyana. On his return to Georgetown, his application of his concept of "the lattice effect" created a significant stylistic turn in his work that had to do with the act of perception and the way it affects the presentation of shape and form. The result attracted such comments as "reworked cubism". Greaves's only response was to suggest that his commentators should view the world through the fronds of palm leaves or from other related objects like jalousied windows, a popular feature of Guyanese architecture.

1979

A Fulbright award in 1979 led Greaves to Howard University to see how "black artists", as self-described, dealt with the issue of race and art. His conclusions remained the same as they had been in 1975: that for all its political correctness, "Black Art" was in danger of becoming a fashion that sometimes hindered the emergence of a real artistic vision.

His own study plan at Howard University was to produce welded sculpture, which presented technical problems of a different order to those of carving in wood or stone. He also decided to work in clay, which previously he felt was too responsive to the touch; he found that it facilitated his interest in form in areas not touched by his other work in sculpture.

1981-85

In 1981 Greaves went on sabbatical leave to Barbados where he studied ceramics with Bill Grace, an eminent ceramist who practiced the Japanese approach to ceramics involving the role of chance, something diametrically opposite to Greaves's approach. The association nevertheless proved to be productive. In 1984-85 he studied with Francisco Gonzalez of Cuba, who was sent to teach classical guitar as part of a cultural agreement with the Government of Guyana. The accent was on technique. Greaves's knowledge of music theory was at this time very rudimentary, but Gonzalez was interested in his progress and, half in jest, suggested that he give up his art work and concentrate more on the instrument and begin studying theory. Under the guidance of Louis LaRoche, cabinet-maker, guitar-maker and cello player, Greaves constructed a "creolized" Spanish guitar.

In 1983 he began to keep separate sketchbooks that are also a repository for his observations on the practices of art, his own and in general. The journals could now be reserved for other interests.

In 1985 he married English-born landscape painter Alison Chapman-Andrews and relocated to Barbados. His marriage to Barbara Klein had ended some years before. Unlike the thousands of Guyanese who emigrated during the harsh years of the Burnham dictatorship, his reasons for moving were essentially private. The art scene in Barbados was more vibrant, with several artists producing work for the flourishing tourist market and putting on many group as well as one-person shows a year. Greaves began showing at the national level, winning prizes in painting and sculpture. Because he was not teaching, as he had been in Guyana, he was able to devote all of his time to producing work. Being based in Barbados eventually led to his work becoming known in the wider Caribbean and internationally.

Another significant feature of the Barbados art scene was the number of expatriate artists on the island, some of them also teaching art in secondary schools on the island. They brought their own aesthetic to bear on unfamiliar themes, and in many cases served as models for young aspiring Barbadian artists. The presence of collectors also helped to stimulate the art scene. In 1990 Greaves became a part-time tutor at the Barbados Community College and in 1996 began to teach stone sculpture, later adding woodcarving to the syllabus. Very little attention was being paid to sculpture at the time. With the exception of Karl Broodhagen's work, consisting of studio portraits and three figurative public monuments, there was little in the community to stimulate an interest in sculpture. This made teaching sculpture even more daunting.

1989

An interest in the origins of Western philosophy led Greaves to worrying thoughts about the nonexistence of speculative philosophy in the Caribbean. While at the University of Guyana between 1975-87 he had made two failed attempts to have an introduction to philosophy taught as a foundation course. It was this interest in philosophical questions that led to the production of the small-scale paintings of the *Caribbean Metaphysics* series. His feeling was that perhaps through the tool of speculative thought we might arrive at some solutions to the interminable debate on Caribbean identity.

1990s

During this period his observations on the political life of the region led to the series *There Is A Meeting Here Tonight*, where irony and scepticism reign. In 1994, to celebrate his 60th birthday, he bought a relatively expensive guitar in New York. Its tone had captivated him just at the point when he was making a serious commitment to the instrument. He became a student of Pam Frost, a trained classical guitar tutor, and began studies in theory and practice for six years. His playing improved enormously, and in 2000 he did a performance for the visiting examiner of the Royal School of Music. He was commended for his performance and for those of his own compositions that he played. In 2001 became the proud owner of an expensive Ramirez guitar.

Throughout the years Greaves has maintained his interest in figure painting. In these, individuals were invariably presented with implements in their hands. This was a reference, perhaps, to his father, like himself, the son of a maker of things. It is a title Greaves prefers to that of artist.

MAJOR EXHIBITIONS

1951-61	Working Peoples' Art Class Annual Exhibitions, Georgetown, Guyana.
1959-62	Department of Culture Annual National Exhibition, Georgetown, Guyana.
1960	Second Group Show of Paintings, with Michael Leila, Ron Savory, and Emerson Samuels, Bookers Universal Building, Georgetown, Guyana.
1967	Final Year Exhibition of Sculpture and Paintings, at Newcastle-Upon-Tyne, Northumberland, UK.
1967	EXPO 67, Canada.
1968-85	Department of Culture Annual National Exhibition, Georgetown, Guyana.
1970	One Man Show, J.F. Kennedy Library Georgetown, Guyana.
	Retrospective Exhibition of Guyanese Art, Guyana Museum, Georgetown, Guyana.
1971	San Paulo Biennial, San Paulo, Brazil.
1972	Coltejar Biennial, Colombia.
	One Man Retrospective of Paintings and Sculpture, Caribbean Festival of Arts (CARIFESTA), Georgetown, Guyana.
1973	San Paulo Biennial, San Paulo, Brazil.
1974	Mural commissioned by Barclay's Bank Main Branch (now the Guyana National Bank of Trade & Industry) in collaboration with Anthony Phillips, Georgetown, Guyana.
1976	Exhibition of Guyanese Art, Caribbean Festival of Arts (CARIFESTA), Kingston, Jamaica.
1977	Exhibition of Guyanese Art, Casa de las Americas, Havana, Cuba.
	Exhibition of Guyanese Art, Festival of Creative Arts (FESTAC), Lagos, Nigeria.
1978	One Man Show of Paintings, J.F. Kennedy Library, Georgetown, Guyana.
1979	Exhibition of Guyanese Art, Caribbean Festival of Arts (CARIFESTA), Havana, Cuba.

1980 Master of Fine Art (MFA) Graduation Exhibition of Sculpture and Prints, Howard University, Washington DC, USA.

1981 Exhibition of Guyanese Art and a member of a mural-painting team Caribbean Festival of Arts (CARIFESTA), St. James Secondary School, Holetown, St. James, Barbados.

1983 One Man Show of Paintings, Sculpture and Calligraphy, Presentation of own Poetry, Pelican Gallery, Bridgetown, Barbados.

1984 Calligraphic Presentation of own Poetry, J.F. Kennedy Library, Georgetown, Guyana.

1986 Exhibition of Guyanese Art, Wifredo Lam Centre, Havana, Cuba.

Exhibition of Guyanese art, Caracas, Venezuela.

1988-91 National Independence Festival of Creative Arts (NIFCA) Exhibition, Grand Salle, Central Bank, Bridgetown, Barbados.

1988 One man Exhibition of Paintings and Ceramics entitled "Hearts, Diamonds and Flowers", with Paintings by Alison Chapman-Andrews (Greaves), Barbados Museum, St. Michael, Barbados.

1989 One man Exhibition of Drawings entitled "Birds of Black", with Drawings by guest Artist Colin 'Abyssinian' Carto, Barbados Museum, St. Michael, Barbados.

1990 One man Exhibition of Ceramics entitled "First Steps", with ceramics by guest ceramist Bill Grace, Barbados Museum, Art Collection Foundation (ACF) Exhibition, Queen's Park Gallery, Bridgetown, Barbados.

1992 Exhibition of Caribbean Art entitled "1492 to 1992", Carpeaux Centre, Courbevoie (France), Corsica, Trinidad, Martinique, Dominican Republic, and Puerto Rico.

Caribbean Festival of Arts (CARIFESTA), Trinidad.

The First Biennial of Caribbean and Latin American Painting, Museum of Modern Art, Santo Domingo, Dominican Republic.

1993	Exhibition entitled "A Caribbean Metaphysic", Queen's Park Gallery Bridgetown, Barbados.
1994	The Second Bienniale of Painting, Museum of Modern Art, Santo Domingo, Dominican Republic Retrospective Exhibition, Castellani House and The Hadfield Gallery, Georgetown, Guyana.
1995	Exhibition entitled "Caribbean Visions", Miami Centre for the Fine Arts. Sept. 9th. 1995, Miami, Florida, USA.
1996	The Third Bienniale of Painting, Museum of Modern Art, Santo Domingo, Dominican Republic. Exhibition entitled "Contemporary Art from Barbados" Hotel Intercontinental, Bridgetown, Barbados
1997	1st International Exhibition of Small Format Prints, Foundation de Arte Contemporaneo, Santo Domingo, Dominican Republic. Exhibition of Prints, Chavon Gallery, Chavon Province, Santo Domingo, Dominican Republic. Show entitled "The Art of Barbados", The Cork Street Gallery, Cork Street, London, UK.
1998	XII Biennial de San Juan, Prints from Latin America and the Caribbean, Instituto de Cultura Puerto-rriquena, San Juan, Puerto Rico. V Biennial of Painting, Cuenca, Ecuador.
1999	Exhibition entitled "The Elders", a two-man show with Bro' Everald Brown of Jamaica, The South London Gallery, 65 Peckham Rd, London, UK. Also Ipswich Gallery, Ipswich, Suffolk, UK. Bienniale of Painting, Bogotá, Colombia. Barbadiana '99, Espace Confluence, Paris, France.
2000	Small Prints Exhibition, 5e Trienniale Mondiale, Chamalieres 2000, Paris, France. Cariforum, Carifesta Travelling Exhibition, Basse-terre, St.Kitts.
2001	Cariforum Carifesta Travelling Exhibition, Santo Domingo, Dominican Republic. Exhibition entitled "Barbados in Two Dimensions", Miracle Mile, Coral Gables, Miami, Florida, USA.

Exhibition entitled "Barbadiana 2001, Contemporary Art in Barbados", Studio de l'Image, 14 Rue des Carnes, Paris, France.
Art Critics International Association (AICA), Exhibition, University of Central Florida, Orlando, Florida, USA.
One man Exhibition entitled "There is a Meeting Here Tonight", Castellani House, Georgetown, Guyana.
The same show, Trinidad Museum, Port-of-Spain, Trinidad.

SELECTED AWARDS

Guyana

1959	National Annual Exhibition, The Burnham Gold Medal, First Prize.
1960	National Annual Exhibition, Third Prize.
1962	National Annual Exhibition, Second Prize.
1970	Retrospective Exhibition of Guyanese Art, First Prize.
1975	National Honours for Art – The Golden Arrow of Achievement (A.A.).
	United States Government International Visitor's Program Award.
1979	Fulbright Scholarship (the First Fulbright Scholar in Art to attend Howard University, Washington DC, USA.).

UK

1965	University of Newcastle-Upon-Tyne, John Bell Simpson Award for Second Year Students.
1966	University of Newcastle-Upon-Tyne, Anabel Winship Smiles Traveling Scholarship.
2002	The Society for Caribbean Studies UK, Bridget Jones Travel Bursary 2002.

Barbados

1987	Art Collection Foundation, Purchase Award.
1990	National Independence Festival of Creative Arts (NIFCA), Gold medal and the Ivan Payne Award for the Best Work (Painting).
	National Independence Festival of Creative Arts (NIFCA), Silver medals (two), for Drawing.
	Art Collection Foundation (ACF), Award for the Best Overall Work, and a Purchase Award.
1991	National Independence Festival of Creative Arts (NIFCA), Gold Medal and the Ivan Payne Award for the Best Work (Sculpture).
	National Independence Festival of Creative Arts (NIFCA), Gold and NIFCA Silver for two Paintings.

Dominican Republic

1994	Gold Medal, Second Bienniale of Caribbean and Latin American Painting.

USA

2002	The Wordsworth McAndrew Award for contributions to Guyanese Culture.

SELECTED BIBLIOGRAPHY

On Stanley Greaves:

Al Creighton, "Reviews: *Kyk-over-Al 45*", *Stabroek News*, (Guyana), Sunday April 23, 1995

Claudette Earle, "Caribbean Man, Stanley Greaves", *Sunday Chronicle*, (Guyana) April 8, 1989

Norman Faria, "Imaginative World of Stanley", *Barbados Advocate*, November 2, 1993

Thérèse Hadchity, "Independence: Perceptions and Attitudes", Catalogue Notes, Barbados Gallery of Art, November 26, 1999

John Henshall, "Elders and Betters", *The New Statesman*, (UK), April 9, 1999

Basil Hinds, "Stanley Greaves", *KAIE Magazine*, (Guyana) May 1966

"The Greaves Exhibit", *Guyana Graphic,* Thursday November 5, 1970

"Retrospect of Art in the Sixties", *KAIE Magazine*, December 1970

"Recall and Update on the Greaves Genre", *Sunday Chronicle*, Nov. 19, 1978 Alim Hosein, "A Master's Voice", *Stabroek News*, Sunday January 31, 1993

"A Master's Voice (ctd)", *Stabroek News*, Sunday February 7, 1993

"Talking to Stanley Greaves – The Creative Temper", *Stabroek News*, Sunday, February 5, 1995

"The Creative Mind – technical and stylistic aspects", *Overcoming the Void*, Castellani House Publication, Guyana, 1997

"Heritage Culture and the Imagination: Alim Hosein Talks with Stanley Greaves", *Stabroek News*, July 11, 1999

"A Meeting of Provoking Trilogies", *Sunday Stabroek*, August 12, 2001

Valerie Jones, "Portrait of Two Artists", *The Nation*, (Barbados), Friday, March 31, 1989,

Manuel Alvarez Lezama, "Gold in the Caribbean", *The San Juan Star*, (Puerto Rico) October 27, 1996

Mirabel, M. Titina and V. John, "Analyse d'une Oeuvre", *Arthème*, No.5, January 2000

Marion O'Callahan, "Meeting Stanley Greaves," *Express* (Trinidad), Monday September 17, 2001

Raschid Osman, "The Stanley Greaves Exhibition," *The Citizen*, (Guyana), Wednesday November 15, 1978

Veerle Poupeeye, *Caribbean Art,* London: Thames & Hudson, 1998

Richard J. Powell, *Black Art and Culture in the 20th Century*, London: Thames & Hudson, 1997

Ulric Rice, "Birds of Black", *Evening Beat*, (Barbados), Wednesday September 6, 1989

Eddie Rodney, "The moral and political content of Greaves' early work", *Overcoming the Void*, Castellani House publication, 1997

Rupert Roopnaraine, "Reflections on the Art of Stanley Greaves", *Kyk-over-Al*, (Guyana), No. 39, December 1988

"Caribbean Metaphysic – Another Reality", Catalogue Essay for Exhibition of the same name, Queen's Park Gallery, Barbados, Pct. 3, 1993

"Visual Arguments, Stanley Greaves at 60", Catalogue Essay for the Retrospective Exhibition, "Celebration 60", (Guyana), 1994

"Stanley Greaves of Guyana, a Caribbean Master", *El Dorado In Flight Magazine*, Guyana Airways, February – April, 1995

"Stanley Greaves: a painter of his time, – works from the 80s and 90s", *Overcoming the Void*, Castellani House Publication, Guyana, 1997

"The Art of Stanley Greaves", Catalogue Essay, The Elders Exhibition, South London Gallery, 1999

"Of Dogs, Gods and the Vote", Catalogue Essay, *There is a Meeting Here Tonight*, Barbados, 2001

Lillian Sten-Nicholson, "Diatribe for the Diaspora", *Daily Nation*, (Barbados), March 24, 2002

Allison Thompson, "Transforming the Barbadian Vision", *Sunday Advocate*, September 18, 1994

"Contemporary Art in Barbados", *Advocate*, (Barbados), Sunday October 27, 28, 29

Elsa Turner, "Caribbean Visions at CFA: a Quest for Identity", *The Miami Herald*, The Arts, Sunday September 10, 1995

Anne Walmsley, "The Elders: Brother Everald Brown and Stanley Greaves", BWIA In Flight Magazine, *Caribbean Beat*, March/April, 1999

"Foreword", The Elders Exhibition catalogue, South London Gallery, 1999

Interview with Stanley Greaves, *Bomb* magazine, New York, Winter 2003/4

Nick Whittle, "Reflections on the work of Stanley Greaves and Colin Carto", *Banja Magazine*, Issue, No. 5, 1989/90

Denis Williams, "Visual Arts 1981", *Sunday Chronicle*, Nov. 29, 1981

Yolanda Wood, "Guyana el Camino de su Arte", *Revolución y Cultura*, No. 8, (Cuba) Agosto, 1986

"De la Plástica Cubana y Caribeòa", Editorial, *Letras Cubanas*, Cuba, 1990

By Stanley Greaves:

"Art, Nationalism and Education", *Praxis* (magazine of the West Indian Student Society, Vol. 1, No. 1, University of Newcastle, UK, March 1965)

The Work of Constantin Brancusi, B.A. (Hons) thesis, University of Newcastle, June 1967

"Art and the Small Man", *Dawn*, Vol.1, No. 2, Georgetown, Guyana, c. 1973

"Ivan Forrester, the People's Painter", Catalogue Notes, Georgetown, Guyana, c. 1976

Broadcast Notes for University on the Air, University of Guyana, c. 1977:

"The Amerindian Contribution to the Creative Arts,"

"Artists and the Masses"

"Public Art"

"Art Groups"

"On Ideas about Beauty"

Iconographic Determinants in my Work, MFA thesis, Howard University, Washington DC, USA, June 1980

"An Outline of the Art Movements of Jamaica and Guyana", History Seminar paper, Secondary School Teachers Seminar, Queen's College, Georgetown, Guyana, 5-8 August, 1980

"The Artist in a Developing Society", Feature Address, The Convocation of Artists, organized by the Bahai of Guyana, Georgetown, 25 April, 1981

"In Appreciation: Art in Barbados", Report to the Department of Art, Barbados Community Collage, July 1982

"Through the Eyes of the Artist", Exhibition Review, USIS Publication, Georgetown, Guyana, 1984

"The Black Artist", a talk presented for "Black Week 1984", Georgetown, 1984

"Art in Guyana", Lecture, Georgetown, Guyana, 1984

"African Retentions in the Visual Arts in the Caribbean", *Stabroek News*, Georgetown, January 23, 1987

"Greaves on Edna Manley", *Stabroek News*, Georgetown, February 20, 1987

"More on Africanism in Caribbean Art – Greaves Responds to Al Creighton", *Stabroek News*, Georgetown, March 1987

"Art in the Caribbean", Lecture to visiting students from University of Michigan, Bridgetown, Barbados, May 15, 1989

"Fusions", Opening Address, Exhibition of paintings by Joyce Daniel, Queen's Park Gallery, Bridgetown, Barbados, February 1990

The Art of Aubrey Williams, unpublished ms., Bardados, 1990

"Memorandum to the West Indian Commission", Dover Convention Centre, Barbados, June 1991

"Open Letter to Ras Akyem and Ras Ishi", in response to their "rapping Art to Two Rases," *Sunday Sun*, Barbados, August 1991

Art in the English Speaking Caribbean, unpublished ms., Barbados, March 1993

"The Role of the Artist in Society", contribution to Panel Discussion, Ocean View Hotel, Barbados, March 1993

"Art in Progress – Wifredo Lam, Leroi Clarke, Aubrey Williams,

James, Boodhoo, Hector Hipolite", *Trinidad and Tobago Review*, September 1993
"Interview", with Dennis DeCaires, De Montfort University, UK, Barbados, November 1995
"The Santo Domingo Biennale", Address to Artists, Castellani House, Georgetown, November 1996
"Opening Address", Aubrey Williams Retrospective Exhibition, Barbados Gallery of Art, Bridgetown, January 1999
"The Sustainable in Art", *Sunday Stabroek*, Georgetown, May 9, 1999
"The Last Walk" (Poem), *Kyk-over-Al*, Nos. 49/50, Guyana, June 2000
"A Vision of Land and Landscape", *Kyk-over-Al*, Nos. 49/50, Guyana, June 2000
"A Vision of Land and Landscape in the Poems of Martin Carter" in *All are Involved: the Art of Martin Carter,* edited by Stewart Brown, Leeds: Peepal Tree Press, 2000
"The Photography of Bobby Fernandes", Catalogue Notes, Retrospective Exhibition of Photographs by Bobby Fernandes, Castellani House, Georgetown, Guyana, March 2000
"De Profundis", "School Days", "Play", "New Day", "Rice Pot", "Dream of Demerara", "Silences II" in *Caribbean New Voices 1,* Anthology edited by Stewart Brown, London: Longman Caribbean, 1995
Horizons, Selected Poems, Leeds: Peepal Tress Press, 2002

Selected Further Reading

John Berger, *Art and Revolution, Ernst Neizvestny, Endurance and the Role of the Artist in the USSR*, London: Penguin, 1969
Herschel B. Chipp, *Theories of Modern Art,* University of California Press, USA, 1968
Arthur C. Danto, *Philosophizing Art*, Berkeley: University of California Press, 1999
The Madonna of the Future, New York: Farrar, Straus and Giroux, 2000

Ian Freestone and David Grimster, Editors, *Pottery in the Making: World Ceramic Traditions,* London: British Museum Press, 1997

Charles Harrison & Paul Wood, Editors, *Art in Theory, 1900-1990,* Oxford: Blackwell, 1992

Robert Hughes, *Nothing if not Critical,* London: Penguin, 1990

Kelley, Robin D. G., *Freedom Dreams – the Black Radical Imagination* (Beacon Press, Boston, 2002.

Wassily Kandinsky, *Complete Writings on Art,* edited by Kenneth C. Lindsay and Peter Vergo, USA: Da Capo Press, 1994

Edward Lucie-Smith, *Movements in Art since 1945,* London: Thames and Hudson, 1969

Brendan Prendeville, *Realism in 20th Century Painting,* London: Thames and Hudson, 2000

Phillip Rawson, *Drawing, (Appreciation of the Arts 3),* London: Oxford University Press, 1969

Herbert Read, *Icon and Idea,* London: Faber and Faber, 1954

Modern Sculpture, London: Thames and Hudson, 1964

Anne Walmsley, *The Caribbean Artists Movement, 1962-1972: A Literary and Cultural History.* London: and Port of Spain: New Beacon Books, 1992

INDEX

(entries in bold indicate either the location of the reproduction of the art work referred to in the text or a major reference.)

Discussion of groups and series in Greaves's work:

Discussion of Greaves's paintings

About the Author

Rupert Roopnaraine was born in 1943 in Kitty, Georgetown, Guyana. He won a scholarship to Queen's College in 1954 where he excelled in cricket, where he captained the team and represented Demerara in the Inter-county Cricket Finals. In 1962 he was awarded a Guyana scholarship to attend the University of Cambridge where he studied Modern Languages and was awarded a Cambridge 'Blue' for representing the University in English county cricket. In 1970 he was awarded a scholarship to Cornell University, New York, where he obtained an MA and Ph D in Comparative Literature. From 1966-1996, he has worked as a university lecturer in the UK, Canada, the USA and at the University of Guyana.

He joined the Working People's Alliance in 1977 and quickly became one of the leaders of the party along with Walter Rodney, Clive Thomas and Eusi Kwayana. He was an activist politician and at the height of the years of PNC repression was arrested on charges of burning down the PNC headquarters. He also narrowly escaped death when he was attacked by PNC party thugs, only reaching safety with the help of sugarcane workers who led him through the cane fields to escape. After the assassination of Walter Rodney he became leader of the WPA. He has been a member of the Guyanese parliament for many years, with a virtually unique reputation for the incorruptible representation of people across all racial groups.

He is unquestionably one of the leading Caribbean intellectuals of his generation, though political activism has restricted his output. Nevertheless, he is an outstanding art critic (champion of the work of Stanley Greaves, Ras Ishi and Ras Akyem), literary critic (author of a pioneering essay on Martin Carter), film-maker (*The Terror and the Time*) and poet. He is the author of *The Web of October: Rereading Martin Carter* (1986) and a suite of love poems, *Suite for Supriya* (1993), both published by Peepal Tree.